The Architecture of Vision

Leadership in Your Professional Practice

Craig Park, FSMPS, Assoc. AIA
&
Barbara Shuck, FSMPS, CPSM

ALSO BY CRAIG PARK

The Architecture of Value:
Building Your Professional Practice

The Architecture of Image:
Branding Your Professional Practice

CRAIG PARK AS CONTRIBUTOR

Marketing Handbook for Design & Construction Professionals

BARBARA SHUCK & CRAIG PARK AS CONTRIBUTORS

A/E/C Business Development:
The Decade Ahead

We dedicate this book to the memory of our fathers. They inspired us to lead.

COPYRIGHT & ATTRIBUTIONS

Copyright 2023, Craig Park and Barbara Shuck. All rights reserved. No part of this book may be used or reproduced in any manner without permission of the author, except in the case of brief quotations embodied in articles or reviews.

ISBN 978-0-9893382-1-9

Books are available at special discounts when purchased in bulk for education, business, fundraising, or promotional use. We can create special editions or book excerpts to specification on request. For details, contact either of us. For more information, see
www.the achitectureofvision.com.

For more information, please contact:

Craig Park, FSMPS, Assoc. AIA
CRAIG**PARK.**CONSULT
843.321.8988
craig@craigpark.com
www.craigpark.com

Barbara Shuck, FSMPS, CPSM
EVEREST MARKETING SERVICES, LLC
602.686.4616
barbara@everestmarketingservices.com
www.everestmarketingservices.com

Published by:
Laquilan Leadership Press
Georgetown, SC 29440
843.321.8988

Cover Photo:
Walt Disney Concert Hall 2.0 Imagined
© 2023. Craig Park. All rights reserved.

TABLE OF CONTENTS

INTRODUCTION | A Path to Leadership i
PART I | INSPIRATION: The First Pillar.................................1
Chapter 1 | **VISION**: Meditation on Leadership............9
   VIEWPOINT – AMANDA BOGNER, PE, BEMP.............17
Chapter 2 | **INTROSPECTION**: Why You Lead 25
   VIEWPOINT – CHRISTINE HILL..32
Chapter 3 | **EMPATHY**: Will They Follow?.......................41
   VIEWPOINT – CRAIG GALATI, FAIA, FSMPS...............50
Chapter 4 | **GENEROSITY**: Sharing Leadership 59
   VIEWPOINT – CRAIG JANSSEN, LEED AP BD+C 67
Chapter 5 | **PATIENCE**: Trusting in Time 75
   VIEWPOINT – DAWN SAVAGE, FSMPS......................82
Chapter 6 | **WISDOM**: Learning from the Path............89
   VIEWPOINT – KATHLEEN HELD, CPSM......................95
PART II | INNOVATION – The Second Pillar..................101
Chapter 7 | **DISCIPLINE**: Committing to Goals...........115
   VIEWPOINT – LANCE JONES, PE 122
Chapter 8 | **EFFORT**: Defining the Practice.................129
   VIEWPOINT – LEE SLADE, PE 136
Chapter 9 | **AGILITY**: Expanding Horizons...................145
   VIEWPOINT – LINDA CROUSE 155
Chapter 10 | **INFLUENCE**: Developing Leaders..........165
   VIEWPOINT – MARJANNE PEARSON 172

Chapter 11 | **PURPOSE**: Creating A Culture 185
    VIEWPOINT – MARK VALENTI, CTS 192
Chapter 12 | **PERSPECTIVE**: Leaving a Legacy 201
    VIEWPOINT – MIKE REILLY, FSMPS 207
PART III | INTEGRITY – The Third Pillar 217
Chapter 13 | **TRUST**: Speaking the Truth 227
    VIEWPOINT – NANCY USREY, FSMPS, CPSM 233
Chapter 14 | **IMPACT**: Leading with Intention 243
    VIEWPOINT – REBECCA JONES 251
Chapter 15 | **VALUES**: Acting with Humility 259
    VIEWPOINT – RON WORTH, CAE, FSMPS 267
Chapter 16 | **COURAGE**: Effort & Mindfulness 277
    VIEWPOINT – SAMANTHA SANNELLA 283
Chapter 17 | **HARMONY**: Alignment & Resonance ... 291
    VIEWPOINT – STEVE OSBORN, PE, SE 298
Chapter 18 | **CHARACTER**: The Responsible Person .. 309
    VIEWPOINT – TIM BARRICK, FSMPS 316
AFTERWORD | Your Leadership Journey 325
    Integral Leadership Assessment (ILA) 331
    Creating Your Development Framework 339
ENDNOTES | Additional References 343
BIBLIOGRAPHY | Recommended Reading 347
ABOUT OUR CONTRIBUTORS 353
ACKNOWLEDGEMENTS 363
ABOUT THE AUTHORS 369

INTRODUCTION | A Path to Leadership

When you see an eagle, you know a portion of genius — lift your head!
William Blake

THE IDEA BEHIND THE ARCHITECTURE OF VISION came from a belief that individuals and organizations can enhance leadership by focusing on three essential pillars — Inspiration, Innovation, and Integrity. With an understanding and development of fundamental traits related to each pillar — through a practice of awareness, acceptance, and action — each of us can become visionary leaders. This leadership development process benefits the individual, their firm, their clients, and their communities.

WHAT IS LEADERSHIP?

Marine Corps Lt. General John A. Lejeune said, *"Leadership is the sum of those qualities of intellect, human understanding, and moral character that enable a person to inspire and control a group of people successfully."*

For a professional service firm, the definition of leadership can be as simple as Lejeune's inspirational command and control model. However, leadership is often more complex, encompassing a wide range of traits that allow an individual to guide, direct, and inspire others toward achieving the organization's goals, objectives, strategies, and tactical efforts.

It is important to note that in professional services, different individuals and roles — partners, principals, managers, and even individual contributors — have leadership responsibilities in achieving the firm's objectives. As author Mark Sanborn said in his same-tiled book, "You don't need a title to be a leader." We agree, and reinforce that point in the book's last chapter, Character – The Responsible Person.

A leader in professional services should have a balance of technical expertise and leadership skills and be able to guide and direct the team while ensuring that the firm delivers high-quality services to its clients based on three pillars of leadership: Inspiration, Innovation, and Integrity.

Inspired and motivated team members are more engaged, creative, and committed to the organization's goals. An inspirational leader fosters a culture of collaboration within the firm. They encourage their team to think creatively and to take calculated risks that lead to new and better ways of doing things. Encouraging creativity results in improved client service, increased efficiency and effectiveness, and a competitive advantage for the firm.

An innovative leader drives the development of new services and creative solutions to meet and exceed market needs. Professional services struggle with differentiation. Innovative leadership provides the basis for competitive advantage. Encouraging innovation builds a culture that distinguishes the firm from otherwise like services.

Integrity is critical in a professional service firm, where trust and credibility are essential. A leader with high integrity sets the tone for ethical behavior and ensures that the organization operates consistently with its values and principles. Integrity helps to build trust and confidence with clients, stakeholders, and the broader community, which can be invaluable for the firm's reputation and long-term success.

HOW WE ORGANIZED OUR BOOK

We organized this book around three themes defining the successful leader's ability to address these goals.

- First is **INSPIRATION**, the realization of the role of the leader as the ability to motivate — the mentoring role distinguishes many leaders. Inspiration can be a sudden brilliant, creative, or timely idea, or it is the process of being mentally stimulated to do something, especially something creative.
- Next is **INNOVATION,** the ability to define a vision through creative effort that establishes a practice as unique from its competition. Vision is the entrepreneurial spirit that imbues many celebrated leaders. Innovation expands on inspirational creation by developing and implementing a new process or service to improve efficiency, effectiveness, or competitive advantage.
- Finally, **INTEGRITY** defines leadership. Integrity demonstrates the leader's true nature through words and actions. Integrity is the quality of honesty and strong moral principles, achieving being whole and undivided.

Each part has a corresponding set of six chapters based on related traits.

INSPIRATION	INNOVATION	INTEGRITY
Vision	Discipline	Trust
Introspection	Effort	Impact
Empathy	Agility	Values
Generosity	Influence	Courage
Patience	Purpose	Harmony
Wisdom	Perspective	Character

The Architecture of Vision

The more we looked at and talked with other leaders, the more critical the need for a more extensive and granular framework became clear. We know that not everyone has fully developed all these traits. We share here what we have observed and experienced so future leaders are more aware of their place along the path to leadership.

THE IMPORTANCE OF A FOCUS

Each chapter starts with a **FOCUS**. The focus is the salient central idea we want the reader to take away and be able to apply to their leadership journey.

This idea sets the tone and direction for each component of the leadership development process. In simple terms, the central idea defines the problem, the solution, and the result. It clarifies the goal, the process, and the desired outcome, creating a roadmap for career success.

Our book is based on the need and methods to become a better leader. Each section is based on the foundations of innovation, inspiration, and integrity — the pillars of a well-rounded leader. Each chapter defines traits that define a fully developed leader.

SMALL STEPS TOWARD GROWTH

As noted above, each chapter includes the PROGRESSION section with reflections framed on **Awareness, Acceptance**, and **Action** concepts. These are crucial steps needed to build a greater understanding of each leadership trait, designed to create greater awareness and provide actionable steps to improve your leadership abilities.

In the late Marta Monahan's insightful book, *Strength of Character and Grace: Develop the Courage to be Brilliant,* she suggests that making five small changes in behavior daily leads to significant personal improvement over time. According to Monahan, this

Introduction

approach involves identifying a few specific behaviors to change each day and consciously attempting to change those behaviors.[1]

We agree that focusing on small steps in the behaviors associated with a few traits makes it easier to make lasting changes and see measurable progress. Examples of behaviors include setting a daily goal, practicing mindfulness, or expressing gratitude. Individuals develop new habits and improve their well-being by making small daily changes.

Over time, as we make these small changes daily, they build momentum and help us achieve bigger goals. The same approach builds leadership capabilities and strengthens personal potential.

PUTTING LEARNING TO WORK

We based our approach to personal leadership development on a process that has worked for us in our personal development journey. Using a protocol of awareness, acceptance, and action significantly helped us develop our leadership capabilities. This approach includes:

- **AWARENESS:** Developing awareness involves becoming more conscious of one's thoughts, emotions, and behaviors, as well as their impact on others. By promoting self-awareness, leaders better understand their strengths, weaknesses, and areas for improvement, leading to greater effectiveness and better decision-making. Additionally, leaders who are more aware of their biases and assumptions are more inclusive and empathetic in their interactions with others, leading to stronger relationships and a more positive work environment.

- **ACCEPTANCE:** Acceptance involves acknowledging and embracing one's strengths and weaknesses. By accepting

---

[1] Monahan, M., *Strength of Character and Grace: Develop the Courage to be Brilliant*, Vittorio Media, 2010.

their limitations, leaders focus on leveraging their strengths and delegating tasks outside their areas of expertise. Additionally, leaders accepting others' differences foster a more diverse and inclusive workplace culture, leading to increased creativity, innovation, and better problem-solving.

- **ACTION:** Action involves using awareness and acceptance to make meaningful changes and improvements. By setting clear goals, creating plans, and taking action to achieve them, leaders become more effective and achieve greater success. Additionally, leaders who give agency to address issues and challenges in the workplace foster a culture of accountability and continuous improvement, which leads to better outcomes for the firm and its clients.

Basing personal development on awareness, acceptance, and action helps leaders and aspiring leaders become more conscious, inclusive, and practical, resulting in a more positive workplace culture and better outcomes for the firm and its clients.

SUPPORTING COMPONENTS

Although we arranged the chapters under the three overarching themes, they are interrelated. Each chapter concludes with additional components to help the reader integrate the ideas supporting each trait.

- The first — **SYNTHESIS** — looks at the intersection and convergence between the learnings from the other pillars of leadership and their importance to the relevant trait.

- Each chapter includes a section titled VIEWPOINT — individual insights drawn from interviews with many of our contributors.

Introduction

- Next, each chapter includes a section titled **PROGRESSION** — an integral three-part approach to starting personal leadership development — using Awareness, Acceptance, and Action essential questions to begin your path to better leadership.
- We conclude with **SYNOPSIS** — a summary of the benefits of developing each leadership trait.
- We also include a blank page for you to use to note your **REFLECTIONS & INSIGHTS**.

LEADERSHIP DEVELOPMENT ASSESSMENT

In the **AFTERWORD** conclusion, we provide an assessment tool, the **Integral Leadership Assessment (ILA),** a holistic leadership assessment tool that evaluates leaders and aspiring leaders across seven stages of leadership development.

We based the ILA on an adaptation of Ken Wilber's 4-Quadrant framework,[2] which provides a well-rounded view of the progression of an individual's leadership capabilities. The ILA focuses on personal and professional growth by identifying areas of strength and development across various dimensions, including worldviews, value systems, relationships, and organizational impact.

The ILA framework illustrates the natural path to professional leadership. Each person is at a level defined by one of seven stages of leadership development:

1. **Reflective:** Managing Self – You rely on your title or position to get things done
2. **Interpersonal:** Managing Others – You have positive relationships with your team members

---

[2] Adapted from Ken Wilber's *A Theory of Everything: An Integral Vision for Business, Politics, Science, and Spirituality,* Shambala, 2000.

The Architecture of Vision

3. **Managerial:** Managing Managers – You set clear goals and expectations for your team
4. **Technical:** Managing Process – You invest time and resources in developing your team members
5. **Strategic:** Team Leadership – You have a clear vision and purpose for your team
6. **Collaborative:** Group Leadership – You have a growth mindset and continuously seek to improve yourself and your team
7. **Visionary:** Enterprise Leadership – You have a sense of purpose and meaning beyond yourself and your organization

You can use the ILA for yourself or as a 360-degree tool, sharing with others up and down within your organization to provide a more complete view of your level of leadership development.

We conclude the book with guidelines for **Creating a Leadership Development Framework**, providing an outline to inform leadership growth within any professional service firm. By understanding individual and collective behaviors, any professional practice can apply this structure to create a leadership development program unique to each professional practice.

WHY WE WROTE THIS BOOK

We wrote this book as a reference guide for experienced leaders (e.g., Veterans, Boomers, Xers) considering transition, and especially for the younger generations (e.g., Millennial/Y, Z, Alpha) of aspiring leaders. We wrote for both individuals seeking to become better leaders, and for firms seeking a framework for leadership development.

We wanted to address a personal path to leadership development that framed the process with a clear understanding of the traits of the leadership persona, including:

Introduction

- **Features that serve to identify an individual**
- **A person's distinguishing qualities**
- **How a person acts or conducts oneself, especially toward others.; how one responds to a particular situation**

Our goal is to provide readers with information, perspective, and applications to inform and improve their potential as leaders and for personal and professional growth in their firms.

Organizations that encompass licensed or degreed professionals working in a specific field — and the administrative, operational, finance, human resources, marketing, and sales staff that support their efforts — have different leadership development needs.

As noted, at the same time, we developed this book to serve as a resource for organizations that want to develop their leaders. We have developed training modules and programs that can be used by organizations that value the importance of leadership development and are looking for formalized programs aimed at helping the next generation of leadership.

There are many excellent books on leadership. We share many of our favorites in the **BIBLIOGRAPHY – Recommended Reading** at the end of this book. However, in our work and research, we found few that focused on the unique challenges of the professional service firm.

In the final **ENDNOTES** chapter, we share other development resources you and your firm can tap to build your own leadership program. And conclude with three important steps on the leadership journey.

FILLING A VOID

As marketing leaders for professional service firms, we have both worked in organizations that developed and promoted technical staff but have yet to see the development of the non-technical but equally professional personnel who are vital to the aspects of human resources, finance, operations, marketing and business development functions of the company.

So, when we use the term intra-professional leadership development, we refer holistically to all aspects of the professional service firm's functional roles, not only those with licensure, as a metric for developmental progress.

We found a perceived vacuum in leadership development and the need for more visibility of growth opportunities. It behooves the individual to self-study — to be entrepreneurial in reaching out and saying, "*I want to take this on!*" — knowing that developing leadership skills is integral to professional growth.

Our motivation for writing was to reaffirm why leadership is essential and should be of personal importance to the readers. Professionals need to adopt a unique leadership style. If one wants to advance, leadership is an integral part of self-development.

There are certainly people who are happy being an employee. And they fill a valuable role. There is nothing dismissive about that. But for organizations to grow, it takes innovation, inspiration, and integrity to develop and grow, to be successful and sustainable.

We support our model with the experiences of the more than two dozen people we spoke to who are respected leaders in various fields. It is essential to notice the range of roles in our contributors. They all have a leadership component to what they do. They all have a perspective on why leadership is essential.

OUR RESEARCH

In our research, we found that all the traits related to leadership — essential for a leader in professional services to possess — include aspects:

Introduction

- **Adaptability:** The ability to adapt to changing circumstances and be flexible in their approach to problem-solving, including being open to innovative ideas and ways of doing things.

- **Communication**: The ability to communicate with clients, colleagues, and other stakeholders, including listening actively, speaking clearly, and writing persuasively, clearly, and effectively.

- **Emotional intelligence:** The ability to read and respond to the emotions of others, manage their feelings, and maintain positive relationships with clients and colleagues.

- **Positivity:** Leaders are notably optimistic, grounded in the knowledge that their vision is achievable., and convey that 'can do' attitude in all their interactions.

- **Professionalism:** Being ethical in all dealings with clients, colleagues, and other stakeholders, including maintaining strict confidentiality in all professional interactions.

- **Strategic Thinking**: The ability to make decisions that align with the organization's long-term goals, including anticipating and responding to market changes and client needs.

- **Teamwork:** The ability to foster collaboration among team members, including delegating tasks effectively and providing mentoring, support, and guidance to team members.

These aspects weave throughout the discussions of the primary leadership traits. Leadership is vital to creating a culture that allows individuals to find inspiration, allows innovation to happen, and reinforces the importance of integrity.

OUR BACKGROUND AND EXPERIENCE

We have spent most of our careers in the architecture, engineering, and construction (A/E/C) industry. While the idea behind this book came from our experience, we believe the same developmental opportunities apply to any professional service practice — whether an accountant, attorney or specialized certified consultant who provides actionable advisory services. Therefore, the reader should consider A/E/C references as metaphorical, contextual, and not unique to those practicing in the construction industry.

Leadership, marketing, and operational talent typically define a professional service's quality, uniqueness, and scale. However, leadership development issues relate directly to the people across the organization and their view of leadership values. Leadership is not a formula. Leadership is not a to-do list. Leadership is situational, experiential, and motivational.

OUR CONTRIBUTORS

We included anecdotal input from many who have walked the path to leadership. We began our book by surveying over one hundred A/E/C industry leaders. We had the pleasure of receiving input from twenty-three — and speaking in depth with eighteen. They include:

- **Tim Barrick**, FSMPS, Principal/CMO, RATIO, Indianapolis, IN

- **Amanda Bogner**, PE, BEMP, President, Energy Studio, Omaha, NE

- **Linda Crouse**, LEED AP, Principal/Chair of the Board, BAR Architects, San Francisco, CA

- **Michael Davis**, Founder/Chief Executive Officer, DAVIS, Phoenix, AZ

- **Craig Galati**, FAIA, FSMPS, Principal/President, LGA Architecture, Las Vegas, NV

- **Kathleen Held**, CPSM, President/Chief Executive Officer, Cini-Little International, Germantown, MD

Introduction

- **Christine Hill**, President, AOI, Omaha, NE
- **Craig Janssen**, LEED AP BD+C, President, Idibri, a Salas O'Brien Company, Dallas, TX
- **Delcine Johnson**, President, Johnson & Pace, Longview, TX
- **Lance Jones**, PE, President, LSW Engineers Arizona, Phoenix, AZ
- **Rebecca Jones**, Chief Executive Officer, SafeworkCM, Lancaster, CA
- **Grenee Martacho**, Chief Executive Officer, Concord General Contracting, Phoenix, AZ
- **Steve Osborn**, PE, SE, President & Chief Executive Officer, CE Solutions, Fort Wayne, IN
- **Marjanne Pearson**, Founder, Talentstar, Santa Rosa, CA
- **Kevin Power**, PE, President, KPE & EngTech, Omaha, NE
- **Michael Reilly**, FSMPS, President, Reilly Communications, Boston, MA
- **Samantha Sannella**, Senior Managing Director, Cushman & Wakefield, Toronto, ON
- **Dawn Savage**, FSMPS, Senior Director, Business Development, ICF, Sacramento, CA
- **Dena Silver**, retired President, M. Silver & Co., Raleigh, NC
- **Lee Slade**, PE, Managing Principal/Board Chair, Walter P Moore, Houston, TX
- **Nancy Usrey**, FSMPS, CPSM, Associate Vice President/Strategic Pursuit Director, HNTB, Dallas, TX
- **Mark Valenti**, CTS, retired President and Chief Executive Officer, The Sextant Group, Pittsburgh, PA
- **Ron Worth**, CAE, FSMPS, Assoc AIA, retired Chief Executive Officer of IAAO & SMPS Kansas City, MO

Their stories, perspectives, and insights provide wayfinding points along the leadership path and appear throughout the book. Each chapter concludes with a VIEWPOINT section where they share the wisdom and knowledge gained from experience and feature an in-depth discussion of leadership. We have provided brief bios of each in the **ABOUT THE CONTRIBUTORS** chapter at the end of the book.

The Architecture of Vision

FINDING THE LEADER IN YOU

The key to leadership is not in the position but acknowledging when you realize everyone is a leader. Supporting authentic leadership at all levels is essential. People follow when they hear something new that is compelling — a vision. They are more inclined to listen (and contribute) when their leadership role is acknowledged.

The concepts of leadership and vision are universal throughout the professional service industry — every practice, firm, business, team, project, initiative, and personal need. We aim to help you better understand those leadership issues facing professional practices everywhere. We provide background and tools to apply these concepts to your personal development and firm. We want to help you achieve your goal of becoming and succeeding as a visionary leader in your own right.

We've created resources, presentations, and workshops as additional resources for both individual and organizational development. You can find more information at www.architectureofvision.com.

YOUR JOURNEY STARTS HERE

We began our book with the hypothesis that inspiration, innovation, and integrity form the three pillars of leadership and the six significant traits underlying each pillar. The surprise came when we found many common elements in each interview with the leaders we met. You will find that the story tells itself through the voices of these leaders who shared their viewpoints, experiences, and perspectives. We found more alignment with each interview than anticipated, even though their experiences differed widely.

We hope that in this book, you find helpful tools, insights, and inspiration for your leadership journey.

— **Craig Park** & **Barbara Shuck**

July 2023

PART I | INSPIRATION: The First Pillar

Leaders become great, not because of their power, but because of their ability to empower others.
John Maxwell

FOCUS: An inspirational leader motivates and empowers their teams to achieve their goals and fulfill their potential.

INSPIRATION IS THE FIRST PILLAR OF LEADERSHIP in a professional service firm. Many aspiring leaders grapple with a range of challenges that, if left unaddressed, can hamper their growth and effectiveness in leadership roles. One of the primary hurdles they face is understanding and bridging the gap between individual performance and organizational leadership. While personal achievements may have been their earlier benchmark for success, leadership demands the ability to inspire, guide, and leverage the strengths of an entire team. Grasping the nuances of group dynamics, managing conflicts, and driving collective goals become paramount.

Many emergent leaders underestimate the importance of self-awareness, empathy, and effective communication. Building strong interpersonal relationships, understanding the needs and motivations of their team, and adjusting their leadership style accordingly are crucial for success. Learning more about inspirational leadership traits equips aspiring leaders with the tools and insights to navigate these challenges. They can transition from individual contributors to impactful leaders by focusing on these core competencies, fostering personal and organizational growth.

HOW INSPIRATIONAL LEADERSHIP MANIFESTS

Inspired leaders motivate and energize the team, foster creativity and innovation, attract top talent, and help to retain employees. As a leader, it is crucial to cultivate an environment conducive to inspiration for the benefit of the team and the practice.

Inspirational leaders have a clear vision and mission, and they communicate it effectively to their team, inspiring them to work toward a common purpose. They lead by example, demonstrating integrity, passion, and commitment to their cause, and they foster a positive and supportive work environment. They encourage creativity, innovation, and collaboration and recognize and celebrate their team. Inspirational leaders create a sense of purpose and meaning for their team, helping them develop their skills and abilities and achieve their personal and professional aspirations.

Inspiration is where we internalize the why of leadership and apply it to our entrepreneurial or organizational mission, vision, goals, objectives, and strategies that motivate us to grow and empower our teams. Inspiration is vital to leadership in a professional service firm for several reasons.

- **Inspiration motivates and energizes teams.** People are more motivated and enthusiastic about their work when they are inspired. As a leader, it is vital to inspire your team so they bring their best efforts to the table every day.

- **Inspiration fosters creativity and innovation.** Inspiration sparks innovative ideas and approaches, leading to the creation and development of new markets or services.

- **Inspiration attracts top talent.** Organizations attract good people if they feel inspired and make a meaningful impact. The practice attracts top talent by cultivating an environment conducive to inspiration.

- **Inspiration helps to retain employees.** People who feel inspired by their leaders and work are likely to stay with the organization. Retention is critical in a professional service firm where keeping top talent is crucial to success.

INSPIRE TO LEAD

Inspirational leadership is an essential element for success in any professional service firm. Inspiring leaders help motivate and encourage employees to perform to the best of their abilities and achieve their goals. Inspirational leaders emphasize the importance of compassion, wisdom, and mindfulness in their leadership style.

Compassion is understanding and empathizing with others' suffering, which is crucial for creating a supportive and caring work environment. Wisdom involves making sound, ethical decisions that benefit the organization and its stakeholders. Mindfulness is being present and aware of one's thoughts, emotions, and actions, which is essential for effective decision-making and communication.

An inspirational leader in a professional service firm embodies these qualities and demonstrates them through their words and actions. They are empathetic and compassionate toward their employees, clients, and stakeholders and actively seek to understand their needs and concerns. They also have the wisdom to make sound decisions that benefit the organization while staying true to its values and mission.

Furthermore, an inspirational leader cultivates mindfulness and self-awareness. They are aware of their biases and limitations and actively work to overcome them. They are also mindful of their employees' strengths and weaknesses and provide the necessary support and guidance to help them achieve their full potential.

Another aspect of inspirational leadership in a professional service firm is the concept of interdependence. A leader who recognizes the interconnectedness between their vision, actions, and values — and those of the firm they lead — works toward creating a harmonious and collaborative work environment where everyone feels valued and respected.

INSPIRATIONAL IMPACT

Influential leaders inspire their followers by establishing a vision separate from themselves that people believe. A leader who insists on their way — without providing context or insight — appears self-serving and may struggle to motivate their team. To be successful, leaders must reconcile their vision with a group vision that all share. Authentic and inspirational leaders focus on achieving shared success rather than serving their interests.

Effective leadership is crucial for the success of an organization. Leaders who inspire their team to achieve greatness and share a vision for the future are essential. A dictatorial leader — even one who may see themselves as "benevolent" — who makes decisions without considering the input of others can negatively impact the organization's growth. Inspirational leaders encourage their teams to understand the market they serve, learn their clients' vocabulary, and command higher fees. The balance between technical knowledge, strategy, and interpersonal skills is vital for effective leadership. A leader's vision should expand the operational model to create success.

DEVELOPING INSPIRING LEADERS

As we delve into some inspirational leadership traits in the following chapters, we must remember that these are only some of the aspects necessary to develop. The well-rounded leader looks for opportunities to expand other positive traits during their career, including:

- **Communication:** Communicating their vision and ideas effectively to their team and stakeholders.

Inspiration

- **Flexibility:** Adapting to changing conditions and in their approach to problem-solving.
- **Accountability:** Taking responsibility for their decisions and actions and holding their team accountable for their performance.
- **Continuous Learning:** Continuous learning and developing their skills to stay relevant and practical.

Developing all these traits helps an inspiring leader create a positive and productive work environment for their team to achieve success.

We identified six traits of inspirational leaders — **Vision, Introspection, Empathy, Generosity, Patience,** and **Wisdom** — that we explore in the following chapters. Each trait's aspects and related behaviors build on an individual's strengths and contribute to personal growth.

The Architecture of Vision

SYNTHESIS

Inspirational leadership, innovation, and integrity are closely interrelated in building an enduring professional service practice. Effective, inspirational leadership creates a positive work culture that encourages innovation and fosters employee integrity.

Innovation is crucial, as it constantly evolves, and businesses must adapt to remain competitive. Inspirational leaders who foster a culture of innovation by encouraging their employees to think creatively, take risks, and experiment with innovative ideas are likely to drive success.

Inspirational leaders who lead with integrity set the tone for ethical behavior within the organization. They communicate the importance of ethical conduct and hold themselves and their employees accountable for upholding these values. A culture of integrity promotes trust among clients, employees, and stakeholders, which is essential for building and maintaining a solid reputation in the business.

Inspirational leaders who prioritize innovation and integrity create an environment where employees feel empowered to develop new and creative solutions while staying true to the organization's values and principles. They encourage employees to take calculated risks, learn from their failures, and continuously improve their work.

The three pillars of leadership that span inspiration, innovation, and integrity are critical for success. Inspirational leaders who cultivate a culture of innovation and integrity create environments that foster creativity, promote ethical behavior, and build trust among stakeholders. Inspiration leads to competitive advantage and long-term success for the organization.

Inspiration

SYNOPSIS

Inspirational leadership is vital for success in professional service firms, as it fosters motivation, creativity, and innovation within teams. Inspirational leaders with a clear vision and mission empower their employees by cultivating a positive and supportive work environment that encourages personal and professional growth.

By developing essential traits such as vision, introspection, empathy, generosity, patience, and wisdom, leaders can inspire their teams to achieve greatness and contribute to the organization's long-term success.

By embodying compassion, wisdom, mindfulness, and interdependence, leaders can inspire and motivate their employees, guiding the organization toward success while staying true to its vision, mission, and values.

Inspirational leaders prioritize goal-setting, strategic planning, team-building, mentoring, and continuous learning. They also ensure efficient resource allocation and risk management and are quick to pivot when required. Beyond the tangible outcomes of increased profitability and business growth, effective leaders foster trust, high morale, and a culture of continuous improvement and leave a lasting legacy.

The following chapters delve deep into the essence of inspirational leadership, breaking down its complexities into six important traits. By understanding these elements, you can embark on a journey of growth from being an individual contributor to a transformative leader.

Chapter 1 | VISION: Meditation on Leadership

You have been assigned this mountain so that you can show others it can be moved.
Mel Robbins

FOCUS: Pointing the way, leaders look beyond what the team members see and guide them toward individual and collective success.

Vision is an essential trait of the inspirational leader because having a vision provides a clear direction and purpose for the leader and theirs. The essence of leadership is vision. Vision guides, provides direction, and infuses a sense of purpose.

However, the challenge many emerging leaders face is defining this vision and ensuring it resonates with their team. A well-articulated vision not only inspires but also aligns actions with the organization's mission. Leaders without a clear vision may often find themselves struggling to engage their teams effectively.

If you expect employees to show up to work each day and be productive, they must see and understand the vision. As a leader, I need the vision to focus on to keep sight of the bigger picture.
— **Grenee Martacho**, CEO, Concord GC

Once a vision is established, translating it into reality becomes the next hurdle. Effective leadership doesn't just revolve around dreaming; it

The Architecture of Vision

also encompasses the practical steps required to bring that dream to fruition. Navigating between the vast realm of possibilities and the limitations of practicality is often challenging. Tools and models can offer the necessary frameworks, but leaders must strike a balance between innovation and feasibility. They need to foster an environment of unrestricted brainstorming, ensuring a free flow of ideas without judgments, which might limit creativity.

One of the underutilized resources for many emerging leaders is the wisdom of those who have come before them. Whether it's competitors, clients, or past leaders, there's a wealth of knowledge available that can shape and refine a leader's vision.

The challenge, however, is discerning which elements of that knowledge to incorporate and which to adapt or set aside. Each leadership journey is unique, and while learning from others is invaluable, it's equally crucial to ensure that the adopted strategies and visions resonate with the current team and organizational ethos.

Notable Singaporean politician, Jessica Tan, said, *"As a leader, you need to set the right direction, make sure that we're getting the right answer and not having people all doing something that's wrong."*

Understanding that while visions might pre-exist, every leader has the responsibility and privilege to enhance, adapt, or even completely reshape them for the organization's betterment.

WHY VISION IS CRITICAL

Vision is more than thinking about or planning the future with imagination and wisdom. A well-crafted vision inspires and motivates people to work toward a common goal, align their actions and decisions with the organization's mission, and foster a shared purpose. A visionary leader creates a compelling picture of the future, promotes innovation, and inspires others to join in creating it.

Noted business author and consultant Warren Bennis said, *"Leadership is the capacity to translate vision into reality."*

A clear and inspiring vision helps leaders overcome challenges, focus on what is essential, and confidently make tough decisions. It also provides a framework for setting goals and measuring progress. When leaders articulate their vision to resonate with their followers, it fosters a sense of trust, empowerment, and engagement, leading to higher productivity, creativity, and innovation.

Vision is critical to inspirational leadership development because it provides the roadmap for success and creates a shared understanding of what the organization strives to achieve.

PLANNING FOR THE FUTURE

As one of the critical traits of leadership development, a leader must have a perspective conducted in the face of market realities. Start with the idea of what is possible — the known market for the practice — at a macro-level, then move forward to implementing ideas at the intermediate stage, and finally, realize the method by delivering on the vision in the micro context of the needs of clients and potential clients. It takes a unique combination of unlimited "what could be possible" thinking with more pragmatic limiting "what is practical" thinking.

Various analytical models like SWOT, STEP, STEER, and EPISTEL provide supporting frameworks for establishing the world of possibilities. In Chapter 9 – **AGILITY**, we explore how using the inspirational Appreciative Inquiry SOAR model,[3] an inclusive and positive approach that focuses on Strengths, Opportunities, Aspirations, and Results can develop objectives, strategies, and tactics for engaging the entire organization in achieving desired goals.

---

[3] Web reference: https://en.wikipedia.org/wiki/Appreciative_inquiry

The Architecture of Vision

Engaging regularly in a freewheeling, no-holds-barred, no-wrong-answers brainstorming "idea factory" meeting is a great way to develop a vision. Set out a strategic premise and let creativity loose. Without exception, there will be some good, some bad, and some "what if we could..." ideas. It is important to avoid setting implicit or implied limits and not raising judgments or doubts about anyone's suggestion. Inspiration and innovation often come from the least likely idea.

LEARNING FROM OTHERS

Looking outside the standard sphere of influence is also crucial. Checking out the competition and even clients and their competitors provides valuable insight. Benefits and value drive a vision that resonates.

Visionary leadership is essential in any firm, regardless of its size. The absence of vision is disastrous, leading to slow and random decision-making, lost and uninspired employees, and lackluster performance. Employees need to know where they are going and how they contribute, making it crucial to have a leader who communicates big ideas and points in the direction forward. In professional services, a leader must deliver great work consistently and efficiently, always with an eye on the client's needs. For the solopreneur, the client is the leader who drives the direction.

Remember that nothing is inevitable in the face of uncertainty and cataclysmic events like the pandemic. Looking at the possibilities and having a broad perspective is crucial in a global economy. A good leader must have the ability to look more broadly and lead their staff, even if they are only working within a small region or community.

LEARNING FROM LEADERS

The leaders we have most admired bring a sense of vision, thus the primary reference to Vision in the title of this book. These leaders had an idea. Whether they started or entered the organization, they were "all in" when they took the leadership role. We agree with Kenneth Blanchard's situational leadership model, which posits that you come into a position like a CMO and not be the CEO but still bring an inspiring innovation component to your job, which gets the people to follow because they see the value of observing.

Whether someone creates the business or is new to the company, there are times when an organizational vision already exists. An example would be each new annual president in a professional association, like the Society for Marketing Professional Services (SMPS). A company or organization may have started with someone else's vision. A new leader may come in later in the company's evolution. Each leader's primary role is to create, continue, or expand the vision for the better.

A leader may look at that vision again, determine if it is correct, and then take it forward. It can be something other than their vision. That vision often exists outside the role. A leader must keep it going. There is always an expansive component to vision.

LEARNING FROM ENTREPRENEURS

Three is often the number associated with an entrepreneurial vision. There are many stories of three entrepreneurs who kickstarted the idea and built an organization around them. You look at the three who started Apple: Steve Jobs, Steve Wozniak, and Robert Wayne. There are many similar examples in architecture, so we have many three-letter acronyms named firms. Often, they were friends in school or an early job, and each brought a different aspect to the leadership role.

There are many examples of a designer (the creative), an operations expert (getting things done), and a marketer (the storyteller). The one thing they have in common is enthusiasm for a vision, an idea, and the framework for the company. The idea is that each practice *"Think Different,"* as Steve Jobs said. A great leader brings excitement to the room, inspiring the followers to move that vision forward.

The Architecture of Vision

It is that visionary trait and others that we look for in this book. We explore how you learn and apply those to your own development. Great talents often find themselves in a position where they become leaders. Continual learning is an organic part of that process.

DEFINING THE PATH

Vision plays a vital role in inspirational leadership development because it provides a sense of direction and purpose for both the leader and the followers. A clear and inspiring vision helps the leader to rally and engage others around a shared goal, making it easier to achieve success together. A concept that resonates with the values and aspirations of the followers inspires them to work harder and make sacrifices to achieve it. A leader lacking a clear picture may struggle to rally others and find leading and making decisions effectively challenging.

A company's leadership plays a significant role in the success or failure of the organization. Decision-making, employee perceptions, and the company's place in the market are all affected by leadership. Good leadership drives success, but if it is lacking, there is a higher risk of failure.

> *Leaders must see the entire scene to move forward, including truth, politics, debate, understanding, and selflessness.*
>
> — **Michael Davis**, CEO, DAVIS

The 2020-21 pandemic showed that nothing is certain in an interconnected global economy. Every business leader learned that the interrelationship between organizations, companies, and markets is essential and that markets do not like uncertainty.

TAKING A GLOBAL PERSPECTIVE

The global interrelationship between organizations and companies is a critical factor that impacts success and growth. The success or failure of a company is often a result of a complex interplay between several factors, including leadership, strategy, operations, and marketplace position. Leaders that understand this interplay work toward finding the right balance for their unique circumstances.

While large organizations are more cognizant of their place on the world stage, leaders of small- to mid-sized firms also understand that the interconnections that drive economic demand for their services is a crucial component of a business's success. A lack of awareness can create a considerable gap, leading to rethinking decisions and taking corrective measures to avoid systemic failure.

VISIONARY IMPACT

Vision involves seeing things as they are without personal biases, prejudices, or preconceptions. Having a vision helps leaders gain a deeper understanding of their motivations. Vision enables a better understanding of the motivations of others and the ability to see the interconnectedness of all things. This kind of transparent and holistic perspective is essential for effective leadership. It enables leaders to make decisions based on a well-rounded and impartial view of the situation rather than by narrow or self-serving interests.

A vision based on intentionality — framing the mission's future state in contemporary terms — focuses on developing a clear and positive motivation for one's actions. In the context of leadership, this might involve having a clear and inspiring vision for the future and a strong desire to serve the greater good. A leader with the right intention acts with integrity and authenticity, putting the needs of others before their own and working toward a common goal that benefits all.

The Architecture of Vision

SYNTHESIS

Like inspiration, vision is a crucial element of leadership in the context of innovation and integrity. Inspirational leaders must have a clear and compelling vision of where they want the firm to go and how it will differentiate itself from competitors. The vision must align with the firm's values and principles and be communicated effectively to all stakeholders.

Innovation is essential in today's rapidly changing business landscape, and inspirational leaders must encourage a culture of innovation within the firm by creating an environment where employees feel empowered to produce innovative ideas and take risks. A leader with a strong vision inspires and motivates employees to push beyond their comfort zones and embrace innovative ideas and approaches.

Integrity is also critical to successful leadership. Leaders must demonstrate a commitment to ethical behavior and uphold the firm's values in all their actions. Integrity means making tough decisions with the firm's long-term interests in mind, even if it means sacrificing short-term gains. An inspirational leader with a clear vision creates a culture of integrity within the firm, where employees understand the importance of ethical behavior and are willing to hold themselves and their colleagues accountable.

In the context of innovation and integrity, vision is a critical element of inspirational leadership in a professional service firm. A leader with a clear and compelling vision inspires and motivates employees to embrace innovation while maintaining ethical behavior and upholding the firm's values.

VIEWPOINT – **AMANDA BOGNER,** PE, BEMP
President, Energy Studio

Leadership does not have to be loud and boisterous; it is quiet and contemplative.
— Amanda Bogner

The Heart of Leadership: Vision, Values, and Strategy

Leadership ensures that all the pieces and parts work together in unison and at maximum potential. From a leading people standpoint, it is uncovering their strengths, ensuring they have the highest potential to explore and build those strengths. It ensures that their roles, jobs, and opportunities match those strengths. Leading a company is defining the vision and mission and aligning that with core values. Hence, the whole organization moves seamlessly toward that guiding light of what we are trying to achieve.

My role is to set the vision and articulate that vision to our staff. Our leadership team helps determine the strategy to achieve the vision. Everyone on the team has a similar moral compass. We are consistent in the application of our core values. If you have people within the company — whether in leadership roles or not — that differ significantly or do not identify with those core values, it just does not work.

Empowering Teams

Regarding inspiration, my role is to help inspire project teams in our work to achieve more. We created a compelling business case and a compelling service offering. We work with good clients. We have a long-term vision of what we are trying to achieve. That has brought us excellent employees. It has brought us amazing clients that continue to engage us on projects. I do not think that when I started Energy Studio in 2011, I recognized inspiration as one of

The Architecture of Vision

our critical foundational elements. But now we know you need it to be a successful company.

No one gives you integrity. Integrity is one of those things where a leader must come with professional and personal integrity. It links back to the concept of moral courage. One of the weaknesses leaders need to overcome is accepting blame for failures. The buck stops with that leader. A leader must work to improve the situation and give credit for corrections and successes. Rarely is one person responsible for remarkable success.

A Leadership Imperative

Another area for improvement is the unwillingness to admit missing skills, knowledge, or abilities. Another is setting realistic expectations, where we want to stretch teams and encourage ideas that improve our companies and organizations but do not promise the moon or deliver on that promise. Overcoming those weaknesses takes much introspection, sitting down, and being honest.

Is it ever the leader that is driving innovation? Specifically, the leader casts a vision that allows the company's members to innovate to achieve that vision.

All our leaders should have integrity. In our firm, we have a similar moral compass. We share core values, and integrity is one of our core values. It means something specific to our line of work. You have it, or you do not.

Leaders must possess all the makings of what an organization needs to succeed. There is not going to be one person that is the silver bullet. So, the weaknesses one must overcome will be as unique as our fingerprints. Self-awareness is important. By being self-aware and knowing your strengths versus liabilities, you build a leadership team that is complementary to each other and fills the gaps.

We use Gallup's Strengths Finder program with our team. We have six people, and of the thirty-four themes in Strengths Finder, we have over twenty covered. They are not all leaders, but knowing we have that diversity is extraordinary. We look at problems in diverse ways and develop solutions differently. We leverage those strengths and are working on what fits together nicely. I have a few strategic forces; some other partners have them in spades. So, we meld their strengths with my maximizer, harmony, and executing strengths and have a well-rounded combination in our leadership team.

Transition and Transparency

I never set up Energy Studio for me to be this figurehead. Even when it was just me, before anyone joined the team, everything I wrote was always "we," as if I had a couple. Now I am thinking about how I will transition the leadership roles over the next ten years so that I step away. I have tried over the last couple of years to give everyone opportunities for ownership of our project work. I empower people to own the communication pathways on projects and be proactive. We coach on the importance of being proactive in communication, knowing our team might offer a different perspective. I want all their voices in the room.

We do quarterly self-assessments, so everyone gets feedback regularly. I have been having one-on-one conversations with everyone every couple of months. That is an opportunity for people to understand business operations. It is a transparent conversation. How do we win work? How does the company function? It is like pulling back the veil so everyone has a better view.

I have had few mentors. I have worked with many senior engineers, but no one was trying to help me cultivate a career. One mentor was more for technical skill type of development. She gave me opportunities to be in rooms that were critical to my success now and allowed me to spread my wings.

The Architecture of Vision

But I have not heard anyone talk to me about what would happen in 10 years, grooming me for this role. I just went and learned by collaborating with people. I struck out alone because I needed better alignment than where I had been.

I learned a lot about project management. I did not know much about business development. I did not know much about all those aspects of running a business. I learned how to do the work. I knew the how.

The Business Learning Curve

Running the business has been a big learning curve. We are not perfect by any means. But I am opening the conversation up to what you want to do in 10 years. What do you think your next 20 years are going to look like? Today, I have a great group of friends who are sounding boards, great advisors, and great cheerleaders when I need them. They are not in our industry. Each person brings something different to the table. They are not mentors, but they are suitable substitutes.

We have all these great ideas for what we want to offer our clients. And we have great clients but only sometimes know how to tell the right story. We are just a group of engineers who just like doing the work. Marketing is a critical component of the leader's vision and the execution of the work. Without the marketing component, nothing happens. You have all these great ideas and need someone to sell them to. You wait for the phone to ring. People must realize that it is continuous and ongoing, something you must always keep doing. Different than projects, marketing always continues.

Vision

PROGRESSION: VISION: Developing Personal Goals

Pointing the way, leaders look beyond what the team members see and guide them toward individual and collective success.

AWARENESS: *Think about these statements on understanding the importance of* **Vision.**

1. Keep a professional journal for notes, impressions, and ideas. Daily entries will provide valuable insight as you create your leadership vision.
2. What is your personal vision?
3. What is your professional vision?
4. Where do you see yourself in one-to-three years?
5. Where do you see yourself in five-to-ten years?

ACCEPTANCE: *Now, reflect on how you reacted when reading these statements. Reflect on what "acceptance" of your truth and what* **Vision** *means to you.*

1. Share your personal and professional vision with a close friend or significant other and listen without judgment.
2. Mark your calendar for one week and review your vision statements. Do they still resonate?
3. Mark your calendar for three months and decide if your personal and professional vision statements remain true. If not, adjust them and repeat this acceptance process until you are satisfied with the work.
4. Review your personal and professional vision statements annually, get insights from those you trust, and revise as you wish.

The Architecture of Vision

ACTION: *Follow these steps to incrementally put that awareness and acceptance into action to strengthen your ability to develop leadership with* **Vision.**

1. Invite someone you admire to coffee or lunch and ask about their personal and professional vision statements. Avoid judging yours against theirs. Do not compare to — learn from.

2. Identify a public figure or leader you admire and read a biography. What surprised you? Find one element that impresses you about that person and keep that thought or word in front of you so you see it regularly on Post-It notes, desktop notes, or the notes app on your phone.

3. Make an appointment on your calendar to reflect on that element monthly in your leadership journal.

4. Read Simon Sinek's **Start with Why: How Great Leaders Inspire Everyone to Take Action**. Sinek's work dives deep into the power of understanding and articulating the 'Why' behind actions, which forms the bedrock of Vision.

Vision

SYNOPSIS

Vision is the hallmark of exemplary leaders. Leadership is the art of guiding, influencing, and directing a group of individuals or an organization towards achieving a shared objective. It is a complex interplay of vision, communication, and strategy that fosters growth, innovation, and goal realization. A 'leader', on the other hand, is an individual who embodies these principles of leadership. They are the driving force, the visionary who is "all in" when they step into their leadership role. Whether originating from a company or joining an existing one, leaders have the responsibility to initiate, sustain, or elevate the organization's vision.

In firms, good leadership is marked by clear direction, innovation, and a robust ethical framework. There's a commitment to transparency, fostering an environment of unrestricted brainstorming, and recognizing and nurturing talent. For individual leaders, a clear and compelling vision is paramount, accompanied by the ability to inspire and motivate. Leaders must also have the ability to adapt to changing circumstances, as showcased during unpredictable events like pandemics. They must be globally-aware, recognizing the interconnectedness of markets and the importance of a broad perspective even in localized settings.

Leaders are known to initiate and uphold a compelling vision that serves as a roadmap for the organization's success. This vision, when communicated effectively, aligns all stakeholders, ensuring collective movement towards the set goals. Leaders foster a culture of innovation and integrity. They embrace and encourage new ideas, balancing them with the firm's long-term interests. Their decisions, even if tough, are anchored in ethical considerations. Visionary leaders achieve higher productivity, increased creativity, and innovation in their firms, and a workforce that feels valued, understood, and motivated.

The Architecture of Vision

REFLECTIONS & INSIGHTS

Chapter 2 | INTROSPECTION: Why You Lead

*Leadership is not just about giving energy.
It is about unleashing other people's power.*
Paul Polman

FOCUS: You lead because there is a need for leadership.

Aspiring leaders face numerous challenges in the dynamic and competitive landscape of modern organizations. In the pursuit of inspiring and motivate teams, they often grapple with the balance between holding onto their authentic self and adapting to the requirements of their role.

Perhaps the most significant challenge is their ability to build genuine trust and relationships, which stems from their self-awareness, emotional intelligence, and the recognition of their values, drivers, and purposes. Blind spots in their awareness can hamper their effectiveness, leading to poor decision-making and strained relationships.

Introspection — looking inward and examining one's thoughts, feelings, and motivations — aids leaders in understanding themselves better. By being aware of their strengths, weaknesses, and biases, leaders can make better decisions, foster innovation, and drive growth in their organizations. Furthermore, introspective leaders will likely be more resilient, open-minded, and receptive to feedback.

They view setbacks not as failures but as opportunities for growth and learning. This mindset benefits them personally and inspires their teams, creating a culture where innovation thrives.

The Architecture of Vision

To actualize the benefits of introspection, leaders must actively make space for reflection in their daily routines. Whether through meditation, journaling, or quiet contemplation, this dedicated time allows them to assess their actions, decisions, and overall direction. Feedback from peers and team members provides invaluable insights, while regularly reassessing personal values and goals ensures alignment with their leadership vision.

By embedding these practices in their lives, leaders evolve into more inspirational, innovative, and integrity-driven figures, adept at navigating leadership challenges and steering their teams toward success.

THE POWER OF SELF REFLECTION

Leaders who spend time thinking about their values, drivers, and purposes have better emotional intelligence skills to understand others, which is critical in building trust and relationships. Leadership is not just a title but a responsibility and process that requires emotional intelligence skills to inspire and motivate teams.

Blind spots, where leaders are unaware of weaknesses, should be a component of leadership introspection to build awareness. Good leaders recognize their personal "why" and how they want to be influential leaders. They do not punish mistakes but instead create a dynamic environment that allows employees to experiment, fail, learn, and grow. Leaders use their lessons learned as case studies to inspire and motivate their team members.

Introspection requires individuals to invest effort in clearing space, opening up, and examining themselves without judgment. Introspective leaders accept things as they are and approach failure with a growth mindset, asking themselves what they learn from the situation and whether they are willing to obtain outcomes that differ from their expectations. Taking a step back and reflecting on conditions helps detach from specific outcomes. Leaders avoid pushing too hard and instead allow results to reveal themselves.

For influential leaders, reflection helps to allow ourselves white space or margin. Time and attention away from the situation allow new thoughts and perspectives to rise. Life's riches happen in the margins — when one does not focus only on outcomes, problems, having our way, and exerting our power.

Introspection is powerful before, during, and after leadership moments. What did I learn? How does this make me a better person? Do I need to go back and apologize? Did I need to go back and relearn something? How did this lesson serve me well — or not? Introspection gives the space to say, "Yeah, that was not my best work, but it is okay. I learned something."

INSIGHTS FOR INSPIRATION

Introspective leadership traits are crucial in fostering inspiration in a professional service organization. Here are some ways in which reflective leadership supports the development of innovation:

- **Self-Awareness:** Introspective leaders have a deep understanding of their strengths and weaknesses, allowing them to make better decisions and allocate resources more effectively, identify opportunities and challenges, and determine which ideas are worth pursuing.

- **Open-Mindedness:** Introspective leaders are likely to be open-minded and receptive to innovative ideas and perspectives, which is essential for innovation, requiring individuals to challenge conventional wisdom and think creatively. Introspective leaders are likely to be comfortable with ambiguity and uncertainty inherent in the innovation process.

- **Willingness to Learn:** Introspective leaders are committed to learning and personal growth, which helps them stay on the forefront of their industry and identify new opportunities for innovation. They are also likely to seek feedback from others and use it to improve their performance.

- **Resilience:** Innovation is often challenging and uncertain, requiring individuals to be resilient despite setbacks and failures. Introspective leaders are likelier to have a growth mindset and see setbacks as opportunities to learn and improve. Resilience helps them stay motivated and persistent in the face of obstacles.

By cultivating these traits, leaders encourage their teams to take risks, experiment with innovative ideas, and drive growth and success for the organization.

MAKING SPACE FOR REFLECTION

Introspection is a continuous process. The real work starts with assuming a leadership role. Taking a moment to reflect and accept things without judgment allows us to look at failures as learning opportunities, which is part of business insight and wisdom. Reflecting on successes, failures, and experiences helps us realign our vision and become better human beings.

Allowing ourselves the mental/internal whitespace and margin to reflect on our careers and lives helps us identify significant opportunities and realign our goals. The next step after reflection is assessment, which involves identifying what we learned and how it makes us better individuals. By doing this without judgment, we learn from our mistakes and become better leaders.

Introspection is a crucial component of leadership development. As leaders, we must learn from our mistakes and take time to reflect and learn from them. Unfortunately, some leaders may be unforgiving and make it difficult for us to learn from our mistakes. However, it is essential to give ourselves some space and time to learn from our mistakes to avoid repeating them in the future. By acknowledging and learning from our mistakes, we demonstrate leadership to our team.

TAKING TIME FOR REFLECTION

The importance of reflection and introspection as a daily practice helps leaders stay centered and focused. Several steps aspiring leaders take to leverage introspection in their daily work include:

- **Schedule Regular Reflective Time:** Set aside specific times during the day or week to reflect on your thoughts, feelings, and actions through journaling, meditation, or quiet contemplation.

- **Seek Feedback:** Ask your colleagues, team members, and clients for feedback. Use their feedback to reflect on your strengths and areas for improvement.

- **Practice Active Listening:** Fully engaging in conversations and seeking to understand others' perspectives helps you gain insights into their needs and motivations and inform your actions and decisions.

- **Analyze Your Decision-Making Process:** Analyzing and considering the factors influencing choices helps to understand biases and how they may impact decisions.

- **Regularly Assess Your Values and Goals:** Consider how they align with a leader's role and use this knowledge to guide decision-making and actions.

- **Learn From Mistakes:** Reflect on past mistakes and learn from them, which helps growth and avoids repeating the same mistakes in the future.

The Architecture of Vision

By leveraging introspection, aspiring leaders develop greater self-awareness and make thoughtful decisions that align with their values and goals, helping them inspire their teams toward more success.

SYNTHESIS

Inspirational leaders who practice introspection consistently evaluate actions, decisions, and behaviors to identify areas for improvement and learn from their mistakes. This reflective practice helps them to stay true to their values and maintain integrity in all aspects of their work.

When it comes to innovation, an inspirational leader who practices introspection drives innovation. By examining their thought processes and biases, the leader identifies opportunities for innovation and makes decisions that lead to new and creative solutions. This type of introspection encourages experimentation, risk-taking, and learning from failure, all critical components of innovation.

An inspirational leader who prioritizes integrity in their work is likely to make ethical decisions, act in their client's best interest, and maintain their team's trust.

When leaders practice introspection, they recognize when they act in ways that compromise their integrity and take corrective action. By practicing reflection, leaders maintain their integrity, drive innovation, and inspire their teams to achieve their full potential.

The Architecture of Vision

VIEWPOINT – **CHRISTINE HILL**
President, AOI

There is a delicate balance between management and leadership. Sometimes, one must work harder to stay on the leadership side of the equation.

— Christine Hill

The Role of Leadership in Uncertain Times

Leadership is about inspiring and motivating others to accomplish goals. 2020 was a pivotal year from a leadership perspective. I have been through plenty of challenging times. I have been through plenty of challenges. I never had to figure out what we would do when every one of our client campuses closed. How are we going to take care of our employees? Are they going to have jobs? Are we going to have a company after this? I have never had to do that before.

2020 was all about digging deep and finding the inspiration to say, "It is going to be okay. Here is what we are going to do." Finding the mission, defining it, motivating the team, and getting them to believe in my plan. It was about ensuring the group knew what to do and their mission and solidifying a team of leaders, so we were all in step. 2021 is about hope. It is about stability.

Integrity, Substance, and Strategy

We know we had done it before because we were adaptable. We look for opportunities and get there first. Leadership is about inspiration, and leadership is about motivation, but also, leadership is about substance. You must be credible. I share information that substantiates what I am saying. I use data, facts, and truth to pick a path and develop a strategy. So that is where I am right now. We have a direction. We have an approach. And there is a lot of enthusiasm.

Integrity is at the top of the list because integrity is all about trust. And you build on trust. We use a phrase around the office: "We're going to do the right thing, even if it costs us money." It does not matter whether it is safety or being honest with a client. You must be transparent. You must be open. I have never regretted going back and making something right. I have regretted not going back and making some right. Integrity is about setting an example for everybody else. It is an investment in your reputation.

Creating Safe Spaces for Ideas

I love innovation. I am at an age where I enjoy watching younger generations have ideas and get to run with them. When you get to say, "That's a great idea. Let us do it!" It excites people when they take ownership and become heroes. The idea of saying "Yes" inspires me! I look for opportunities to say yes. I use the phrase, "We're in no bad ideas mode. We are absolute, even if they are bad ideas would appear because we're in no bad ideas mode." Integrity and innovation come from a safe environment. If someone feels it is safe to be innovative, it is safe to say something crazy. That might work. It is safe to produce an idea that nobody has done before. It is safe to question authority. It is safe to say, "Hey, I'm struggling with this."

Integrity, innovation, and inspiration all work together. As leaders, we celebrate and embrace their innovative ideas. We use them to inspire younger generations, which translates to organizational stability.

One of the most significant areas for improvement is that leaders need to have the stamina and the focus to see strategies to completion. We all tend to feel that is as far as we go, so I must start something new. We are off to the next thing but have yet to finish the first.

People often tell leaders what they think they want to hear. Either because they do not believe we are going to listen, or we are not listening, or it is just too hard. Somebody once told me that when you become the boss your jokes are funnier. Leaders must find ways to create meaningful, honest employee engagement and not demotivate.

One of my favorite things is to create opportunities for others to lead. We use our AOI Gives program to support those people who, by their actions, show us they have leadership potential. We assembled a team from each business unit that forms our annual AOI Gives committee. Their job is to pick something out in our community that we come together around through fundraising efforts. I encourage them from behind the scenes, but they self-organize and determine the goal, set the program, and make it happen. And, each year, they knock it out of the park. It lets us say, "I want you to lead this." And then coaching from behind and encouraging from back is something we do.

Building the Next Generation of Business Leaders

Mentors say things you do not even want to admit to yourself. A good mentor will let you be your whole self and completely open and authentic about your thoughts and struggles. They are good mirrors that are incredibly encouraging, validating, and truthful. I have had mentors open doors for me. Women need both male and female mentors. It is critical to have both. I have always had people I have looked to and reached out to listen to, especially when they get stuck.

Regarding our brand, I see myself as a company representative with a unique ability that could strengthen the AOI brand and draw not only partnerships and opportunities but also workforce candidates. Putting a name or a face to a brand makes it more personal.

Marketing is both external and internal. We are constantly marketing to our employees through internal communications, things like core values, what we have accomplished, and, more importantly than what we did, that we did this together. Each group highlights things of which they are particularly proud. We share our success with our clients. We use third-party surveys to learn about how we are perceived. Marketing is critical, whether it is a client-focused communications strategy or an employee engagement strategy.

PROGRESSION – **INTROSPECTION**: Filling a Void

You lead because there is a need for leadership.

AWARENESS: *Think about these statements on the importance of* **Introspection.**

1. Why do you want to be a leader?
2. Ask a close friend or colleague in a leadership position what motivated them to become leaders. Reflect on their thoughts through your journal entries.
3. What is your biggest fear?
4. What are the negative aspects of being a leader that you want to address or avoid?

ACCEPTANCE: *Now, reflect on how you reacted when reading these statements. Reflect on what "acceptance" of your truth about what* **Introspection** *means to you.*

1. Use your journal to reflect on a situation when you did not get the desired results. How did it make you feel? Did you take any action to avoid the same problem?
2. What are three mistakes, and how did you deal with the outcome?
3. What are some actions that help you face your fears?

ACTION: *Follow these steps to incrementally put that awareness and acceptance into action to strengthen your ability to develop leadership with* **Introspection.**

1. Consider your current position in your career and identify at least three leadership opportunities you investigate to apply for or volunteer for in the next six months, including

a promotion at work or an organization that interests you personally or professionally.

2. After you have checked out the opportunities, prioritize them and identify the next step you take in your leadership journey.

3. Make an appointment, apply for the position, and confidently follow through.

4. Read the Arbinger Institute's **Leadership and Self-Deception.** This book discusses how our own self-deceptions can hinder leadership and provides insight into self-awareness.

The Architecture of Vision

SYNOPSIS

Effective leadership in firms is visible through a culture of innovation, resilience, and open-mindedness. Such organizations foster a learning environment where mistakes are seen as growth opportunities and employees are encouraged to challenge conventions.

Good leaders are self-aware, understanding both their strengths and weaknesses. They are receptive to feedback, open to diverse ideas, and maintain a growth mindset. They value introspection, which helps them remain grounded in their values and maintain integrity.

Leaders actively seek feedback to improve and grow. They make decisions that balance both short-term results and long-term vision. Their actions drive innovation, foster team collaboration, and inspire trust. The results of their leadership include improved team morale, increased organizational productivity, and a culture where continuous learning and innovation thrive. To become truly effective, leaders must develop several competencies:

- **Self-Awareness:** Recognizing personal strengths, weaknesses, biases, and drivers.
- **Emotional Intelligence:** Understanding and managing personal emotions while recognizing and influencing the emotions of others.
- **Open-Mindedness**: Being receptive to diverse perspectives and new information.
- **Resilience:** Possessing the ability to bounce back from setbacks and viewing challenges as opportunities.
- **Reflective Practice:** Regularly engaging in introspection to align actions with values and to learn from experiences.

Leadership is not just about holding a position of authority; it's about introspection, growth, and influencing others positively.

Introspection

REFLECTIONS & INSIGHTS

Chapter 3 | EMPATHY: Will They Follow?

A brave leader is someone who says I see you. I hear you. I don't have all the answers, but I'm going to keep listening and asking questions.
Brene Brown

FOCUS: You lead at anything you do with anyone you do it with.

ASPIRING LEADERS OFTEN GRAPPLE with the balance between achieving business goals and maintaining humane touchpoints. Empathetic leadership, especially in professional service firms, can transform organizational culture and innovation.

Empathetic leaders inspire by cultivating an environment where creativity, risk-taking, and experimentation are valued. Such leaders encourage diverse perspectives, ensuring psychological safety for all team members, provide resources for innovation, and more importantly, understand the essence of learning from failure rather than penalizing it.

Empathy allows me to understand the needs of others. It opens the mind to understand the root cause behind actions or performance and enables me to help them improve.
— **Kathleen Held,** CPSM, President & CEO, Cine-Little

Personal growth is pivotal for a leader. One primary challenge faced by many leaders is developing true empathy, which goes beyond mere sympathy. Empathetic leadership requires an intricate blend of self-awareness, kindness, effective communication, honesty, mindfulness, and a razor-sharp focus on the needs of employees and clients alike.

Moreover, a journey towards client empathy is instrumental in enhancing the client experience. This involves steps like qualitative research, diverse client recruitment, and the use of empathy maps, ensuring that leaders address client emotions, needs, and motivations holistically.

At its core, leadership is about people. Aspiring leaders need to understand that empathy is not just beneficial but vital for maintaining robust client relationships and fostering a positive work culture. Being an empathetic leader means actively listening, valuing diversity, being adaptive to individual needs, and promoting collaboration among team members. Such a leadership style enhances trust and productivity and catalyzes creativity and innovative problem-solving.

EMBARKING ON THE EMPATHY JOURNEY

In essence, the journey of empathetic leadership is continuous, demanding self-reflection, introspection, and genuine understanding. But the rewards are unparalleled regarding trust, innovation, and organizational success.

An empathetic leader in a professional service firm provides inspiration by creating an environment that encourages and rewards creativity, risk-taking, and experimentation. Here are some ways that an empathetic leader does this:

- **Encourage Diverse Perspectives:** Recognize the value of diverse perspectives and encourage team members to share their ideas, opinions, and experiences, leading to new insights and innovative solutions.

- **Foster a Culture of Psychological Safety:** Create a space where team members feel comfortable sharing their ideas and taking risks without fear of retribution, leading to more experimentation and innovation.

- **Resources and Support:** Give team members funding, time, and access to the expertise they need to pursue innovative ideas.

- **Recognize and Reward Innovation:** Celebrate innovative ideas and efforts, even if they do not always succeed, fostering a culture of innovation and encouraging team members to pursue innovative ideas.

- **Embrace Failure:** Failure is often a necessary part of the innovation process and encourages team members to learn from mistakes and use them as opportunities for growth and improvement.

By implementing these strategies, an empathetic leader creates an environment that fosters inspiration and encourages team members to pursue new and creative ideas.

Leading with empathy is the key to gaining dedicated followers. A caring relationship with those who follow you creates trust and a platform for high performance.

— **Tim Barrick**, FSMPS, Principal/CMO, RATIO

Meditation and introspection help leaders clear their minds of ideas and allow thoughts to rise, making them more open to change, inspiring ideation, and unusual ways of seeing. It is a continual process, and self-reflection is a vital part of self-development, allowing leaders to look at failures as learning opportunities and realign their vision.

Assessment without judgment is also essential, allowing leaders to learn from their mistakes and become better individuals. Empathy and self-reflection help leaders become better human beings and build great relationships.

DEVELOPING EMPATHY

There are several steps to self-awareness and personal development that apply to developing empathetic leadership:

- **Awareness:** Develop a deep awareness of employees' needs and challenges, which requires an understanding of the human experience and the ability to see things from the perspective of others.
- **Kindness:** Be compassionate and understanding toward employees and show genuine care about employees' well-being.
- **Communication:** Speak in a way that is respectful, kind, and compassionate, avoiding language that is harsh, critical, or judgmental.
- **Honesty:** Demonstrate actions consistent with values and beliefs, supporting employees' needs.
- **Mindfulness:** Be present and fully engaged in interactions with everyone in the organization.
- **Focus:** Center attention on employees and their needs, tuning out distractions and staying intentional in interactions.

MAPPING THE EMPATHY JOURNEY

The path to empathy and compassion takes increasing understanding, awareness, and effort.

Empathy

In professional service practices, leaders and developing leaders understand the importance of empathy rather than sympathy when addressing clients' needs. Empathy allows leaders to fully comprehend clients' emotions, needs, and motivations, enabling them to provide tailored solutions that enhance clients' experiences and empower them. Steps to take in practicing client empathy include:

- **Conduct Qualitative Research** to understand clients' behaviors, motivations, and concerns.
- **Recruit Diverse Clients** To Ensure Accessibility And Inclusivity In Addressing Their Needs.
- **Encourage Team Members and Stakeholders** to observe research sessions and interact with clients.
- **Use Videos of Clients** when presenting research findings to stakeholders for greater impact and understanding.
- **Create Empathy Maps** to capture users' emotions, hopes, and fears, and identify gaps in knowledge.
- **Invest in a Diverse Team** to ensure a broad range of perspectives and experiences.
- **Incorporate empathy** into design guidelines and establish protocols that encourage empathetic practices.

By fostering empathy in their practice, leaders create more meaningful and effective solutions for clients, ultimately improving their experiences and driving the success of the professional service practice.

See Figure 1 – Empathy Map, next page.

The Architecture of Vision

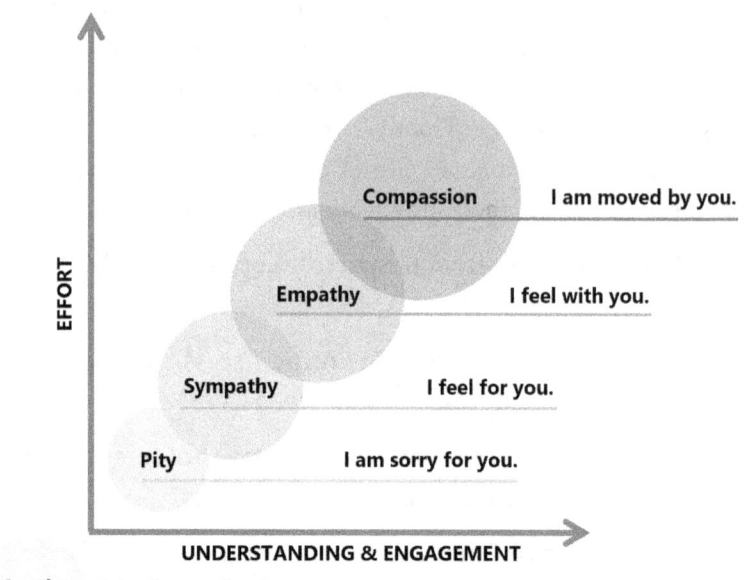

Figure 1 – EMPATHY MAP   Source: Nielsen Norman Group

The size of the circles indicates the ability to positively impact others.

EMPATHY AT WORK

Empathy is crucial for leaders' relationships with clients and their relationships with the professional and administrative staff reporting to them. Practicing empathy in these relationships can lead to a more positive work environment, higher staff satisfaction, and increased team performance. To apply empathy with their staff, leaders should:

- **Listen Actively:** Encourage open communication and listen carefully to staff concerns, needs, and ideas. This helps leaders understand their team members better and address any issues.

- **Be Approachable:** Create a culture where staff members feel comfortable sharing their thoughts and feelings

Empathy

without fear of judgment. This fosters trust and open dialogue.

- **Encourage Diversity:** Value and promote diversity within the team to ensure a range of perspectives and experiences. This can lead to more creative solutions and a deeper understanding of clients' needs.

- **Offer Support:** Be available to provide guidance, resources, and assistance when needed. This demonstrates a genuine interest in the staff's well-being and success.

- **Recognize Achievements:** Acknowledge and celebrate team members' accomplishments to boost morale and motivation.

- **Foster Collaboration:** Encourage teamwork and collaboration among staff members. This improves team dynamics and facilitates knowledge sharing and learning from each other.

- **Be Adaptive:** Understand that each team member has unique needs, strengths, and weaknesses. Tailor your leadership approach accordingly to maximize their potential and help them grow professionally.

By practicing empathy with their staff, leaders can create a supportive and inclusive work environment where everyone feels valued and respected. This, in turn, promotes staff engagement, productivity, and overall success for the professional service practice.

MAKING IMPACTFUL CONNECTIONS

Empathy is an important leadership trait because it allows leaders to understand and connect with their team, which leads to a more positive and productive work environment. Empathetic leaders recognize and respond to the needs and concerns of their team

The Architecture of Vision

members, creating a sense of trust and mutual respect. Employing empathy allows leaders to:

- **Build Trust:** When leaders show empathy toward their team members, it helps to build trust between them. Trust allows team members to feel more comfortable sharing their thoughts and feelings, which leads to better collaboration and communication.

- **Foster Engagement:** Empathetic leaders connect with their team members on a deeper level, increasing engagement and motivation. When team members feel their leader cares about them and their work, they are likely to invest in the organization's success.

- **Improve Decision-Making:** When leaders are empathetic, they consider the perspectives of others and make decisions that are in the team's best interest, leading to better outcomes and more effective decision-making.

- **Enhance Creativity:** When team members feel that their leader is open to their ideas and perspectives, they are likely to be creative and innovative, leading to fresh solutions and approaches that benefit the organization.

Developing empathy creates a more positive and productive work environment, builds trust and engagement, improves decision-making, and enhances creativity.

Empathy

SYNTHESIS

Empathy is an essential trait of inspirational leadership in a professional service firm because it helps leaders connect with their team members on a deeper level.

Where innovation is about creating new and better solutions to meet clients' needs, an inspired leader leverages inspiration and empathy to understand those needs better. Inspiring leaders take the time to listen to clients and team members, understand their pain points and challenges, and use that information to develop innovative solutions that meet their needs.

Integrity is also essential to inspirational leadership, and empathy is critical in fostering a culture of integrity within a professional service firm. When leaders are empathetic, they demonstrate that they value and respect their team members, which helps build trust and strengthen relationships. Trust, in turn, creates a culture of honesty, accountability, and transparency, all essential components of integrity.

The Architecture of Vision

VIEWPOINT – **CRAIG GALATI,** FAIA, FSMPS
President, LGA Architecture

Leadership is developed from within and not copied. Every person has different traits that make them good leaders. Tapping into your strengths and surrounding yourself with those with other powers is authentic leadership.

— Craig Galati

The Evolution of a Leader

I define leadership as service. A leader's job is to serve those following them, putting them in positions where they thrive and work together. It is not about charging up the hill with the flag. It is about helping people to find the best way to go up the mountain.

Today, I am in the transition of leadership. I am mentoring two younger partners to lead. One of them has already been named the next president. So, my role today is to teach them along the way. I sometimes must set a bit more direction than I want to, but I make this an organic effort through dialogue to get to wherever I want to go.

What has worked well for me is that I only let the conversation end once we agree. It is so easy — especially for young leaders — to want to jump at that first thing. I did not have anybody to mentor or coach me. I had to make decisions. And I made a lot of mistakes and had a lot of failures along the way. That is how you learn. If I move them and teach them about keeping the idea alive, we consider multiple viewpoints simultaneously. Once we do that, we make better decisions.

After we transition, I will still be active in business development and marketing and coach the younger leaders as needed. I want to stay within my welcome. It is going to be a delicate balance. Being the new leader is hard when the old one is still there.

Core Tenets of Leadership

Integrity is the easiest one to answer. You must be who you are. You must walk the walk of your talk. You must demonstrate honesty and integrity to everybody to have a leadership position. People will only follow someone who is true to their word. People follow people who are true to themselves and who they say they are. They like to work in (and with) companies aligned with that same personal integrity.

Inspiration is harder for me because teaching people to aspire to something is more important than just being inspired by what you say. You use inspiration to sell, to get people excited about something. The real key as a leader is to help people find something they want — a vision or a role — and then teach them to aspire to that end and not wait for somebody to inspire them to do something. Aspirational thinking is a strong character builder for leaders and organizations.

When I think of innovation, I think about not being afraid to fail trying new stuff. You know it will not all work, but sometimes it will. We have been trying something innovative that grew out of COVID. Not knowing what else to do, it is turning out to be some of the most successful stuff we have done as a company. It is generating excellent brand awareness. And I thought it would fall on its face.

Facing Uncertainty with Innovation

Due to the pandemic, in April 2020, we lost all our projects. We did not have any more projects. They all stopped at once. We needed help figuring out how to get a hold of clients. Or how to talk to clients. Or how to meet clients. We need help finding new leads or figuring out how to prospect. So, we decided very strategically that we would not sell now. So, we created a series of web-broadcast fireside chats. This format allowed us to bond with our clients differently. We were not there to sell to them. We were there to bring out their points of view.

By November, after we had done nine or ten of these fireside chats, the phone started to ring, and work returned. These fireside chat programs were the impetus for us to be able to stay front and center with our clients. When they were ready, they said, *'These are the people who have been with us, who care about what we care about.'* The programs have been getting our brand out there. We have been able to interject who we are through our questions and how we interact with the clients. The coolest thing is collaborating with these people. We unobtrusively bond with them. We do not ask for work or sell ourselves. We do not have to pitch. And they see us as people.

The Intangibles of Effective Leadership

In my own experience, there are two important factors for leaders. First, you must learn how to tame your ego. Use the ego for what it is suitable for to keep yourself confident front and center. Do not take yourself too seriously. The second is communication. You should always strive to communicate effectively. I have heard people talk too much, but communication is different. It is a two-way street. If you want to teach people and see them grow to lead and serve, communication is one of the things they must master.

It is crucial to lead by example. Only ask somebody to do something you would do. That gives you a lot of credibility. Leadership is not thinking you are above anybody else. Be impeccable with your words. Do not talk behind the back of anyone. If you feel the need to say something, say it to them. Too many leaders have been undermined by those who thought they were not faithful to who they were.

Leadership happens at many diverse levels. People practice leadership in any capacity, and they should. Rather than make decisions for the people I work with, I ask, 'What do you think? How would you do this?' That helps build confidence in themselves and confidence in my leadership style. By doing that, you build leadership capacity in your people. And you gain respect from within. It recognizes that no person knows it all and teaches them to use the resources around them.

The Lasting Impact of a Good Mentor

Lou Marines, former AIA executive director and Advanced Management Institute director, has been my mentor and coach. Even today, he is working with the firm, helping us facilitate a strategic session, and mentoring one of our younger partners.

He taught me so much about myself. He could call us out on many things we were not committed to. He challenged us to dig deep, to produce something we wanted to do and why. You need people like that, someone who calls you on the carpet very professionally and helps you focus on where you need to be. He questioned me a lot about the why of the things I said I wanted to do. And I remember those conversations now, close to 20 years later.

PROGRESSION – **EMPATHY**: Making Connections

You lead at anything you do, with anyone you do it with.

AWARENESS: *Think about these statements on building an understanding of the importance of* **Empathy**.

1. When someone shares emotions through tears, how does that make you feel?
2. How do you comfort others?
3. How do you feel before a difficult conversation?
4. What decisions have you made that have made you feel uncomfortable?
5. Do you use silence in conversations? If so, when?

ACCEPTANCE: *Now, reflect on how you reacted when reading these statements. Reflect on what "acceptance" of your truth about what* **Empathy** *means to you.*

1. What should others understand about you?
2. How do you deal with negative emotions? Positive ones?
3. When are you most present?

ACTION: *Follow these steps to incrementally put that awareness and acceptance into action to strengthen your ability to develop leadership with* **Empathy**.

1. Spend time with someone you know less well, and ask them about themselves, how they are, and what their life is like.
2. Experience what it is like to be unable to do something or not know how to interact with where you are.

3. Talk to people about the essential things in their lives.
4. Listen and do not interrupt.
5. Read Daniel Goleman's **What Makes a Leader?** Goleman's exploration of emotional intelligence makes a compelling case for the importance of empathy in leadership.

The Architecture of Vision

SYNOPSIS

The hallmark of good leadership — especially in professional service firms — is rooted in empathy. Empathetic leaders are those who not only understand the intricate dynamics of the business but also the human emotions that interplay within it. Such leaders create environments where diverse perspectives are championed and innovation thrives. They are adept at fostering a culture of psychological safety, ensuring team members can freely express themselves without fear. These leaders stand out by recognizing and celebrating innovation, understanding the inevitable nature of failure in the innovation process, and using it as a stepping stone for growth.

Actions speak louder than words, and this is particularly true for leaders. Empathetic leaders take proactive steps like conducting qualitative research to deeply understand client behaviors, motivations, and concerns. They prioritize diversity in client recruitment, ensuring inclusivity. By encouraging team members to observe and engage with clients directly, they ensure a holistic understanding of client needs. The results of such actions manifest in tailored solutions that enhance client experiences, fostering trust, and building long-term relationships.

Becoming a truly effective leader requires more than just business acumen. It demands a commitment to personal development, specifically in areas that foster empathy. Leaders must develop a profound awareness of their team's needs and challenges. This includes honing skills like genuine kindness, compassionate communication, unwavering honesty, mindfulness in interactions, and a focused approach to addressing the unique needs of everyone within the firm. Furthermore, an empathetic leader actively listens, is approachable, values diversity, and adapts their leadership style based on individual team member's strengths and weaknesses.

Empathy

REFLECTIONS & INSIGHTS

Chapter 4 | GENEROSITY: Sharing Leadership

The reluctance to solicit feedback, to offer both praise and criticism, and to create an environment in which everybody is doing the same, is one of the biggest problems in business.
Kim Scott

FOCUS: Showing a readiness to give more than is strictly necessary or expected.

ASPIRING LEADERS OFTEN CONTEND with balancing the needs of their team members, clients, and stakeholders while also navigating the pressures of managerial roles. Another challenge lies in cultivating genuine generosity without seeming forced or transactional. Leaders may know the importance of sharing their expertise and knowledge, but they might be unsure how to do so effectively and authentically.

The culture of an organization greatly influences its output and morale. Creating and nurturing a culture promoting collaboration, innovation, and risk-taking requires more than good intent. Aspiring leaders might find it challenging to implement these cultural changes, especially if they go against established norms.

Ensuring one's leadership style aligns with personal values can also pose a dilemma. Balancing selflessness with the need to set boundaries and understanding the true essence of generosity beyond mere fiscal measures can be difficult to navigate.

By understanding that generosity goes beyond monetary facets, leaders can shape their leadership styles more effectively. The tangible and intangible benefits of generosity offer a fresh perspective. Generosity aids in building trust, fostering collaboration, and enhancing a firm's reputation, providing leaders with actionable insights into how their actions directly influence team cohesion and the firm's brand.

The essence of genuine leadership is rooted in commitment, availability, and understanding that leading is more than just a position — it embodies values and actions. Mastering the intricacies of generous leadership equips leaders with knowledge, strategies, and reflective insights to overcome prevalent challenges and lead with authenticity and efficacy.

THE POWER OF GIVING

Generous leaders give their time, resources, and expertise to help others succeed. They prioritize the needs of their team members, clients, and other stakeholders and are committed to building relationships based on trust, respect, and mutual benefit.

Generous leaders prioritize the needs of others above their own, share their knowledge and expertise, provide support and encouragement, act with empathy and understanding, and lead by example. Generosity builds trust, fosters collaboration, encourages creativity, enhances a firm's reputation, and develops essential leadership skills.

Generous leaders also promote an inspired culture by encouraging the sharing of ideas, providing resources, promoting collaboration, supporting risk-taking, and celebrating success. Generosity is essential in connecting with people who follow the leader and setting the tone for those followers. Generosity is not just a choice but a requirement for good leadership.

Generosity

CHARACTERISTICS OF A GENEROUS LEADER

- **Puts Others First:** Leaders prioritize the needs of others above their own and are willing to go beyond to help them succeed.

- **Shares Their Knowledge and Expertise:** Leaders are willing to share their knowledge, skills, and expertise with others, whether through mentorship, training or simply being available to answer questions.

- **Provides Support and Encouragement:** Leaders provide support and encouragement to their team members, clients, and other stakeholders, always looking for ways to help them overcome challenges and achieve their goals.

- **Acts with Empathy and Understanding:** Leaders are empathetic and understanding and take the time to listen to others and understand their perspectives and needs.

- **Leads by Example:** Leaders lead by example, demonstrating the behaviors and values they expect from others and are committed to building a culture of generosity and collaboration within the firm.

A generous leader focuses on building relationships, supporting others, and creating a positive and collaborative work environment.

GIVING TO LEAD

Generosity plays a vital role in leadership and leadership development in several ways:

- **Building Trust:** Generosity helps leaders build trust with their team members, clients, and other stakeholders. By being generous with their time, resources, and expertise, leaders demonstrate that they care about others and are committed to helping them succeed.

- **Fostering Collaboration:** Generosity encourages collaboration among team members. When generous with their knowledge and skills, leaders help others improve and grow. Generosity, in turn, leads to a more cohesive and effective team.

- **Encouraging Innovation:** Generosity also promotes innovation. When leaders share ideas and resources, team members are likely to think creatively and develop innovative solutions to problems.

- **Enhancing Reputation:** Generosity enhances a firm's reputation. When leaders are known for their generosity and willingness to help others, they build a positive image for the firm in the eyes of clients, potential hires, and other stakeholders.

- **Developing Leadership Skills:** Generosity is an essential component of leadership development. By practicing generosity, leaders learn to be more empathetic, collaborative, and innovative.

SUPPORT THROUGH INSPIRATION

A generous leader understands the value of Inspiration and builds culture in several ways:

- **Encouraging the Sharing of Ideas:** Promoting an open culture where team members share their ideas and perspectives without fear of judgment or criticism allows everyone to feel comfortable sharing their ideas, and they are likely to produce innovative solutions to problems.

- **Providing Resources:** Supporting allocation of resources — time, money, people, and equipment — includes providing training and development opportunities,

Generosity

allocating funds for research and development, or providing access to innovative technology.

- **Promoting Collaboration:** Generosity fosters collaboration and teamwork, which leads to more innovative ideas. When team members work together, they combine their skills and expertise to develop new and creative solutions.

- **Supporting Risk-Taking:** Encouraging team members to take chances and try new things helps create a culture of innovation where team members feel empowered to experiment and take risks.

- **Celebrating Success:** Recognition of those who contribute to innovation helps create a sense of pride and accomplishment among team members and encourages them to continue innovating.

By providing the necessary resources and support, encouraging the sharing of ideas, and celebrating successes, a generous leader helps foster a culture of innovation that benefits the entire organization.

FINDING THE HEART OF THE LEADER

A generous leader embodies all the positive personal traits necessary for effective leadership. It is not necessarily about money but time, availability, and commitment. Great leaders give their time and energy to mentor and coach team members, attend industry and social organizations, and support the organization's goals. This commitment builds a leader's brand, feeds on itself, and often results in opportunities to serve in a leadership role within the voluntary effort.

For a leader to be generous, their efforts must be consistent with their leadership values. Giving time and energy has a value commensurate with that investment. Leaders must be clear about how much they are willing to give. Being a leader requires selflessness and goes beyond time or money. It is about commitment — how the organization and its stakeholders value generosity.

Leading by example is one of the traits of a good leader, and generosity is one of those areas where it sets the tone for the follower's bond. Generosity is essential in making connections with people who follow you.

They are likely to follow you if they feel you are generous. Helpful leaders also prioritize availability and an open-door policy to support their team members. It is only sometimes about being important enough to make time but more about recognizing that generosity is a requirement of good leadership.

THE BENEFITS OF GENEROSITY

A generous leader embodies positive personal characteristics, provides time and energy, and supports the organization's goals. Generosity is not just a choice but a requirement for good leadership.

As a professional service firm leader, it is essential to embody generosity. When thinking about organizational leadership, staff members look to their leaders for acknowledgment of their work. Generosity comes from monetary compensation, a pat on the back, or celebrating someone's achievements in public.

Leaders should also strive to learn, master, and teach. Teaching others what they have learned is a crucial component of generosity. This learning, mastering, and teaching process is continuous and multidimensional, and it helps leaders become better professionals. Sharing leadership is vital for personal and professional growth. It allows older leaders to mentor and coach younger ones and ensures their knowledge and experience are valued.

Leaders should not hold onto their knowledge tightly but instead share it generously with others. Doing so provides a purpose for themselves in retirement and creates a space for younger leaders to grow. Leaders who embody generosity generate a culture of learning and growth within their organization.

Generosity is an essential trait for leaders of professional service firms. It goes beyond monetary compensation for excellent work, although that is important. Generosity also comes in the form of acknowledgment, celebration, and guidance. As a leader, it is vital to recognize the hard work of your staff and celebrate their achievements, such as when a colleague receives professional awards. This kind of celebration makes the individual feel valued and boosts morale for the entire firm.

Generosity is a cycle of learning, mastering, and teaching. As a leader, it is vital to continue learning and mastering new skills and teach and guide others. By sharing knowledge and skills, leaders improve and become better professionals. As a result, the staff benefits as well. It is important to be generous with your leadership and not hold it tightly. Giving time is especially important for older leaders who may want to stay and provide valuable mentorship and coaching to younger staff.

SYNTHESIS

Generosity, innovation, and integrity are all essential traits that an inspirational leader of a professional service firm should possess.

Generosity is essential because it demonstrates that the leader cares about their team members and is willing to invest in their growth and development. A generous leader may provide opportunities for professional development, offer support and guidance, or provide additional resources to help their team members succeed. This generosity creates a sense of loyalty and motivation within the team, as they feel valued and supported by their leader.

Finally, integrity is essential for building trust with clients and team members. Inspirational leaders should be transparent and honest in their dealings with others and hold themselves and their team members accountable for their actions. By demonstrating integrity, the leader establishes a reputation for reliability and builds long-term relationships with clients and team members.

By integrating these traits, a professional practice's inspirational leaders create a culture encouraging generosity, innovation, and integrity. This culture attracts and retains top talent, positioning the firm for long-term market success.

VIEWPOINT – CRAIG JANSSEN, LEED AP BD+C
President, Idibri, a Salas O'Brien Company

Leadership is, first and foremost, about unifying people around a common purpose. Secondly, it enables the team to be successful.
— Craig Janssen

Guiding Principles in Leadership

I am purpose-driven. I always want to know what we are trying to achieve. That is my guiding principle. Our team's guiding principle is helping people communicate well in larger spaces. Part of leadership is allowing our clients to share their messages, experiences, and vibe effectively. Leadership is not the end goal of technical excellence but a byproduct. The core of success for us is — when we look back — that they were successful projects that made a difference in the community and helped people to engage and connect.

That principle goes for leadership, too. Leadership is about unifying people around a common purpose. And secondly, I am enabling the team to be successful. If you are a leader, are you hierarchal — people exist to serve me — or do you serve them? My bias is very strong toward purpose-driven service. I love to help the team to be successful. I do not exist to tell them what to do every day. Nor do I exist to be in the lead in the promotional aspects of the firm. When I diminish my role, I enable others the most.

Key Elements of Effective Leadership

Inspiration is congruent with how I defined the sense of purpose. We are at our best and most motivated when inspired to achieve something. It is the difference between passion and purpose.

The Architecture of Vision

Passion is a quickly depleted energy source, whereas purpose is a continuous energy source. Passion burns hot,

Innovation is highly situational and contextual, meaning more than just some things that need innovation. That is the biggest challenge in the design industry. Do we always have to redo a new thing?

Integrity is fascinating. And there is a parallel path that aligns integrity, purpose, and inspiration without anything additional and nothing less. Integrity is acts performed with honor. Honor means everything from financial integrity to honesty to how you treat everyone around you.

Lessons from the Experts

I read *The Speed of Trust* by Stephen M. R. Covey about 15 years ago. Covey talked about trust dividends and the tax on distrust. There is a dividend in acting with integrity. Not simply for moral reasons but for very pragmatic reasons. When you treat people with respect, you get care in return. Integrity is as much a business model as it is a moral positioning.

Marketing must primarily be about your brand. And your brand must be about your promise to your clients. If that's true, marketing is inextricably linked with leadership. Without a brand promise, you are developing a brand promise or focusing on profitable opportunities. Everything is moderated and modeled against profit versus promise.

And in the absence of promise — the marketing side — you are only left with the goal of profitability. Unfortunately, that means that the focus is only on finding opportunities for profit without tying the results back to your promise to your clients. If you do that, it screws up everything else. It is not that you do not make a lot of money. You are not contiguous without separating brand promise from profit. Leadership sets the story, and marketing explains it.

The Importance of Humility and Empowerment

The most impactful leaders — those who align with fulfilling their sense of purpose in a clear, articulate, and long-lasting way — are humble, which is different from not having tremendous self-confidence. Primarily, leaders must acknowledge it is not about me. Pride is a leader's greatest downfall. You must have humility, admitting that you are not all-powerful. And in that acknowledgment, by definition, you have created space for others to grow.

A few years ago, we hired some marketing experts to figure out what we were about. They interviewed everyone in the company. We were going to have this excellent brand analysis. And it did have that. But what I read page after page was, 'Craig's a good guy, but we will never grow if he does not get out of the way. Craig must be at the center of every decision. We do not get stuff done.' I needed to switch from specialist to enabler. It is very seductive to be the guru.

A Framework for Empowerment

So, I stepped back. The more I did, the more other people rose, elevating their profile. We reward people who disseminate information and power as fast as they can. We devised a framework called collect, automate, democratize, and empower. It is a great model where everyone gets to contribute to the idea that an organization should build a collated set of information and then be able to aggregate the information from multiple sources. Next, you automate it — organizing it in automated data sets using artificial intelligence.

We democratize that data so that everyone has equal access to everything. Democratize is how we celebrate people giving away information — and penalize people who hoard information. We create that opportunity to democratize and then finally empower, giving them the authority to share knowledge. It helps if you empower people. Empowering is the hardest part for many leaders.

Generosity

PROGRESSION – **GENEROSITY**: Share with No Expectation

Hoarding experience, knowledge, trust, and the idea of a generous leader do not co-exist.

AWARENESS: *Think about these statements on understanding the importance of* **Generosity.**

1. What examples of generosity do you see in leaders you admire?
2. List at least five ways you are generous in your professional role.
3. What are the consequences of being generous?
4. What keeps you from being generous?

ACCEPTANCE: *Now, reflect on how you reacted when reading these statements. Reflect on what "acceptance" of your truth about what* **Generosity** *means to you.*

1. How do you feel when someone else is generous to you?
2. What are opportunities for you to be generous with a colleague or peer?
3. How much time or money do you want to spend on being generous?

ACTION: *Follow these steps to incrementally put that awareness and acceptance into action to strengthen your ability to develop leadership with* **Generosity.**

1. Practice one random act of kindness a week for a month; that is, do something nice for someone without them knowing it. If they find out, it does not count.

2. Become a mentor formally with someone outside of your firm or practice.

3. Become a mentor in an informal capacity with someone inside your firm or practice.

4. Read James Hunter's, **The Servant: A Simple Story About the True Essence of Leadership**, The concept of servant leadership revolves around the idea of serving others, closely tied to generosity.

Generosity

SYNOPSIS

At the heart of effective leadership in firms lies generosity, which isn't merely about giving financially but prioritizing the needs of the team, clients, and stakeholders. Effective leaders exhibit a profound sense of empathy, ensuring they actively listen to and understand diverse perspectives and needs. More than just preaching values, true leaders embody and demonstrate the behaviors and ethics they expect from their teams. They focus on fostering collaboration and unity, understanding that a cohesive team is more efficient and innovative.

Leaders cement trust with their teams and stakeholders by generosity in sharing time, knowledge, and resources. Leaders instigate a culture of innovation by encouraging the free flow of ideas and being open to risks.

A generous leader who gives time, resources, and expertise selflessly elevates the firm's image in the eyes of clients, competitors, and potential hires. Through mentorship, training, and an open-door policy, leaders ensure their team members' continuous personal and professional growth.

This cycle enriches the leader and ensures that the team and the firm continually evolve. While generosity is crucial, understanding its limits is equally important. Leaders need to gauge how much to give, ensuring it aligns with both the firm's objectives and their personal leadership values.

Beyond individual interactions, leaders must be adept at shaping the broader organizational culture. This involves promoting collaboration, celebrating successes, and making resources available for innovation. Leaders must introspect regularly to ensure their actions are congruent with their values. This consistency between belief and action is fundamental for sustained leadership success.

The Architecture of Vision

REFLECTIONS & INSIGHTS

Chapter 5 | PATIENCE: Trusting in Time

Good judgment comes from experience; experience comes from bad judgment.
Dr. Kerr L. White

FOCUS: Developing the capacity to accept or tolerate delay, trouble, or suffering without getting angry or upset.

PATIENCE EMERGES AS AN IMPERATIVE quality when considering leadership as a multifaced journey. While the marketing of professional services often promises swift answers, true leadership requires patience to ensure the process's integrity and results.

Aspiring leaders frequently face the allure of speed, which, if unchecked, can sidestep vital learning opportunities. Impatience not only hampers decision-making but also strains relationships and workplace culture.

Leadership is tricky; you always continue learning and growing in your position.
— **Grenee Martacho**, CEO, Concord GC

Patience in leadership operates at several pivotal levels. It aids in building genuine trust, crafting an environment conducive to the professional growth of team members, effectively managing change, and ensuring comprehensive decision-making. These benefits are especially evident in the professional services sector, where projects follow a structured journey from conception to execution.

The Architecture of Vision

However, a significant generational challenge surfaces; younger professionals, often driven by a different pace and life experience, might undervalue the importance of patience. Leaders foster stronger ties within their teams and enhance their decision-making acumen and strategic vision through understanding and embracing patience.

Intentional patience stands out as more than a passive trait; it is a deliberate action that demands consistent practice. Leaders must be prepared to face the inherent challenges of their roles by slowing down, embracing uncertainties, and valuing the non-linear path of progress. Leaders can build their reservoir of patience by investing in mindfulness, empathy, setting realistic expectations, and other strategies. Consequently, a patient leader is poised to promote innovation, uphold organizational integrity, and strike a harmonious balance between short-term results and long-term aspirations, ensuring sustained success.

THE NEED FOR PATIENCE

One of the biggest learnings of leadership is the need for patience. If one follows processes and practices, answers will come quickly. Professional services rely on the practice model, where each project goes through a series of definable steps to get from concept to execution based on definable goals. The objective of developing patience is to feel that one is moving at the right pace. Impatience leads to lessons not learned.

Patience helps build trust, develop others, manage change, and make better decisions. It requires intentional effort and practice, including mindfulness, empathy, setting realistic expectations, active listening, taking breaks, and practicing delayed gratification. Leaders who cultivate patience are likelier to make well-informed decisions, build stronger relationships, and foster a positive work culture.

WHY PATIENCE MATTERS

Patience is an essential quality for inspirational leadership and plays a crucial role in these several areas of professional practice:

- **Building Trust:** Patience helps build trust among team members, clients, and stakeholders. When leaders take the time to listen to team members and understand their perspectives, they make sense of trust and respect that strengthens relationships and creates a positive work environment.

- **Developing Others:** Patience is also essential for developing others. Leaders must be patient while coaching and mentoring team members. Leaders are willing to provide constructive feedback and give staff time to implement the changes needed to improve their skills and performance.

- **Managing Change:** In professional services, change is constant. It is essential to be patient when addressing change and allow time for it to take effect. Leaders support and guide team members during transition and are patient while adapting to new processes and methods.

- **Making Decisions:** Patience is also essential as a leader. Gathering information, evaluating options, and considering different perspectives lead to better decision-making outcomes. Rushing into decisions without patience leads to costly mistakes and negative consequences.

Patience is something that older generations often appreciate more than younger generations. A young person's timeline is different, and they lack the whole-life experience that many (but not all) older professionals have. When we learn that we do not control everything, we are likely to learn from events as they happen. Being patient emphasizes the importance of learning from both good and bad experiences.

TRUST IN THE PATH

In leadership, patience is a trait that a leader needs to demonstrate and convey its importance. Leaders base process changes on a timeline to meet an expectation or need. Followers should understand that a certain level of patience needs to be part of the understanding.

It is essential to communicate with impatient team members and help them understand issues such as resources, conflicting requirements or demands, and outside influences. A good leader adjusts the process, reframes the question or challenge, and identifies incremental steps to a solution. Leaders understand the processes that are the framework for the practice.

In any organization, the more the aspects impacting the practice are understood, the better the organization adapts to unknowns. Patience is not just waiting to see how time passes but also recognizing processes, humanity, and existing situations. The better one becomes at leadership, the more one understands the need for patience. Leadership is a journey, not a destination. Leadership is an ongoing process of learning, adapting, and evolving. A crucial part of that journey is cultivating the quality of patience.

INTENTIONAL PATIENCE

As leaders face complex challenges and ever-changing environments, remaining patient and focused on the big picture is essential. When impatient, leaders tend to make hasty decisions, miss critical details, and overlook valuable insights. Patient leaders are likelier to make well-informed decisions, build stronger relationships, and foster a more positive and productive work culture.

Patience

It is essential to recognize that patience is not simply a passive trait. It requires active effort and intentional practice. Leaders who cultivate patience must be willing to slow down, listen deeply, and be open to new perspectives. They must also be willing to accept uncertainty and ambiguity, knowing that progress is rarely linear and that setbacks and challenges are inevitable.

Like all leadership traits, developing patience requires intentional effort and practice. Some strategies leaders use to create their patience include:

- **Practice Mindfulness:** Being present now and fully aware of your thoughts and feelings helps leaders increase their awareness of their emotional states and improve their ability to manage their reactions to stressors.

- **Practice Empathy:** Developing the ability to understand and share the feelings of others helps leaders by increasing their understanding of the perspectives and needs of their team members and clients.

- **Set Realistic Expectations:** Being practical helps reduce stress and frustration, which often leads to impatience. Be clear and realistic about timelines, goals, and outcomes.

- **Listen Actively:** Fully engaging with and understanding what someone else is saying helps leaders gain valuable insights that help to reduce misunderstandings and frustrations.

- **Take Breaks and Practice Self-Care:** Stepping away for a moment helps leaders recharge and reduce stress, which leads to more patience. Encourage team members to do the same.

- **Practice Delayed Gratification:** Delaying immediate rewards for long-term benefits helps leaders by

The Architecture of Vision

strengthening their ability to focus on long-term goals and resist the temptation to take shortcuts or make hasty decisions.

By developing their patience, leaders improve their decision-making, build trust with team members and clients, and lead their firms to more success.

SYNTHESIS

Patience as a quality in a professional service firm's leadership significantly impacts innovation and integrity within the practice. Patience fosters innovation by allowing leaders to take the time to explore innovative ideas and possibilities. When leaders are patient, they encourage their team members to experiment, take calculated risks, and try novel approaches. Patience leads to the development of innovative solutions, processes, and services that set the firm apart from competitors.

Patience is also critical for maintaining integrity in the leadership of a professional service firm. Patient leaders take the time to consider the consequences of their actions, evaluate their options, and make decisions that align with the firm's values and principles. Patience helps build a culture of transparency, honesty, and ethical behavior essential for the firm's long-term success.

Patience is also essential for balancing short-term and long-term goals. Patient leaders resist the temptation to focus only on immediate results and instead take the time to develop strategic plans that align with the firm's vision and values. Patience helps ensure that the firm is on track to achieve its long-term goals while also delivering results in the short term.

Patience is an essential quality for promoting innovation and integrity in leadership. It helps foster a culture of experimentation and ethical behavior while balancing short-term and long-term goals. By being patient, leaders make better decisions and lead their firms to long-term success.

VIEWPOINT – **DAWN SAVAGE**, FSMPS
Business Development Director, ICF

Being a leader and leadership is the same. The former focuses on the individual, and the latter on the significant resulting impact.

— Dawn Savage

What Defines a Leader

A leader is someone that you want to follow. Leadership is not a title. In addition to wanting to follow that person, they inspire you to act and demonstrate a commitment to what they ask.

We lead up, and we lead down. For example, I work with a vice president who has managed an extensive program but needs to learn about business development. My job is to help her make informed decisions about current opportunities and to help educate her for the future. I must help lead her to a conclusion but wait to decide, enabling her to get there independently. For me, that is that leading up. I also have a team with direct reports and some who do not. I guide them through planning, engagement, and capture and proposal strategies.

Core Qualities of Leadership

Inspiration aligns with my view of leadership. You can be a manager but not a leader. Suppose you do not inspire someone. In my mind, you are not a leader. The ability to influence becomes paramount. If I do not inspire, I do not influence.

Integrity is personal. If you do not have integrity, I do not have respect for you. I am never going to follow you as a leader. We have a high ethical standard. We own it. We talked about it. It is part of our mission statement. We talk about our integrity and the integrity of our work. Integrity is in our DNA.

I need help with innovation. Just because you are a leader does not mean you are innovative. Is somebody very innovative in their approach, or are they just creative thinkers? People are drawn to that naturally. But being innovative is optional to be a leader.

Overcoming Weaknesses

Leaders should acknowledge and address weaknesses, even if they have not necessarily overcome them. For example, I could improve on the details. I want to get better, but at this point, I am not going to. By acknowledging that weakness, I partner with somebody great at detail and build the organization with them. We complement each other. As a leader, you must recognize your weaknesses before acknowledging anybody else's. When your weaknesses impact your ability to lead and influence, you must overcome them to lead more effectively.

If you are not a good communicator, you must figure out how to overcome that to be a leader. Where you could improve in a group setting, like in a big presentation, by acknowledging this is not my strength, I will follow up in writing. You get some coaching to become more comfortable with presenting. Those are ways leaders overcome their weaknesses.

Building Leaders Within the Organization

The first step to building leaders is acknowledging that you want to make opportunities available to the staff. Then, you must walk the talk as a company. Provide opportunities. Provide training, internally and externally, that supports the employees seeking that training. Support takes various forms, from time to financial backing to mentoring and guidance. Leadership only comes naturally to some. You need to build those skills. As a company, we must provide the opportunity. There may be little opportunities early in a career and more significant opportunities as they gain experience and confidence.

The Role of Mentorship

Mentoring is huge. Whether it is direct mentoring, where you recognize and acknowledge it, or indirect, where the process may need to be more formalized, it is critical. Both excellent and ineffective mentors have some characteristics, qualities, activities, and behaviors that impact the mentor/protégé relationship. Mentoring allows you to see things in yourself and others you would like to improve or emulate. You also see some that you do not want to do.

The mentor often gets more out of the process than the protégé. Mentoring provides a sounding board for areas where we are struggling. I improve by acknowledging my shortcomings. I recognize that I need to grow by defining my goals, and the mentor helps me discover how to get there. A mentor can be incredibly influential. They might not give you an opportunity, but they might be the connection to somebody else.

Valuing Diverse Roles in Leadership

Everyone wants their department, function, or role to be valued. We have that expectation of company leadership. We want our company's leaders to value and recognize our work in our skill areas. For marketers and business developers, there is a recognition that leaders can be experts in some rooms. However, good leaders acknowledge others' expertise and value it. Because of our roles, we sometimes have an unintentional bias where we discount leadership that sees marketing and business development as something other than the growth engine. If you ask somebody in accounting, project management, or human resources, they have their own perspective on the leadership value of their role.

PROGRESSION – **PATIENCE**: Trusting in Time

Leaders go slow to go fast.

AWARENESS: Think about these statements on understanding the importance of **Patience**.

1. Study the Eisenhower Matrix (Urgent, Important, Not Urgent, Not Important) from Stephen Covey's book *The 7 Habits of Highly Successful People* and reflect on your daily activities.[4]
2. Keep track for a week to notice how you typically spend your time.
3. Notice your decision-making process: are you quick to respond or slow to decide?
4. How do you feel when a colleague moves too slowly on a task?

ACCEPTANCE: *Now, reflect on how you reacted when reading these statements. Reflect on what "acceptance" of your truth about what* **Patience** *means to you.*

1. How do you feel about standard operating procedures and required procedures? Identify at least three that you find appropriate and three that you find frustrating.
2. Consider the current situation and describe if you want it to move faster or slow down. What do you notice?
3. Track your level of patience for a week, identifying when you feel that things should be moving faster or if something should be moving slower. What do you notice?

---

[4] Covey, S. R, The 7 Habits of Highly Successful People, Simon & Schuster, 2020.

The Architecture of Vision

ACTION: *Follow these steps to incrementally put that awareness and acceptance into action to strengthen your ability to develop leadership with* **Patience.**

1. Make yourself wait at least 24 hours before making a decision that will significantly impact you.
2. Stop doing things that are not important.
3. When you feel pressure to decide quicker than you would like, take a moment to breathe and relax.
4. Schedule 10-minute mindfulness breaks to stop working, move, and connect with colleagues outside activities requiring focus and energy.
5. Read John Maxwell's **Good Leaders Ask Great Questions**. By asking questions and actively listening, leaders exhibit patience and seek to understand.

Patience

SYNOPSIS

With firm and individual leaders, patience is a hallmark of effective leadership. It's not just about waiting; it is a profound understanding of processes, humanity, and prevailing circumstances. Patience is integral in cultivating trust, facilitating professional growth, managing change, and refining decision-making.

While young professionals may approach patience differently due to their unique life experiences, learning from positive and negative experiences becomes pivotal in leadership. The importance of patience is further emphasized by the assertion that leadership is not just about reaching a destination; it is an ongoing journey.

Leaders who embrace patience foster a work environment where trust flourishes. They actively listen, providing constructive feedback that aids in skill and performance enhancement. This patience also becomes essential in managing change, particularly in professional services where change is a constant. Instead of rushing decisions, patient leaders gather information, evaluate options, and consider various perspectives, which leads to superior decision-making outcomes. As a result, these leaders are more adaptable, making better-informed decisions that promote a positive work culture.

To evolve into effective leaders, individuals need to develop several competencies. Intentional patience is critical – it isn't a passive trait but requires active effort. Being present enhances emotional awareness and the ability to manage reactions to various challenges. Effective leadership in firms is marked by an intentional practice of patience, which fosters trust, encourages professional growth, and ensures informed decision-making. By honing competencies like mindfulness, empathy, and active listening, leaders are better positioned to navigate the challenges of their roles and lead their organizations to success.

The Architecture of Vision

REFLECTIONS & INSIGHTS

Chapter 6 | WISDOM: Learning from the Path

We desperately need more leaders who are committed to courageous, wholehearted leadership and who are self-aware enough to lead from their hearts, rather than unevolved leaders who lead from hurt and fear.
Brene Brown

FOCUS: Trust in the soundness of an action or decision based on the application of experience, knowledge, and good judgment.

ARISING FROM PERSONAL GROWTH AND REFLECTION, wisdom is integral to effective leadership. Leaders with this quality gain invaluable perspectives by connecting their current challenges to past experiences. They listen attentively, enabling their followers to feel valued and motivated.

While wisdom is often associated with age and experience, it is essential to note that younger individuals can also bring forward profound insights. Thus, creating a culture of shared organizational wisdom necessitates embracing diverse perspectives, ensuring the wisdom remains impactful and relevant.

A wise leader listens. When followers are heard, they feel inspired to do better and excel. Have the wisdom to listen for sounds of the future.
— **Dena Silver,** retired President, M. Silver & Co.

The Architecture of Vision

Leaders who prioritize wisdom create environments conducive to growth and success. By reflecting on past actions, assessing their outcomes, and executing learned lessons, they foster innovation and provide valuable insights into their leadership journey. This involves recognizing their own "aha" moments and sharing them, creating a ripple effect that inspires others. It becomes crucial to recognize the balance between sharing personal insights and allowing others to learn through their own experiences. A wise leader appreciates the role of diverse perspectives in generating organizational wisdom, ensuring it remains dynamic and evolves throughout one's career.

CHARACTERISTICS OF WISE LEADERSHIP

Wisdom is a crucial trait resulting from personal growth in one's career development. Leaders gain perspective by reflecting on their past experiences. As they encounter new challenges, they see connections to previous situations.

Wisdom is an essential quality that develops over time through personal growth and reflection. Leaders with wisdom, generosity, and patience inspire and guide others toward success. It is critical to recognize that wisdom is not limited to older generations. Younger individuals also offer valuable insights. By embracing diverse perspectives and creating a learning culture, leaders develop and maintain shared organizational wisdom that remains relevant and impactful.

LEARNING FROM THE PAST

As Bob Dylan wisely said in one of his early songs, *"Here I sit so patiently, waiting to find out what price you have to pay to get out of, going through all these things twice."*[5] However, some may need to go

---

[5] Dylan, Bob, *Stuck Inside of Mobile with the Memphis Blues Again,* Blonde on Blonde, 1966

Wisdom

through the same situations repeatedly before they learn from their past.

Leaders must provide the time and space required to learn and develop wisdom. Some of the most valuable lessons emerge when they reflect on their past actions and evaluate their outcomes. They gain insight into what they did not know then but understand now. Wisdom aligns with perspective, with the "aha" moments that leaders experience when they recognize how all the pieces fit together.

> *Wisdom is the knowledge, experience, and good judgment over time, as well as the soundness of action or decision.*
> — **Rebecca Jones,** CEO, SafeworkCM

Reflection, assessment, and execution of lessons learned often provide inspiration, innovative ideas, and insight into a leader's work. Acknowledging lessons learned and sharing them with others are also elements of leadership. Leaders who share their successes and failures inspire others to learn and grow.

Wise leaders learn to balance sharing their insights with allowing others to learn through their mistakes. While older generations may want to impart their knowledge, younger individuals may prefer to learn by making mistakes, generating wisdom.

Learning from different perspectives and generations contributes to organizational wisdom. Younger individuals who bridge generational gaps and apply new learning to existing knowledge are valuable organizational contributors. Understanding must remain relevant and dynamic to stay effective and engaging, continuing to evolve throughout one's life.

It is important to note that wisdom is not solely associated with age. Many young people possess understanding beyond their years, and leaders must learn from them and create opportunities for them to share their insights. A diverse and equitable organization is one where individuals from multiple generations come together to share their perspectives and learn from each other.

> *Wisdom comes from knowing the importance of seeing the entire scenario before you move forward, which involves truth, politics, debate, understanding, and selflessness.*
>
> — **Michael Davis,** Founder/CEO, DAVIS

Organizational wisdom draws from a variety of opinions and experiences. When leaders prioritize diversity and inclusion, they create an environment where everyone feels valued, and the combined understanding of all contributes to the organization's success.

GAINING WISDOM

There are several steps that one can take in leadership development to become more conscious of wisdom as a positive trait:

- **Seek Out Mentors:** Find people who embody wisdom and who you respect as leaders. These mentors offer guidance, share experiences, and model wise leadership behavior.
- **Reflect on Past Experiences:** Take time to reflect on past experiences, both positive and negative. What was learned? Think about how those lessons inform current and future decision-making.
- **Practice Mindfulness:** Practice mindfulness techniques such as meditation, journaling, or mindfulness exercises to cultivate self-awareness and clarity of thought. Reflection

Wisdom

helps leaders make more informed decisions and cultivates greater wisdom.

- **Encourage Diverse Perspectives:** Seek out diverse perspectives from colleagues and team members. Encourage them to share their thoughts and ideas and actively listen and consider their input. Seeking other views helps us see issues from multiple angles and make more informed decisions.

- **Read Widely:** Read widely on diverse topics, including leadership, psychology, philosophy, and history. Learning helps develop a broader perspective and enhances a better understanding of the world.

- **Seek Feedback:** Ask for feedback from colleagues, mentors, and team members on leadership style and decision-making. Be open to constructive criticism and use it to refine approaches and methods.

By taking these steps, leaders cultivate greater self-awareness, broaden their perspective, and develop the wisdom necessary to be influential and respected leaders.

The Architecture of Vision

SYNTHESIS

Wisdom as a leadership trait relates directly to aspects of innovation and integrity in leadership development in several ways.

First, wise leaders make informed and effective decisions that balance short-term and long-term goals. Leaders with wisdom draw upon their past experiences, insights, and knowledge to make well-informed decisions that foster innovation and drive the firm forward. At the same time, wise leaders understand the importance of maintaining integrity in all aspects of their work, including decision-making.

Next, wisdom enables leaders to identify and capitalize on opportunities for innovation. Wise leaders recognize emerging trends, anticipate changes in the market, and develop new strategies that keep the firm ahead of the curve. They also foster a culture of innovation by encouraging their teams to think broadly and experiment with innovative ideas.

Finally, wise leaders maintain the highest standards of integrity in their work. Leaders leverage their wisdom and understand that trust is essential to success. They work tirelessly to build and maintain trust with their clients and colleagues. They lead by example, setting high ethical standards and holding themselves and others accountable for upholding them.

Leaders with wisdom leverage their insights and experiences to drive innovation and maintain the highest standards of integrity in all aspects of their work. By embodying these qualities, leaders inspire their teams and create a culture of excellence that supports the firm's growth and success.

VIEWPOINT – **KATHLEEN HELD,** CPSM
CEO, Cine-Little International

Leadership is the ability to listen and guide the team, help them be the best they are, and be their champion.
— Kathleen Held

Leadership Fundamentals

Leadership is being able to listen and provide guidance to the team and help them be the best they are. Oh, and championing them along the way.

I spend a lot of time talking to our staff and encouraging them to improve. When they feel that an area is not their strong suit, I always tell them I push them past their comfort zone. And then continually expand whatever that comfort zone is to make them a more well-rounded individual.

Inspiration is big. I am constantly pushing our staff to have elastic thinking — thinking from the bottom up, not the top down — about how what we do impacts everything around us and how everything around us impacts what we do. I constantly challenge our team to think creatively.

Organizational Structure and Leadership

We like to think of ourselves as having great integrity. We are always trying to set the bar higher with our thought leadership. I acknowledge my weaknesses and tell my staff I do not know everything. I need their input. Many people are scared to give the CEO input on what they do better or what they are doing good. I need that just as much as my staff does. It is a two-way conversation.

As CEO, and to provide leadership opportunities, I eliminated the president title and delegated that role to five director-level people now doing what the President had been doing. I want them to invest their time in the leadership of the firm.

Learning and Development

I learned a lot from SMPS about leadership. From leading a chapter to national roles, SMPS provided a great pathway to leadership. Now I am sitting where it is not only my marketing teams that need to run smoothly. Every other aspect of the organization — from accounting and HR to the technical aspects of food service consulting — I must be knowledgeable about every part of the practice as a leader. In all my conversations, the client is always at the front of my mind because marketing is my background.

Leadership and Marketing

Even before I became CEO, I was always intrigued by how marketing could touch other aspects of the company. For many years, I fought with HR to have a say in hiring because I felt that when you market a company, you sell to the people. It took a little time, but now I participate in hiring anyone above the project manager. It is important to me that everyone understands the clients, their needs, their hot buttons, and the trends in the industry. It is logical for marketing to lead a company because you touch on many aspects of the client experience. You are not as siloed in your thought process.

PROGRESSION – **WISDOM**: Learning from the Process

Wisdom is not a leadership destination; it results from thousands of experiences, good and bad.

AWARENESS: *Think about these statements on understanding the importance of* **Wisdom.**

1. Write in your journal every day for a month and describe a new insight you gained, a new skill you learned, or a new person you met.//
2. How do you feel when you complete a project or task?
3. Describe at least ten steps where you accomplished something important to you. Note all your feelings, including struggles, fears, frustrations, and moments of joy.

ACCEPTANCE: *Now, reflect on how you reacted when reading these statements. Reflect on what "acceptance" of your truth about what* **Wisdom** *means to you.*

1. Reflect on your career and notice the challenges you have overcome. What do you appreciate about the struggles and how you responded, adapted, learned, and grew?
2. Reflect on the relationships that have provided the most value to you and those that did not. What patterns do you notice?
3. Think about your decision-making process and style. Would you change anything about it? When would you move faster, and when would you prefer to slow down?

The Architecture of Vision

ACTION: *Follow these steps to incrementally put that awareness and acceptance into action to strengthen your ability to develop leadership with* **Wisdom.**

1. Try something new at least once a week for a year.
2. Talk to someone you do not know well and ask them to describe the most critical lesson they have learned. Listen well.
3. Do something the hard way, unlike how you usually do it. How did it challenge you, and what did you learn?
4. When working on a team, ask yourself and others if you have a good variety of voices and perspectives involved. Build diverse teams.
5. Embrace uncertainty. Recognize when you do not have all the information and decide to move forward.
6. Read Stephen Covey's **The 7 Habits of Highly Effective People**, Covey's timeless principles offer insights into developing wisdom in leadership.

Wisdom

SYNOPSIS

Wisdom emerges as a cornerstone in effective leadership within firms and individuals. Such leaders are characterized by their ability to reflect upon and derive lessons from past experiences, facilitating deeper connections to current situations. They excel in listening, ensuring every team member feels heard, valued, and inspired to outperform. Importantly, wisdom isn't merely the domain of the seasoned; younger leaders, too, can offer fresh, invaluable insights.

Therefore, a wise leader's hallmark is one who champions diverse perspectives, fostering a continuous learning culture that ensures organizational wisdom remains dynamic, relevant, and impactful.

Leaders steeped in wisdom proactively create environments where reflection, innovation, and growth thrive. By revisiting past actions and critically assessing outcomes, they are adept at recognizing patterns, drawing insights, and guiding teams with an informed perspective. These leaders internalize and actively share their learnings, setting precedents for others to emulate.

This sharing, however, is a delicate balance—while they generously impart knowledge from their own journey, they also understand the importance of letting others navigate, learn, and even falter in their unique paths. This ensures the organization's collective wisdom is enriched, stays pertinent, and drives consistent success.

Leadership rooted in wisdom is not merely about accruing experiences but reflecting, adapting, and applying those experiences to cultivate growth, inclusivity, and innovation at an individual and organizational level.

The Architecture of Vision

REFLECTIONS & INSIGHTS

PART II | INNOVATION – The Second Pillar

Innovation distinguishes between a leader and a follower.
Steve Jobs

FOCUS: Innovation is the strategic, operational, and interpersonal process to address a need, a goal, or a challenge.

INNOVATION IS THE SECOND PILLAR OF LEADERSHIP in any professional service firm. The role of innovation has different meanings in the professional service firm, where delivering the work of the licensed practice tends toward rote and routine. Professional services are acts of service that support the client's need for something outside their core competency.

THE CHALLENGES OF THE INNOVATIVE LEADER

The innovative leader wears many hats: strategist, visionary, creative, and knowledgeable. These are all traits of the innovative leader. A crystal ball and an internal compass are their tools; revenue, profit, and resultant brand strength are their measure. However, the challenge the innovative leaders face are significant. Seek innovation, and you will be one too.

- **Differentiation from the Competition.** In a crowded marketplace, it is challenging to stand out. Introducing new ideas and approaches makes the firm more attractive to potential clients.

- **Driving Growth.** Innovation leads to developing new services, which drives revenue and expands the firm's client base.

- **Staying Relevant.** The business-to-business ecosystem constantly changes, and professional service firms must adapt to remain relevant. A firm stays current and meets its clients' needs by embracing innovation.

- **Continuous Improvement.** Innovation is about more than just producing big, groundbreaking ideas. It is also about continuously and iteratively improving processes and finding ways to do things more efficiently. An innovative mindset helps drive excellence throughout the firm.

Innovation is a crucial component of a professional service firm. It helps to differentiate the firm, drives growth, keeps the practice relevant, and fosters a culture of continuous improvement. Embracing innovation is essential to the success and longevity of any professional service firm.

SIMPLICITY AND INNOVATION

In his insightful book *Selling the Invisible,* Harry Beckwith noted, "Innovate, yes. But innovate to make things simpler, not more complex. Innovate to eliminate barriers, not create them. Innovate to save people time and make their lives easier, not more complicated."[6]

Regardless of title, leadership in professional practice provides the framework for innovation. In larger firms, leadership includes roles like chief executive officer, chief financial officer, and chief operations officer. More recently, the C-Suite has seen the rise of the chief marketing, information, human resources, learning, and administrative officers. Leadership wears multiple hats in many firms

---

[6] Beckwith, H., *Selling the Invisible: A Field Guide to Modern Marketing,* Grand Central Publishing, 2012.

where the entrepreneurial and technical staff supply the practice and management capabilities.

As companies evolve, the need for innovation becomes a natural extension of leadership at all levels. It is rarely a single individual responsible for developing and communicating the company's value proposition to its client audience.

THE INNOVATION CHALLENGE

Many innovation-related issues define the challenges facing the firm today and apply equally to firms practicing in all professional service areas:

- **Profitable Sustained Organic Growth** has become the business imperative, driving both perceived brand value and intrinsic monetary value for the stakeholders
- **Marketing and Business Development** are expected to produce results
- **Turnover is Increasing** because achieving sustained organic growth is limited by available talent
- **Saturated Markets and Clients** are less responsive and challenge traditional service delivery methods
- **All Aspects of the Practice** contribute to key financial performance metrics
- **Firms Must Leverage Technology** to connect internally and externally if the enterprise is to grow

For a firm to endure and for leaders across all areas of the practice to be successful, they will need to achieve agreement on the following issues:

- **Build and Execute New Business Processes** focused on connecting marketing and operational metrics with financial consequences

- **Collaborate and Share Best Practices** that address the most pressing issues facing the firm, the industry, and clients

- **Direct and Focus Additional Research And Strategic Initiatives** as necessary to stay ahead of the current market economy and meet evolving client needs

The following questions are critical to leadership success. Increasing knowledge and awareness, thereby creating an optimally designed, efficient, highly functioning, and innovative practice, comes from knowing:

- **How are staff and resources most optimally organized?**
- **What are the opportunities for cost control and outsourcing?**
- **How can sales and profitability goals be more effectively aligned?**
- **What are competitors spending on various innovation initiatives?**
- **How to advance a corporate strategy in a decentralized organization?**
- **What is the best way to measure ROI and communicate the results?**
- **What are the newest or most essential technologies to make the firm more competitive?**

As professional service firms seek to maintain growth and profits in turbulent economic times, many look to their leaders to spearhead that growth. Innovation should be at the forefront of any effort if one

Innovation

desires and aspires to become a leader. While many aspire to a title, there first needs to be an understanding of the goals for the role, the skill set required to be successful, and the expectations from the firm, other executives, and staff.

Evidence shows that more firms seek greater diversity in the professionals filling leadership roles, focusing more on the best-qualified and results-producing leaders for critical roles in the executive team.

EXPERIENCE & RESEARCH

The key to becoming a leader who provides value to the firm requires a combination of vision, fundamental skills, and determination. A common thread with most leaders is the impact of mentors. Internal and external advisors helped them focus on the practice's business throughout their careers. A mentor contributes as much if not more than, leadership to the practice.

While innovation is important, leaders must develop and understand the importance of meeting the business expectations of the company's stakeholders rather than just excelling at the creative aspects of developing an effective service or marketing message. The foundation of a leadership mindset is to think and act expansively, spanning service lines, functional lines, and geographic silos to build a profitable business for their companies.

One of the challenges facing leaders in professional service is the changing market dynamics and disruptions that have characterized the market over the past few years. Most leaders rely on reading and researching as many sources of current business information as they squeeze into an already full day. From blogs to business and client-focused journals and the profession's trade press, they read and absorb as much as possible to help gain and apply perspective to the planning and decision processes in their marketing and business development efforts.

Faith Popcorn, the noted futurist, says that *"accurate prophecies are inseparable from paying attention."*[7] There are fast and sure ways to learn the hot issues facing clients in any market. Surf the Internet, obtain copies of the last six to twelve industry publications, and look at the table of contents for industry drivers and challenges.

INNOVATION AND THE CREATIVE PROCESS

Innovation is the outgrowth of a promising idea. Much of what makes organizations resilient and respected — and improves their brand value — is innovation. From the outside perspective, most professional service firms look very much alike. The firm's external brand image may not reflect the innovative qualities the practice might have. There is an assumption that if I hire an architect, they must be creative. If I hire an engineer, they must be accurate. If I hire a lawyer or accountant, they must be honest.

Innovation is the lifeblood of the best firms, whether small, less than 20-person practices or big firms of several thousand people. There are no limits to what creativity and innovation mean to the value perceived by clients. Focusing on providing creative value establishes the firm and its leaders as innovators.

Another aspect of innovation is whether it is practical. Many innovators write "creative science fiction," suggesting ideas that have potential but are challenging to realize in any reasonable period. The best innovations are those based on a practical solution to an existing problem executed on time and within budget and making a difference.

Much like the early space program, when President Kennedy said we would have a man on the moon by the end of the decade and bring them safely back home, they did not have the technology, they did not have "Tang," they did not have any of the right stuff. But because there was a vision and a commitment to that dream. NASA had to innovate,

---

[7] https://faithpopcorn.com/

invent, and solve problems. They still needed to learn to make that happen. That is the definition of innovation: pure creativity expressed as an invention.

LEADERSHIP AT ALL LEVELS

For those in different roles in professional services, whether marketing business development professionals or technical professionals, a creative component goes with each position. Innovation is not just being open — having an open mind to possibilities — but also continuously looking at the world through different lenses, seeing the world in diverse ways.

When you are open to different ideas, you solve problems you could not see if you only operated from an experience-based mindset. In the 2004 best-seller *The Medici Effect*,[8] Franz Johansson wrote about the importance of lowering barriers to thinking creatively, showing how this can help in business by breaking free from fixed thought patterns and associating freely through brainstorming to arrive at creative ideas. Often, managers and employees need help with creative thinking, which is difficult to break through. Leaders who embrace innovation create the cultural opportunity to put the Medici Effect to work.

Innovative leaders work at the intersection of quite different ideas. To develop creative leadership skills — by reading, listening, and doing things outside our comfort zone — we get better at what we do and get better by doing new things. It is a cross-training concept. By embracing innovation and learning to get outside your head, you set yourself up to be a more innovative thinker.

---

[8] Johansson, Franz, ***The Medici Effect***: *Breakthrough Insights at the Intersection of Ideas, Concepts, and Cultures*, Harvard Business Review Press, 2004.

DRIVING INNOVATION

In our interview with Ron Worth, former CEO of the Society of Marketing Professional Services (SMPS) and the International Association of Assessing Officers (IAAO), he talks about how they created a "skunk works" style innovation program inside of his association's marketing group. They aimed to develop innovative ideas for delivering service to their members in ways not tried before.

He empowered them with the tools and resources to let them beta test and get things done. They embraced the "fail fast" idea as the prize. Try new ideas, test them quickly, iterate on the results, and then continue to iterate until the concept is ready to market. It is an outstanding quality of a leader to empower that ability within an organization.

There are two aspects to this approach to innovation. One is having an environment where invention is encouraged. The other is learning to be innovative during a crisis. The pandemic triggered some firms to revamp how they did things. They say, *"We will keep doing these things because they work."*

It is hard to predict, but many organizations may only have embraced new and innovative approaches because of the pandemic. Having an innovation mindset and cultural environment that supports creativity, recognizing a situation that demands change, and being able to test and quickly implement a new plan is the definition of an innovative leader.

ITERATIVE INCREMENTAL INNOVATION

Leaders find a balance because efficiency is comfortable, and innovation is risky. Innovation is like throwing dice. The reality of the — sometimes seismic — shifts in the economic, social, technological, and political landscape means a leader needs to shift with it. That especially applies to design, engineering, and construction, which are historically risk-averse.

Innovation

As an industry, the A/E/C sector is typically very reactive to the needs of client groups with diverse points of view, whether residential, institutional, commercial, retail, healthcare, corporate, or education. They all react differently to change, which drives firms differently because things impact their business or operational model.

There are concepts in innovation that focuses on small change. The Lean Six Sigma[9] and Kaizen[10] approach focuses on optimizing current systems but being open to minor incremental improvements through constantly re-evaluating all the steps in a process.

Many companies in Silicon Valley were early adopters of this approach. Using a "lessons learned" technique, they iterated the outcome of each major (and sometimes minor) effort (i.e., new product, new building, new process, etc.). Focusing on ensuring each new project yielded better results than the previous version and leveraging "what we've learned" allowed them to make the next effort more efficient or better.

As a result, a leader needs perspective. The importance of viewing potential horizons and seeing broadly to convey an innovative concept does not necessarily mean the leader has to be the innovator. But they need to inspire innovation.

Leadership innovation parallels the concepts behind strategic planning. If a leader has a vision for what the firm aspires to be, the

---

[9] Lean Six Sigma is a process improvement approach that uses a collaborative team effort to improve performance by systematically removing operational waste and reducing process variation. It combines Lean Management and Six Sigma to increase the velocity of value creation in business processes.

[10] Kaizen — Japanese for small, incremental improvement — refers to business activities that continuously improve all functions and involve all employees, from the CEO to the assembly line workers. Kaizen also applies to processes, such as purchasing and logistics, that cross organizational boundaries into the supply chain. It has been applied in healthcare, psychotherapy, life coaching, government, and banking.

The Architecture of Vision

point of goal setting is aspirational. Vision conveys aspiration to the organization.

The leader may only partially develop the strategy by saying, *"This is our mountain, and there is the flag. We want to put the flag on the mountain. These are the steps we see and the needed processes will get us there. And these are the individuals, resources, and teams to make it happen."* The goals, objectives, strategies, tactics, timelines, and assigned responsibilities — depending on how granular you want to get — convey the vision.

Approaching planning with a diverse, inclusive, and appreciative inquiry mindset opens the conversation to open-ended questions that yield rich options and team commitment. The appreciative inquiry model includes the following seven steps:

- **Imagine:** *What might happen?* Explore divergent, emerging, and potential business scenarios (i.e., societal, political, economic, technological) that, if relevant, would improve engagement and outcomes. What scenarios — positive and negative — should we plan for?
- **Goals:** *What is important?* How will we measure results and impact? What are our challenges?
- **Impact:** *What matters?* What metrics do we or should we use to measure success? What results if we achieve our goals?
- **Strengths:** *What's working well now?* What lessons learned apply to achieving our goals?
- **Opportunities:** *What could be?* What is possible if we have no limits on resources or time?
- **Aspirations:** *What should be?* How can we rank our opportunities by their potential impact?

- **Results:** *What will be?* How do we measure the results of our approach and efforts (e.g., priorities, commitments, objectives, and metrics)?

Leaders who take this approach develop a much more positive outcome regarding messaging and conveying the vision as motivating toward a goal. Leaders who are open to the gift of feedback — understanding what worked, what did not, and what we do to improve — understand that incremental improvement is part of the innovation process.

Taking an open approach to planning innovation often also means reflecting on things that are not working well. Being honest about low-performing initiatives is a great learning moment and an opportunity for innovation. The chance to change, teach, grow, and improve makes leaders and their organizations dynamic. There is no need to criticize or belabor on problems if the goal is to innovate for better solutions. Being realistic and including some of what has not worked provides a learning path.

As positive as this innovative approach is, the leader does not dismiss competition or other outside issues impacting the ability to execute the vision. Start the framing by understanding the context in which planning occurs. Those competitive issues or structural weaknesses come out in that conversation. Being open to the shared perspective helps. Goal setting requires — even demands — a shared view. The quality that the leader — whether the nominal leader of the organization or the facilitator in a group of leaders — facilitation needs to get everyone involved to reach a forward-looking consensus.

The goal-setting process reflects the leader's style. A leader must make it as transparent, inclusive, and diverse as possible, drawing from internal and external opinions and perspectives.

The Architecture of Vision

LEVERAGING THE COLLECTIVE VISION

Organizations that work together use the collective word "we." Organizations reflect how everyone provides connections to clients, stakeholders, vendors, and affiliates. Those connections include the person who answers the phone and the one who closes the door and turns off the lights. The best leaders understand the importance of starting small and supporting connected and visible leadership regardless of how large the company has grown.

When the leader is the one who started the business, it is hard to let go. Those leaders' personalities are typically defined as "driven." They have goals. They get things done. But they are also less likely to bring people into the conversation before they make a final decision. Successful firms are more collaborative, diverse, and flatter organizations. Giving employees conversational engagement is part of the leader's responsibility. A good leader balances the conversation with getting things done so there is progress and movement.

We identified six traits of innovative leaders — **Discipline, Effort, Agility, Influence, Purpose**, and **Perspective**— that we explore in the following chapters. Each trait's aspects and related behaviors build on an individual's strengths and contribute to personal growth.

Innovation

SYNTHESIS

Innovation is significantly interrelated with the leadership pillars of inspiration and integrity. Leaders must inspire their team members to be innovative and creative by setting a clear vision and purpose for the organization, communicating that vision effectively, and leading by example. Leaders also create a sense of shared purpose and a culture of collaboration that inspires team members to work together toward common goals.

Similarly, leaders with integrity and ethical behavior are transparent and honest in all communications, treating team members and clients with respect and dignity and upholding ethical standards in all business dealings. Leaders who demonstrate integrity are likely to inspire trust and loyalty in their team members and clients, which is essential for building an innovation culture in the professional service firm.

Leaders build successful organizations that thrive in a rapidly changing marketplace by fostering a culture of innovation, inspiring their team members, and operating with integrity and ethical behavior.

The Architecture of Vision

SYNOPSIS

In firms and individual leaders, the hallmark of great leadership is a balance between innovation and efficiency. While innovation entails risks, efficiency leans on the familiar. Successful leaders recognize the importance of adapting to economic, social, technological, and political shifts. This adaptability is particularly evident in the A/E/C sector, where firms are often reactionary, adjusting their operational models based on the changing needs of diverse client groups. A forward-thinking leader, therefore, possesses a broad perspective, inspiring innovation even if they themselves aren't the innovator.

Silicon Valley's "lessons learned" technique is a testament to how top companies iterate and improve upon every project. This iterative approach ensures every subsequent effort is better than the last, with a keen focus on what was learned in the past. Leaders achieve success by clearly conveying their vision, akin to strategic planning. This vision isn't just a distant goal; it's laid out with tangible steps, resources, and teams to realize it. Using the appreciative inquiry model, leaders delve into seven pivotal steps, from imagining potential scenarios to gauging the results of their strategies, optimizing the innovation process, and ensuring continued growth.

By fostering an inclusive and diverse mindset, leaders encourage dialogues that generate rich options and ensure team commitment. Innovative leaders emphasize the importance of progress over perfection, appreciating feedback and understanding that every step, no matter how minor, contributes to innovation. Recognizing and learning from low-performing initiatives fosters a culture of continuous learning and innovation.

Organizations thrive when they leverage all members' collective expertise and perspectives, ensuring everyone has a voice in decision-making.

Chapter 7 | DISCIPLINE: Committing to Goals

We don't have to be smarter than the rest. We have to be more disciplined than the rest. Discipline and hard/smart work – that's the key to success..
Warren Buffet

FOCUS: Set aside the idea of discipline as punishment and think about discipline as the rigor and routine required to develop positive habits.

LEADERS FACE MYRIAD CHALLENGES as they hone their leadership skills. Foremost among these challenges is the development and maintenance of discipline.

Discipline is crucial for several reasons: it directs a leader's efforts towards meaningful outcomes, equips them to navigate unforeseen obstacles, provides metrics for progress assessment, and encourages a continuous improvement mindset. However, discipline's connotations of rigidity and punishment can be off-putting. In leadership, discipline is about commitment, mastering a craft, and inspiring others through consistent actions.

Discipline means structure and planning, which provides the steps to innovate in our field.
— **Delcine Johnson,** President, Johnson & Pace

The Architecture of Vision

Another challenge leaders face is maintaining *focus* amidst complexities. Leaders must strike a balance between advancing current business goals and preparing for future challenges. Getting bogged down in the details can cause a leader to lose sight of the bigger picture, leading to misalignment between their actions and aspirational messages. This inconsistency erodes trust, akin to a brand misalignment where perceived image and self-identity diverge. Leaders must genuinely embody the principles they champion, ensuring their actions and words resonate in harmony.

Finally, the *courage to change* is an integral aspect of leadership. Focused effort and personal discipline differentiate successful leaders in our digital age. Leaders must set clear goals, commit to them, and exhibit the discipline to change behaviors in line with these goals. Combined with disciplined routines, concentrating without distraction equips leaders to produce faster, adding immense value to their organizations.

THE VALUE OF DISCIPLINE

Discipline builds mental and physical capabilities and leads to sustainable performance. Like great athletes, practice leads to perfection. Discipline — committing to goals and practices that help achieve the practice's vision — is the first important trait of innovative leadership development. Key elements include:

- **Discipline Helps Focus the Leader's Efforts.** Innovative leadership development often requires trying new things and taking calculated risks. Discipline and committing to specific goals ensure you work toward something meaningful.
- **Discipline Helps to Overcome Obstacles.** Innovative leadership development is challenging, with unforeseen obstacles along the way. Practicing a disciplined approach

and staying committed to goals helps overcome these obstacles and keep initiatives moving forward.

- **Discipline Helps to Measure Progress.** Commitment make it easier to measure progress and determine whether innovative initiatives are on track to achieving those goals, which is essential for both the leader and the organization.

- **Discipline Supports Continuous Improvement.** Even after achieving a specific goal, leaders should always strive to improve. Discipline helps maintain a focus on constant innovation and personal development.

Disciplined leaders set a clear vision and direction, stay on course, and drive toward goal achievement.

THE IMPORTANCE OF FOCUS

Focus is one term that defines discipline as an essential trait of good leaders. Few, if any, business challenges are completely manageable. There are risks. There are deadlines. Complexity is more the norm than simplicity and clarity. To do anything well takes discipline. Discipline is the execution of high exacting standards.

Focus requires a leader to find the balance between keeping the business going forward, the agility to lead change when things do not stay the same, and the consistency of focus on the future. Leaders who are absorbed in the details must remember to look at the horizon, or else they get so focused on the goals that they forget you must deliver results all along the way. Finding a good balance is critical.

Discipline is a harsh word with a connotation of punishment. But in a leadership development context, discipline is a commitment to a regimen and routine of positive efforts. Discipline is every act needed to master a craft. Discipline is a trait of an inspiring leader that inspires the organization to master its practice. In this context, it is more about a level of discipline than punishment's negative connotation.

At the same time, we all do routine things to get things done and to be efficient. And yet, this working style could be even more disciplined. Inconsistency of the behavior versus the words espoused is challenging for leaders because everybody is always watching.

When there is a disconnect between aspirational words and how a leader behaves, it has a negative impact. Like the firm's brand, a leader's identity is what they say about themselves. Image is how others perceive them. When they are different, there is a disconnect between those two perceptions, creating a gap in brand alignment. Practice what you preach. *"Do as I say, not as I do"* does not work in the context of leadership.

THE COURAGE TO CHANGE

Committing to goals to change behaviors and improve leadership abilities is critical to becoming an effective leader. Setting clear and specific goals helps focus efforts and helps you stay motivated as you work to change your behaviors.

> *Without discipline, one is easily distracted by unplanned disruptions and other people's agendas. It is crucial to remain focused on the things that matter most, the things that move you toward your vision.*
>
> — **Steve Osborn**, PE, SE President, CE Solutions

It is also essential to write down goals. This way, a leader tracks progress and ensures accountability. Additionally, breaking down significant goals into smaller, manageable tasks makes them achievable and helps to build momentum.

Discipline

When it comes to leadership, having a clear sense of purpose and communicating that purpose effectively to others is crucial for inspiring and motivating them. Leaders inspire their teams to work toward a shared vision and foster a culture of excellence by setting and committing to goals that align with a sense of purpose.

Goal setting, planning, and commitment are critical to personal and leadership development. By setting and committing to goals, individuals change their behaviors and improve their abilities personally and as leaders.

THE RESULTS OF FOCUS

In his book, *"Deep Work,"* Cal Newport emphasizes the importance of focus and personal discipline in leadership. He argues that the ability to focus intensely on a task without distractions is becoming increasingly rare and valuable in today's digital age. Newport states that this skill is critical for leaders to succeed in a competitive and fast-paced environment.

Newport suggests that leaders who focus intensely on their work and make considerable progress on important projects will be more successful than those who are easily distracted by the constant flow of information. He also argues that the ability to focus profoundly is a crucial differentiator in today's economy. It allows individuals to produce more quickly and create more value for their organizations. Newport said, *"Focus is the new IQ in the knowledge economy, and individuals who cultivate their ability to concentrate without distraction will thrive."*

Additionally, Newport argues that personal discipline is crucial for leaders, enabling them to apply their focus consistently and effectively

The Architecture of Vision

to their work. He suggests that leaders who establish routines and stick to them better manage their time and achieve their goals.[11]

Discipline defines a commitment to a positive effort. Leaders who practice discipline focus their efforts, overcome obstacles, measure progress, and support continuous improvement. Focus is also essential, requiring leaders to consistently balance the present with the future and deliver results. Committing to specific goals, writing them down, and breaking them down into manageable tasks help individuals and leaders improve their abilities. Finally, focusing intensely and maintaining personal discipline is crucial for success in today's fast-paced and competitive environment.

---

[11] Newport, Cal, *Deep Work: Rules for Focused Success in a Distracted World*, Grand Central Publishing, 2016.

Discipline

SYNTHESIS

A disciplined leadership style is crucial for the firm's success and growth. Discipline involves setting clear goals, establishing processes, and creating a culture of accountability, which, in turn, helps to drive innovation and improve service delivery.

To be effective, disciplined leaders must be inspirational and demonstrate integrity. Inspirational leadership motivates employees to be creative, take risks, and push beyond their limits. Disciplined leadership creates a sense of purpose and direction, which inspires individuals to work towards a shared vision.

Leaders who demonstrate integrity are vital because they foster trust and confidence among employees, clients, and stakeholders. Leaders who are honest, transparent, and ethical in their actions and decisions hold themselves accountable and take responsibility for their actions, which builds credibility and earns the respect of others.

In combination, a disciplined, inspirational, and high-integrity leader creates a powerful and practical approach to innovative practice and helps the firm operate with the highest ethical standards and maintain trust with its clients and stakeholders.

The Architecture of Vision

VIEWPOINT – **LANCE JONES**, PE
President, LSW

Leadership looks much different from the outside compared to when you are in it. Leadership is often challenging but also brings opportunities for great rewards. It is sometimes lonely. A solid and trusted team is essential for survival.

— **Lance Jones**

Fundamentals of Leadership

Vision is a crucial component of leadership. It is critical to create a vision and communicate it to encourage others or to elicit the support of others to help move in that direction. Vision combines creativity, a little luck, and a ton of support. If you master all those, things will go well. It is a balance where all those skills come together in equal proportions.

Because of our size, I often wear multiple hats. A significant part of my role is networking, business development, and client service. Another hat goes on when there are operational requirements, legal issues, or office management. Of course, because I am an engineer, I manage projects too. So, while it is good to do multiple things, it causes distractions, too. That is why it is most important for me to focus on leading the firm.

Integrity is one of the three values we have identified within our company as critically important. How we operate with one another and work with our clients is based on trust. Integrity stands out as the thing you must have to be able to make the right decision based upon what is best for our clients.

Inspiration and innovation are both critical. There is a difference between the entrepreneurial model and the management model. In the entrepreneurial model, we encourage innovation from within, whereas the management model would be to bring someone in and let them drive innovation. Entrepreneurial innovation exists if you try to take over a particular market share or change direction by doing something completely different.

Inspiration is hard. It takes charisma and an understanding of the other person's perspective. Inspiration requires understanding why they do or do not want to follow and what motivates them. What are their pain points, or what are their goals? If you are looking for a common goal, it is because there is either a common enemy or a common good. We want to inspire people to follow the common good because enemies are rarely the thing that motivates us. If you identify that common goal and have everybody rowing in the same direction, it helps.

Communication and Growth

One of the most significant areas for improvement of leaders is being too fixated on their ideas, as opposed to stepping back and letting ideas for development and growth come from other people. When we are too fixated, we squash the innovation and inspiration of other people by pressing for that next great thing — the bright, shiny object that everybody should follow — instead of listening to other people in the organization.

Part of what lets us become leaders is the ability to work with and communicate with others. Part of that may be because we step out more assertively. When you are in a leadership position, it is essential to let other people do their part and to start moving up so the organization backfills behind you. You are not going to be there forever. By allowing others to grow and develop, you will hopefully spy on the person with those seeds you want to help foster.

Organizational Structure

The way we are structured, we have multiple principals within the firm. That structure brings its own set of challenges. It would be easier if we had fewer folks in management. One of the things we do well is give our principals a lot of freedom and latitude in how they work with their clients. Still, the client is the responsibility of the company. Our best marketing is doing an outstanding job with engineering. That is what we try to focus on.

I learned from my mentors that I have an entire office full of people and am responsible for providing continued work and employment for them. Suppose we lose projects — because of the failure of a product we specified — that puts all those people at risk. The understanding of risk was when I learned about responsibility and the weight of leadership. Leadership goes beyond the vision — the part we see and get or give accolades for — it is the part that keeps me up at night.

PROGRESSION – **DISCIPLINE**: Committing to Goals

Set aside discipline as punishment and develop positive habits that build mental or physical capabilities that lead to sustainable performance.

AWARENESS: *Think about these statements on understanding the importance of* **Discipline.**

1. What are three life goals that you plan to accomplish? Why (answer for each purpose)
2. What are three leadership goals that you want to accomplish? Why? (Answer for each goal)
3. Make each goal SMART (Specific, Measurable, Attainable, Relevant, Time-Based)
4. Use any journal or planning system to regularly track goals in the Action phase.

ACCEPTANCE: *Now, reflect on how you reacted when reading these statements. Reflect on what "acceptance" of your truth about what* **Discipline** *means to you.*

1. What excuses will you use not to reach those goals?
2. What hurdles will you have to overcome to attain your goals?
3. What are detours that might get in your way?
4. What is the ONE thing you will do to keep focused on your goals?

The Architecture of Vision

ACTION: *Follow these steps to incrementally put that awareness and acceptance into action to strengthen your ability to develop leadership with* **Discipline.**

1. Post your goals and whys so you see them every day.
2. Share your goals with a friend, mentor, supervisor, or someone whose insights you value.
3. Review your goals at least monthly and notice your progress.
4. Meet with the person you identified in #1 to discuss progress twice yearly
5. Read Joco Willink and Leif Babin's **Extreme Leadership: How US Navy Seals Lead and Win.** The Navy Seals' discipline and its application in leadership contexts provide invaluable lessons.

Discipline

SYNOPSIS

Discipline is one of the cornerstones of effective leadership. Disciplined leaders clearly understand their organization's objectives and the broader industry landscape. They are strategic thinkers who can foresee potential challenges and opportunities.

Effective leaders drive tangible outcomes for their organizations. They set clear, ambitious goals and mobilize their teams to achieve them. Such leaders foster a culture of innovation and continuous improvement through their actions. They are also adept at navigating challenges and making informed decisions even in uncertain situations. As a result, their firms often report enhanced productivity, employee engagement, and profitability. several competencies:

- **Strategic Vision:** The ability to set a clear direction for the future, considering immediate and long-term goals.
- **Emotional Intelligence:** Understanding and managing one's emotions while empathizing with and effectively responding to team members' emotions.
- **Decision-Making:** Analyzing available data and insights to make informed choices, even when faced with ambiguity.
- **Communication Skills:** Clearly and persuasively conveying ideas, fostering open dialogue, and ensuring alignment within the team.
- **Adaptability:** Being receptive to change, learning from experiences, and pivoting strategies when necessary.

By understanding and embodying these elements of disciplined leadership, individuals can propel their journey toward becoming truly impactful leaders.

The Architecture of Vision

REFLECTIONS & INSIGHTS

Chapter 8 | EFFORT: Defining the Practice

Do or do not. There is no try.
Yoda

FOCUS: Effort requires guts and grit to persevere internally and externally.

LEADERS ARE OFTEN CHALLENGED to define the nature of their practice's mission, vision, values, and goals. The concept of "effort" is a foundational aspect of innovative leadership. The benefits include better market alignment and enhanced stakeholder engagement.

Clarifying the practice's objectives and the value it delivers is a critical component of the leader's value. Hence, for innovative leadership, it is crucial that effort is viewed through the client's lens, ensuring both internal and external clients are aligned with the practice's promise.

Aspirational leaders seek excellence and innovation to elevate the profession. Leaders can steer their professional service firms toward genuine success by cultivating positive leadership attributes, addressing negative traits, consistently upgrading skills, and making ethical decisions.

THE IMPORTANCE OF DEFINING EFFORT

Defining the nature of the practice — its mission, vision, goals, and values as "effort" is the second important aspect of innovative leadership development. The effort is vital to the success of leadership because it helps define the organization's purpose and direction.

The Architecture of Vision

- **The Mission** defines the organization's current purpose and the specific benefits it provides its clients.
- **The Vision** describes the organization's aspirations and what it hopes to achieve soon.
- **Values** provide a framework for decision-making and guide the behavior of the organization's employees in service to their clients and their communities.

These three elements help create a shared sense of purpose and direction among the organization's employees, which is crucial for effective leadership and success. Additionally, the firm communicates its intention to clients, stakeholders, and potential employees with a clear mission, vision, and values. A well-defined effort leads to better alignment with the needs of the firm's markets and improved engagement from employees, clients, and other stakeholders.

A FRAMEWORK FOR SUCCESS

Where the mission defines the "what" the practice provides its clients, the vision describes its aspirations. Goals and objectives underpin the strategies — internally and externally — that set the firm's direction. Values — discussed in greater depth in Chapter 16 — define the integrity with which the firm practices. These terms represent the leadership's effort to serve its clients, employees, and stakeholders.

A clearly defined effort provides direction. Innovative leadership development requires a clear sense of direction. A well-defined mission and vision help guide decision-making and ensure everyone in the organization is working toward the same goals.

A well-defined effort inspires commitment. When people understand and believe in the organization's goals, they are likely to be committed to achieving them. Duty is essential for innovative leadership development, as it takes effort and commitment to bring innovative ideas to fruition.

Effort

A clearly understood effort helps align resources. Innovative leadership development requires using resources such as time, money, and personnel. A clear mission and vision help to align these resources and ensure effective effort.

A well-communicated effort helps connect the firm's clients, those clients' clients, and the practice's community with the firm's purpose. Innovative leadership development often requires communication and collaboration across different departments and teams. A clearly defined effort ensures that everyone is working toward the same objectives.

The effort defines the practice's mission and vision and is essential to innovative leadership development. It helps to build a shared understanding of the organization's goals and objectives, which is crucial for creative leadership development.

THE WHAT, HOW, AND WHO BEHIND THE WHY

"What are we going to do?" defines one aspect of the effort. Expanding the definition to *"Whom are we serving?"* — framed by value delivered — sets the service's goal. In innovation, effort is often the niche versus the generalist. Efforts can be local versus regional versus national versus international or global. The question is always: *"What are we trying to be? Who are we serving? What value does that bring to them?"*

Behind these questions is an equally important question: *"Why?"* This question is both a leadership challenge and a dilemma. Defining the effort is an integral part of the vision. Establishing the *"what"* behind the *"why"* is at the core of the business strategy.

Defining the organizational *"why"* — in the voice of the client — is a critical concept behind defining effort. The effort must be highly focused and service-based. Clients do not care about a leader or organization's why in the aspirational or metaphorical sense. They care

The Architecture of Vision

about what you are doing and how it helps them — the intersection between *"what"* and *"how"* is a benefit they find valuable.

For the innovative leader, the effort must be seen through the client's lens and conveyed as insight. Similarly, leaders must communicate the action to all the employees so they embrace the vision of the effort to deliver on the practice's promise. The leader defines effort for both internal and external clients. Internally, it is the people they work with. Externally, it is the people that they work for. Like the sections and chapters of this book, having an effort as a focus is critical to the practice's success.

GENERALISTS v. SPECIALISTS

Many professional service firms choose to be generalists because it is easy. A generalist practice takes on any project. Not all firms are created equal, but the generalist tends to fall into the category where it is more difficult for a potential client to differentiate one from another.

Alternatively, a firm chooses to be a specialist, focusing on a niche that allows it to compete against a smaller cohort of similar firms. While the generalist satisfies the middle sector of client opportunities, they are rarely known for innovation. Leadership makes the call that defines the effort, but notable firms typically provide a more inspirational and innovative approach.

The counterargument to a niche focus is the necessity to generate consistent revenue. If a niche market declines and a firm needs to be more diverse, pivoting to more consistent revenue generation takes work. Market uncertainty is why many firms choose to be more generalist or have defined market silos.

It takes leadership courage to define what the firm does and whom it is doing it for and to live with it to create a sustainable business. That is where innovation comes in. There are always opportunities to develop a niche strategy because those firms innovate with deep knowledge of a subject.

EFFORT AS A HINDRANCE

One reason firms attempt to refrain from growing or not flourishing is that there is comfort in staying focused on the initial effort. Leaders might say, *"Stay in our lane. We know what we are doing."* Leadership finds and hires people like themselves. There are many practices like that in the professional sector.

However, if leadership is aspirational, the practice works in service by doing excellent (not simply good), creative (not just mundane), and innovative (not average) work that serves our clients and advances the profession. Part of the aspiration is to raise the bar for the whole profession. If there is one thing the books in this series advocate, it is aspirational thinking: Finding ways better to serve our client's needs and the profession.[12]

There is an old saying that doing good work will generate one good referral, but doing substandard work will generate ten bad references. The problem compounds because most clients associate the work of service firms with "professional." So, when service quality is less than expected, or clients have a terrible experience, they are less likely to hire a good professional consultant and more likely to go in another direction entirely. That diminishes the whole service sector.

Like many licensed professionals, architects and engineers enforce the ethical practices they must provide. However, many professional services "consultants" are non-licensed and have no enforcement mechanism for their ethical behavior. From the client's perspective, a firm's performance impacts everyone in that sector. In defining

---

[12] Also by Craig Park, *The Architecture of Value: Building Your Professional Practice*, and *The Architecture of Image: Branding Your Professional Practice*, published by Laquilan Leadership Press in 2003 and 2013, respectively.

The Architecture of Vision

"effort," a leader must convey the importance of professionalism and the aspiration to be the best.

THE PATH TO APPLIED EFFORT

In Buddhism, "right effort" refers to the principle of sustained effort to develop and maintain positive qualities and overcome negative ones. Right effort applies to leadership in four ways:

- **First, Develop Positive Leadership Qualities** such as compassion, wisdom, and integrity. By sustaining these qualities, a leader more effectively guides the organization toward its goals and builds trust with employees and clients.

- **Next, Avoid Negative Leadership Traits** such as greed, anger, and ignorance. A leader becomes more effective in fostering a positive and productive work environment by making a sustained effort to identify and overcome these negative traits.

- **Third, Maintain and Improve Skills and Knowledge** necessary for leading a professional service firm. By staying informed about industry trends and developments, a leader can more effectively guide the organization toward success.

- **Finally, Balance the Organization's Activities** and make ethical decisions. By balancing the needs of the organization, employees, clients, and other stakeholders, a leader fosters a sense of fairness and justice.

Centering the practice's mission, vision, and values on the right effort is essential for leaders to move a professional service firm toward success. By developing positive qualities, overcoming negative ones, staying informed, and making ethical and balanced decisions, the strategies that support the overarching vision of the firm can be realized.

Effort

SYNTHESIS

The effort of an innovative leader's mission, vision, and values is essential for its success. The effort involves aligning all activities, decisions, and strategies with the firm's core purpose and values guiding its operations. Alignment helps create a clear sense of direction and purpose and provides a foundation for success.

An effort-based leadership style is integral to inspirational and high-integrity leadership. Inspirational leadership is vital because it helps to motivate employees and inspire them to strive toward the firm's goals. Effort creates a sense of purpose and direction and encourages individuals to work toward a shared vision.

High-integrity leadership helps build trust and credibility between the firm, its clients, and its stakeholders. Leaders who are honest, transparent, and ethical in their actions and decisions hold themselves accountable and take responsibility for their actions, which builds credibility and earns the respect of others.

The Architecture of Vision

VIEWPOINT – **LEE SLADE**, PE
Chairman, Walter P Moore

A leader makes sure there is a clear vision. They lead the development of that vision and then communicate it consistently and powerfully to get people aligned behind it, excited about it, and committed to it.

— Lee Slade

The Imperative of Leadership Development

First, leadership is crucially important. It is a standing board agenda item for us. We realized how important it was for the board to be responsible for ensuring a flow of good leadership talent through the company. We needed to provide leadership at every level related to enabling ownership transition at every level. We have done an excellent job ensuring the ownership transition, but we still need to be there for the leadership transition.

We sent individuals to ACEC Senior Executive Institute, which I graduated from in class five. That is expensive but an excellent leadership development program. To develop the number of leaders that we need — we have about 750 people in twenty-three locations working in fifteen practice areas — we need leadership development down to the managing director level. That helps with succession plans, emergencies, and long-term planning. We focused on providing candidates at the executive level.

The Art and Pitfalls of Leadership in the A/E/C Industry

A leader makes sure there is a clear vision. They lead the development of that vision and then communicate it consistently and powerfully to get people aligned behind it, excited about it, and committed to it. If a leader does nothing else, that is what they must do.

In the A/E/C industry, for varied reasons — usually technical prowess and ego — leaders do the wrong things for the wrong reasons. Sometimes, they get too deep in the weeds, or worse, they believe too much in their own press. We hope we all aspire to the humility of servant leadership. Leadership is something that we must take seriously and think about every time we turn around.

We are developing a leadership development program called Impact, which has fifteen inaugural participants at the point in their careers where they need to build leadership skills intentionally. I am not talking about management. Management is different than leadership. Leaders understand systems thinking, strategic planning, scenario planning, and change management. Leaders must understand what it takes. You do not just wake up one day and go to a class and say, *"Okay, now I've moved from a manager to a leader in our industry."*

You asked who the leaders that you admire in our industry are. Well, the A/E/C industry has so far to go. No one person stands out. We have a lot of good leaders, but we need to do a better job of separating management from leadership and developing stronger leaders.

Navigating Modern Leadership Models

Management and leadership are different skill sets. When I started my career, I was told, "There's one horse, one cowboy," meaning every organization should have one leader and only one leader. I am more of a believer in team leadership. We have developed something we call the balanced leadership model. It has four quadrants of leadership: design leadership, organizational leadership, operational leadership, and client leadership.

Project leadership is essential as opposed to just project management. That is where you start learning how to build teams, influence people to go beyond themselves and collaborate, and get them to do things they do not want. All those good leadership skills become crucial when leading a more extensive group up to the board level.

I am in an interesting, exciting place. I just submitted my statement of interest in being reelected to the board next year. We elect our board every year. So, I need to be reelected to chair every year. We have been moving to a nominal three-year cycle. You want your board, Chairman, or CEO to stay the same because it sends a message to the world that you are stable. On the other hand, we have a powerful CEO form of management.

Leadership in Crisis: A Case Study from the Pandemic

The CEO has real responsibilities. My role as Chairman is to lead the CEO and guide the board to act as the boss the CEO needs. I see that as someone supportive, someone who provides a good vision and accountability and provides resources and all those things.

We want the board to refrain from making operational decisions. We have other operating units for that. We have a marketing council, which focuses on strategy, and an operations council. Those are the bodies that the CEO counts on to get things done. My role is to ensure that we have a strategy, that we are following that strategy, and that the CEO is consistent and accountable in managing the operation.

As the Chairman, I ensure we focus on the right things in the company's leadership. That has never been more important than today. The pandemic changed our response to that of the adaptive and agile leader, showing the organization what we can do. I am creating a half-day session for our Impact program on leadership in crisis, using our COVID-19 response as a case study of what we did and did not do. The takeaway from that is in terms of lessons for future crisis leadership.

The Critical Role of Inspiration

While the leader's inspirational role sounds fuzzy and soft, it is essential. To inspire, there must be a vision. That vision must be robust and articulate. It starts with values. Core values are non-negotiables. Core values are who you are as a company. We try to live our values built not just on integrity — doing the right thing for the right reasons — but also on respecting and treating people right and being willing to own our errors. Values are the most important thing because, without values, you have nothing. Values set the boundaries within which we live and work.

Inspiration, innovation, and integrity work together. But inspiration is the critical element. If you get your team aligned — inspired — around a goal, we will find ways to innovate. We will find ways to get better, do things faster, or do them cheaper. Our clients are more sophisticated than ever. We must innovate. But innovation does not just happen. When you see it, you must reward it. Challenges drive engineers. We love to solve problems, do things better, do them faster, and innovate.

Reputation, Client Experience, and People

We have nothing if we do not have clients. We do not have a position in the marketplace. HR says our most important asset is our people. I am afraid I must disagree. Our people are number three. Our reputation is number one. Our reputation builds on trust. We do what we say we are going to do. We create a client experience. Client experience is number two. That is what differentiates us in the marketplace. So, people, clients, and reputation are all bound together in how we market. Everything we

The Architecture of Vision

do is marketing. I look at everything in the business from the standpoint of client maintenance.

Leaders must learn not just how to delegate but how to trust. Ken Blanchard's *Situational Leadership* is a fantastic model for leaders to understand that sometimes you must be directive, and sometimes you must delegate. Learning how to get the best out of people requires learning how different people respond differently. The first person you must understand is yourself.

Effort

PROGRESSION – **EFFORT**: The What Behind the Why

Effort requires guts and grit to persevere, both internally and externally.

AWARENESS: *Think about these statements on understanding the importance of* ***Effort.***

1. Notice when you avoid certain situations because they seem too difficult.
2. What holds you back?
3. What excuses do you make that keep you from trying, experimenting, or asking for help?
4. Notice how other people learn to overcome weaknesses or challenges. What is the difference between them and you?

ACCEPTANCE: *Now, reflect on how you reacted when reading these statements. Reflect on what "acceptance" of your truth about what* ***Effort*** *means to you.*

1. What situations do you regularly face, and now that you are aware of your tendency to avoid them, would you be willing to do something different to develop guts and grit?
2. What help do you need to move forward?
3. What is the first step to moving forward?
4. What is a reasonable period for you to make progress?

ACTION: *Follow these steps to incrementally put that awareness and acceptance into action to strengthen your ability to develop leadership with* ***Effort.***

1. Read biographies of people who have dealt with challenges and overcame them. (See the reading list at the back of the book)

The Architecture of Vision

2. Create a list of affirmation statements that inspire you to push through challenges. Post them so you see them every day.
3. Review your #1 step in the Acceptance phase and start doing the #3 step.
4. Tell a friend, mentor, or supervisor.
5. Use your journal to keep track of your progress, noticing your feelings, accomplishments, obstacles, and feelings that make you want to quit.
6. Do not quit. Finish that effort.
7. Celebrate that accomplishment with your friend, mentor, or supervisor.
8. Pick another challenge to build your perseverance.
9. Read Jim Collins and Jerry Porras, **Built to Last: Successful Habits of Visionary Companies.** This looks into how sustained effort has contributed to the success of visionary companies.

Effort

SYNOPSIS

A clear definition of effort helps effective leaders excel in defining their organization's mission, vision, and values. This ensures a cohesive sense of purpose and direction within the firm. With a client-centric vision, they possess the ability to view efforts through the client's perspective, ensuring that the services and value offered align with clients' genuine needs and aspirations.

Leaders who decide strategically whether to position their firm as generalists or specialists recognize specialization's innovative potential despite market volatility challenges. Rather than resting in comfort zones, good leaders are aspirational, always seeking to elevate the quality of work and innovate, thereby advancing the profession.

Leaders create a shared sense of purpose by clearly defining mission, vision, and values, ensuring the entire organization rows in the same direction. Effective leaders communicate the firm's intent to stakeholders, resulting in improved engagement from employees, clients, and other parties involved.

Through clear effort, they align the firm with market needs, ensuring that the services offered are relevant and beneficial to the clients. By prioritizing excellence and innovation, they contribute to elevating the standards of the entire professional sector.

Leaders should develop the competency to perceive services through the client's lens, focusing on tangible benefits over abstract aspirations. Given the challenges of market volatility, leaders must remain adaptable, especially if they lean towards a niche or specialist strategy. Rooted in the concept of "right effort", leaders must sustain positive qualities like compassion and integrity, overcome negative traits, stay updated with industry trends, and make balanced, ethical decisions for the organization's well-being.

The Architecture of Vision

REFLECTIONS & INSIGHTS

Chapter 9 | AGILITY: Expanding Horizons

In my action, I may soar as high as I now discern with this clear eye.
Henry David Thoreau

FOCUS: Agility is the ability to move quickly and easily and think and understand quickly.

Agility in the face of changing circumstance is one of the challenges all leaders face. With factors like pandemics altering market conditions, leaders are confronted with unforeseen shifts, often rendering their firm's mainstay services obsolete or less relevant. Firms that narrow their focus excessively on specialized services may struggle with adaptability when market demands evolve.

As leadership roles move from generation to generation, the balance between technical expertise and operational leadership becomes vital, and maintaining this balance is challenging. As firms expand, it becomes harder to instill agility across departments without creating silos. In the face of external changes, like economic or political shifts, leaders should quickly reorient their teams toward new goals.

Innovation is contingent on change... pivot, redirect, or reimagine a new process, service, or market. Without agility, the stress outweighs the reward.
— **Dena Silver**, retired President, M. Silver & Co.

Beyond mere reactivity, leaders must cultivate responsiveness to changes, marrying long-term vision with the flexibility to adapt. Leaders should foster inter-professional brainstorming by adopting methodologies like design thinking, drawing from diverse domains for innovative problem-solving.

Leaders need to ensure that, as firms transition across generations, they blend technical and operational acumen, addressing the unique challenges of each generational change.

THE IMPORTANCE OF AGILITY

Expanding horizons or pivoting in the face of changing circumstances is critical to innovative leadership. Agile leaders help their firms in several ways:

- **Adapting to changing market conditions.** Professional service firms operate in a constantly changing environment. Being agile and adapting quickly to new market conditions is crucial for success.

- **Staying ahead of the competition.** By being agile and open to innovative ideas, professional service firms stay ahead of the competition and maintain a competitive edge.

- **Identifying new opportunities.** Professional service firms that are agile and willing to explore innovative ideas and approaches will likely identify new opportunities that drive growth and success.

- **Managing risk.** By being agile and able to pivot quickly in the face of changing circumstances, professional service firms better manage risk and minimize potential negative impacts.

Agile leaders navigate uncertainty and change, make quick decisions, adapt to innovative ideas, and take risks. All of which are crucial elements to succeed in a professional service firm.

UNEXPECTED CHALLENGES

The recent pandemic has changed our perspective on many things. There has been much discussion about the "pivot." A leader's biggest challenge is an unexpected change in conditions. The difference could be economic or political, or competitive market forces. For example, the pandemic hit the commercial office space market hard. The impact affected all aspects of the A/E/C services sector.

If you are in a practice that focuses on a particular market, and something changes that market's model, the speed with which a leader engages their team makes a significant difference between success and failure.

How do we pivot? The key is extending your horizon only a little, which allows the organization to be more agile. A planning horizon of one to three years — instead of the more typical five or ten years — with quarterly and yearly interim reviews gives an organization a set of checks and balances against outside influences that may impact the practice.

From a leadership perspective, an agile approach is a willingness and ability to make decisions quickly. Leaders must be agile, nimble, and responsive to outside influences. The leader is responsible for the health of the enterprise. Organizations — even those that are good to great — that do not adapt to changing environments do not survive. Think, Kodak.

The nature of a globally interconnected world requires companies to be agile, which means their leaders must be agile. Nothing lasts as long as it used to. Change happens faster. Clients want more and better and cheaper. Add technology that impacts all aspects of the organization. Everything is going to change, and that changes everything.

> *Your firm is only as strong as your leadership and reflects how the firm operates through decisions and crises, good and bad. When leadership is a priority, the impact naturally trickles down. Those who progress and move up learn the best way to lead.*
> — **Delcine Johnson,** President, Johnson & Pace

RESPONSIVE ACTION

The impact of change raises the concept of responsiveness. From the standpoint of expanding horizons, it is vital to have a long-term view, but it cannot be so cast in stone that it prevents being responsive, not just reactive. Agility is both a product of innovation and a requirement to be innovative. To be creative, you must be agile.

Chan Kim and Renee Mauborgne, the authors of *Blue Ocean Strategy*, discuss looking for the gaps in response to change. They stress finding service needs and market opportunities.[13] In the case of professional service, that approach often takes a different mindset.

Professional service providers train in whatever their technical skill set is and do that daily. Leaders ask, *"Can we apply our service offering to a new market?"* Or seeing something from a different sector and imagining what would result if applied to their organization.

Inter-professional brainstorming programs are notable examples of drawing innovative ideas from disparate and divergent thinking.

---

[13] Kim, W.C. and R. Mauborgne, Blue Ocean Strategy: How to Create Uncontested Market Space and Make the Competition Irrelevant, Harvard Business Review Press, 2015.

Agility

Bringing disparate thought to problem-solving is a sign of an open-minded leader. The old saying, *"No one is as smart as all of us,"* opens the opportunity for collaborative planning, both a feature and a benefit of agile thinking.

The term design thinking refers to an approach to innovation. In application, design thinking is an empathetic approach to problem-solving. As a methodology, design thinking provides a framework to address a design challenge. Agile leadership involves engaging others in conversations beyond yourself and leveraging their input to pivot and improve the organization.

GENERATIONAL LEADERSHIP

An entrepreneur starts many first-generation firms. They bring design expertise, operations experience, and the business development understanding needed to launch a new service. There are many examples of the three-legged stool model, where each of those traits — design, operations, and marketing — are represented by three different leaders. That is how the company grows.

As firms move into second-generation or third-generation leaders, there tend to be more non-technical professionals in leadership positions. Leadership realizes that the specific skills required are more business operational background and less about the technical knowledge associated with the professional services offered.

From an agility standpoint, technical professionals — who know what they do well — risk not being very agile when they know it is highly specialized. Developing broader operational, financial, and marketing muscles helps with practice agility. That goes for any practice, whether law, architecture, engineering, management, or accounting.

The Architecture of Vision

THE T-SHAPED ORGANIZATION

Employers and educators increasingly prioritize boundary-crossing competencies such as teamwork, communication, perspective, networks, and critical thinking across many disciplines. This model includes many systems and disciplines and requires thorough understanding and communication.

Individuals who bridge the traditional boundaries between disciplines are called "T-shaped Professionals" (see Figure 1). A greater focus on competency-based skills in this model has the potential to close the gap between traditional rote education and the needs of the workplace.

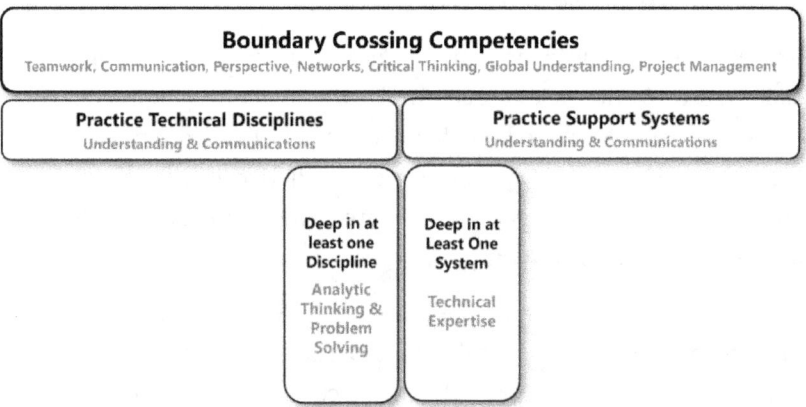

Figure 1 – T-Shaped Professional

First coined by IDEO,[14] a respected international design firm, and studied and developed by IBM in conjunction with Michigan State University, a T-shaped professional has not only deep contextual understanding/knowledge in their discipline (the base of the "T") but also a competency-based skill set needed in the workforce. A person who delves into other disciplines and understands how they all work together to solve real problems is what employers look for in a recruit.

---

[14] https://www.ideo.com/

Agility

Any vision for undergraduate education must focus on preparing students with these fundamental competencies.[15]

Today's employers want multidisciplinary workers capable of responding creatively to unexpected situations. Leveraging the values of the T-shaped professional across all aspects of the organization provides a foundation for flexible and functional leadership development.

The broader your conversations, the more comprehensive your experiences, and the wider the team, the better it will be for the client because everyone benefits from all those differences. The earlier discussion of the T-shaped professional would naturally extend that to the leadership. When you assemble a leadership team, people should have broad knowledge and be specialists in their practice area to make it cohesive. When you have that, the organization is better positioned to be agile in the face of change.

Figure 2 illustrates a T-shaped leadership team model that provides growth opportunities in all aspects of professional practice.

Figure 2 - T-Shaped Leadership Team

---

[15] Web reference: https://en.wikipedia.org/wiki/T-shaped_skills

The Architecture of Vision

From that perspective, as the firm develops and grows, T-shaped professionals naturally become T-shaped leaders — those with deep and broad skill sets — to build the structure of practice leadership.

While C-Suite titles can be aspirational for some, they are used here to illustrate leadership roles in any organization. The T-Shaped leader sees roles and responsibilities as more important than position and power.

In our conversation in Chapter 1 with Amanda Bogner, CEO at Energy Studio, we learned how conscious she was that — even as the firm's leader — she was not exclusively the knowledge keeper of everything. She knew there were good people "around her," not "below her." Leaders are conscious of the importance of the contributions of others.

MARKETING THE SERVICE

The same agility issues apply to marketing and business development. Technical professionals who understand the value of marketing and become doers/sellers or sellers/doers possess an agile mindset that allows them to think outside their more technical framework. By expanding horizons, they are removing limits to personal growth.

In many organizations, the business developer is only a business developer. Suppose the technical professional seller/doer is good at finding and helping build the business, becoming the de facto salesperson of the firm. In that case, they are often seen, erroneously, as non-technical. When a technical person represents the firm, they understand the practice's design and operations. It is a challenge to overcome that perception, but one that is part of the pathway to leadership.

Although good business developers are essential, good leaders acknowledge that winning work also depends on having solid teams for marketing, proposal writing, project management, technical design, and construction coordination. Recognizing and celebrating the team's contribution builds the brand because the ultimate solution delivered to the client is not just the sale. It is the delivery of the result. That is a team effort.

BECOMING AN AGILE LEADER

These leadership traits are easier to identify and implement when you have a small firm. Coaching and mentoring are easier to implement. As a firm grows, the trend is to make them small by focusing on departments to build new leaders within a narrow silo. For developing leaders, it is a challenge not to get so focused on the vertical stem of the "T" and build broader communication. Interprofessional skills are across the top bar of the "T." Those skills are the ones that give the ability to have insightful conversations.

Bill Taylor, the cofounder of Fast Company, said it well, *"The true mark of a leader is the willingness to stick with a bold course of action even as the rest of the world wonders why you're not marching in step with the status quo. In other words, real leaders are happy to zig while others zag. They understand that in an era of hyper-competition and non-stop disruption, the only way to stand out is to stand for something special."*[16]

---

[16] Shared by contributor Craig Galati, FAIA, FSMPS, LGA Architecture

The Architecture of Vision

SYNTHESIS

An agile leader who quickly pivots and adapts to changing circumstances is likely to inspire team members and build trust with clients if they operate with integrity. An inspiring leader who motivates and engages their team members is likelier to create a culture of agility and innovation if they work with integrity. A leader who operates with integrity is likely to inspire trust and respect from team members and clients, contributing to agility and creativity in problem-solving.

Agility, inspiration, and integrity are interrelated in complex and dynamic ways. Leaders who cultivate and embody these qualities help their firms thrive in an ever-changing business landscape. The ability to quickly adapt to changing situations, be flexible, and navigate complex challenges is essential for staying ahead of the competition, responding to clients' evolving needs, and keeping up with technological advancements and industry trends.

Motivating and engaging team members during times of change inspires employees to be more productive, creative, and committed to their work, benefiting the firm and its clients. The fundamental traits of honesty, ethics, and transparency in all business dealings and upholding exacting standards of professionalism and accountability are essential for establishing a solid reputation and sustaining long-term success during normal times, but even more so during changing or challenging times. Agile leaders adapt to changing market conditions, identify new opportunities, stay ahead of the competition, and manage risks.

Agility

VIEWPOINT – **LINDA CROUSE,** LEED AP BD+C
Principal/Board Chair, BAR Architects

Leadership is about communicating goals, processes, and actions and helping others become future leaders.
— Linda Crouse

The Core Tenets of Leadership

Leadership is visionary, inspirational, and strategic. All those factors come into play in understanding how to inspire someone to help them reach their best potential and contribute to the firm. People can be leaders in different ways. To inspire others, you need to understand what skills sets they need to develop to become a leader.

As Board Chair and Director of Marketing at BAR, I set strategy. I am constantly looking at how we are developing leaders, recognizing those with potential, and trying to inspire them. It is not about training but understanding how to get each individual excited about the opportunity to lead. I'm in regular contact with many of our staff to understand their concerns and goals.

I prioritize working with my partners to improve client, consultant, and staff relationships through marketing and firm-wide leadership. We want our leadership to motivate the staff to perform as well as they do. We are only as good as our weakest link if they are not performing.

Innovation, inspiration, and integrity are well aligned. I talked about motivation, but innovation is critical, too. Every leader must be an innovator. You also must be able to surround yourself with innovators, recognize when there is a promising idea, and support it. One of my favorite quotes is *'Winners lose more than losers lose."* because winners take more risks. They may lose, but they win more overall. That is the thing with innovation. You must try a lot of stuff before something sticks.

Integrity is huge. You must be sincere. Honesty and integrity are critical. It helps to have honest dialogue. If you want people's support, you must be truthful and have integrity.

Navigating the Pitfalls

One leadership weakness is making decisions too quickly. There is a delicate balance of being fast enough. If you do not consider enough information, you can get into a mindset of an almost automatic 'No.' So, rather than finding what is wrong with this, try understanding what is right about it and what is needed. That is critical. Leaders must recognize we are not all perfect. We are not able to do everything. Some people are amazing and can do most, but we all have different leadership strengths and weaknesses.

Understanding how to support ourselves by leveraging the strengths of other people in the organization helps strengthen our shortcomings and our organization. Some leaders are great internal leaders but may need better public speakers. Understanding each person's strengths and how best to support and build on those strengths is vital.

Building on Strengths

Leadership development helps with the present day and building the future. We have programs where we look at different qualities and capabilities of what people are doing and how to foster growth best. We also have an excellent training program for various levels of staff and leadership. Our HR director is an expert at helping us figure out broader training programs that target the firm, teams, smaller groups, and individuals with specific training.

We also have a program relating to our people, one on one. We check in with them to understand their needs and include them in the dialogue. You must know how things are going with the people so you can help them, provide opportunities, and recognize those with leadership potential or other talents that may appear in their day-to-day responsibilities.

Our retreats have sessions that include junior staff, intermediate level, and principals. It's often a way of recognizing what the team brings and setting a framework for future opportunities. It helps us identify what training may be needed and what we can do to help them further develop.

We are also constantly training from a perspective of marketing (who you know), sustainability (environmental education), and design (our people and our practice), looking for opportunities for knowledge sharing. It begets leadership because we have broader firm-wide initiatives related to individual goals and development initiatives. We work with our associates and senior associates to develop programs for them to get involved — to demonstrate their passion — and through those programs, we can recognize their leadership abilities.

The Value of Mentorship

One of my early mentors was an early SMPS leader, Margaret Spaulding. She supported my growth from both a marketing and a female perspective. I began my A/E/C career as a receptionist for a small SF-based design firm, then became a marketing assistant at another firm. I took a class through the UC Berkeley Extension, and Margaret was the teacher. I followed up, and we developed a mentor/protégé relationship. She was part of the original "Bird Doggers Anonymous" group (i.e., Bill Hankinson, Jim Rosarito, William 'Sandy' D'Elia, and others) that became the founders of

SMPS. All those people were kind to me and became mentors. I was young, and they inspired me.

My father was also a mentor to me. He taught me to believe in myself, supported what I wanted to do, and be out there and accomplish things. He helped me learn how to relate to people. He was very sociable and a people person with a can-do attitude.

Finally, there was a local San Francisco-area A/E/C management consultant, Patrick Bell. He worked as an advisor to the firm where I started in marketing. He is an excellent listener but also very direct. He was instrumental in hiring me. I met him during my interview, which was extremely thorough. But he always believed in me and supported me through all my seventeen years with the firm. He saw my potential. Knowing how bright he is, it meant a lot that he took an interest in my growth.

And while all those people were inspirational and helpful, I do not believe that I ever had a real mentor the way that we mentor now. Not to get too Yoda about it, but I had to make my way. indeed, indeed, a trial by fire. I just had to do it. My father and mother instilled the belief that 'you do it,' and I believed I could do anything.

I would have loved to have a real mentor to give me feedback and say, 'Oh, think about this or look at this.' We do more training and development work now because of the generational change in the organization. It is quite a different time now, one where we recognize and prioritize the value mentoring and training brings to both the individual and the organization, and it is excellent.

Intersecting Leadership and Marketing

Marketing and leadership are very much tied together. The best marketing is asking questions and listening. It is hearing what people are saying and then relating it to what they say. Those listening skills are also crucial in finding hidden objections or hidden agendas. Understanding people is a vital attribute of a leader and an essential need in marketing. And if you do not naturally have that skill, you best surround yourself by people who do and learn from them.

The Architecture of Vision

PROGRESSION – **AGILITY**: Expanding Horizons

An agile leader recognizes that continuous learning and improvement drive business success.

AWARENESS: *Think about these statements on building an understanding of the importance of* ***Agility.***

1. What are your favorite subjects to learn about, personally and professionally?
2. What is a dream you have for continuous learning?
3. What professional degrees, licenses, or certifications do you aspire to complete?
4. What is your progress for those?
5. How much time or resources do you allocate for continuous learning per day, week, or year? Be specific. What keeps you from finishing those efforts?
6. What are the resources needed to complete a learning dream you have if you still need to start it?

ACCEPTANCE: *Now, reflect on how you reacted when reading these statements. Reflect on what "acceptance" of your truth about what* ***Agility*** *means to you.*

1. What will you sacrifice to complete the items in #3 in the Awareness section?
2. What help do you need to move forward with your continuous learning dream?
3. Are your learning dreams large enough?
4. How will you feel when you accomplish a learning dream?

5. When you are entirely honest with yourself, what holds you back from investing in skills that will improve your career success?

ACTION: *Follow these steps to incrementally put that awareness and acceptance into action to strengthen your ability to develop leadership with* **Agility.**

1. Be available to dedicate yourself to learning every day, week, month, or year. Set aside time in your calendar and keep the time from slipping. Reschedule if you need to and keep your commitment to continuous learning.

2. Dedicate learning time to "hard" and "people" skills that improve your leadership agility.

3. Set a deadline to finish courses, especially free or low-cost online learning.

4. Attend learning opportunities outside your profession to learn how other businesses operate. Share your insights with a friend or mentor or in a company meeting or workshop.

5. Create a list of subjects and topics you want to know more about so you can take advantage of learning opportunities.

6. Read Franz Johansson's **The Medici Effect: Breakthrough Insights at the Intersection of Ideas, Concepts, and Cultures**. The cross-pollination of ideas requires agility, and this book explores that.

The Architecture of Vision

SYNOPSIS

In an ever-changing world, agility is paramount for leadership success. External forces such as pandemics can dramatically alter market conditions, and leaders must quickly adapt to unforeseen shifts.

Being agile allows firms to adapt, stay competitive, manage risks, and seize new opportunities. The recent pandemic serves as a poignant reminder of how unexpected challenges can arise, with many industries being forced to pivot their primary operations to survive.

However, it's not just about being reactive. True leadership lies in marrying a long-term vision that can be adapted in real time. Innovative methodologies, such as design thinking, encourage leaders to draw from diverse fields for problem-solving, leading to more dynamic solutions.

Generational shifts in leadership present their own challenges. As firms grow and transition between leadership generations, there's an evolving balance between technical expertise and operational leadership. Leaders must be careful not to overly specialize, as being too niche can reduce adaptability in changing times.

Leaders with deep expertise in their domain and a broad understanding of other disciplines foster agility and innovation. This model emphasizes the significance of diverse skill sets in the workforce. In marketing, agility is equally critical. When technical professionals understand and participate in marketing, they bring a unique perspective that enhances the firm's positioning.

Emphasizing that successful service delivery to clients is a collective effort, underscores the importance of a holistic team effort, from marketing and proposal writing to project management. True leadership is marked by the ability to stand out and champion unique values, especially in an era marked by competition and disruption.

Agility

REFLECTIONS & INSIGHTS

Chapter 10 | **INFLUENCE:** Developing Leaders

I define a leader as anyone who takes responsibility for finding the potential in people and processes, and who has the courage to develop that potential.

Brene Brown

FOCUS: Influence hides in words and actions. Be mindful.

Aspiring leaders face several challenges in their journey to effective leadership, and understanding the role of influence is pivotal in overcoming these challenges. The essence of leadership is centered around influence: the ability to impact others' character, development, or behavior positively.

One significant obstacle emerging leaders encounter is integrating and valuing fresh perspectives, especially from younger generations or newcomers to an organization. These fresh insights often come with innovative ideas, which can be integral to a company's growth and fostering a culture of innovation. However, existing leaders are responsible for recognizing, nurturing, and creating pathways for these new ideas to flourish, ultimately reinforcing the importance of innovative thinking within the company's culture.

Another critical aspect of leadership is mentorship. Leaders may often underestimate their influence, failing to see their impact on others. Many individuals owe their growth and shifts in career trajectories to informal moments of influence or mentorship. A casual remark or suggestion can profoundly affect an individual's professional path,

The Architecture of Vision

bolstering their confidence and leadership capabilities. Mentoring relationships are organic, stemming from a genuine belief in an individual's potential, and play a pivotal role in helping them recognize their leadership capabilities. Furthermore, feedback mechanisms, both formal and informal, are vital. Leaders must understand the power of constructive feedback and its role in employee growth. If incorporated seamlessly into a company's culture, this feedback loop can lead to a mutual understanding, fostering a sense of belonging and purpose among employees.

For leaders to remain relevant and effective, they must prioritize innovative influence. The rapidly evolving market landscape necessitates leaders who are not only innovative but can also inspire and foster innovation within their teams. This involves motivating teams, building robust professional relationships, navigating complex environments, and, most importantly, overcoming resistance to change. In this context, influence becomes the backbone for driving change and ensuring organizations remain at the forefront of their industries.

THE POWER OF INFLUENCE

All the contributors to this book emphasized the importance of influence: providing pathways to growth for individuals to take on more leadership responsibility. A leader's influence is the capacity to affect the character, development, or behavior of someone, something, or the effect itself.

When leaders offer to listen to the input to younger generations or those who came in from outside the organization, they often receive fresh perspectives. Providing the ability to share with someone with a higher authority and responsibility level gives them the agency to put forward innovative ideas. Encouraging innovative ideas across the organization enforces the importance of innovative spirit and thinking as an element of the firm's culture. That approach is top leadership

Influence

saying this is important and backing it up with skills training and leadership opportunities.

INFLUENTIAL IMPACT

As Christine Hill at AOI said in the concluding Perspective in Chapter 2, providing leadership opportunities is essential to the firm's growth. In her example, while not related directly to the practice of AOI, their annual charity event is associated with the brand of AOI in the community. Giving younger staff leadership opportunities to develop a program idea, manage the process, and make it happen helps build leadership skills.

Leaders often do not see in themselves what other people see in them — this idea of influence centers on the importance of coaching and mentoring, sometimes both informal and formal. A casual influence often shapes a career resulting in life-altering changes to the planned path. Many of our contributors said, *"You changed my life,"* when their mentor said that or did something important. The mentor may not know their influence, only wanting to help. Influence is often a little thing like the leader putting weight toward an opportunity for younger staff and pushing it forward.

Those minor incremental influences help build your firm's reputation, the staff's confidence, and their leadership skills. Leaders use their power better when they understand that the softer side of authority has the most impact. Leaders acknowledge that they can have an effect by leveraging influence and being mindful of it. And when a leader starts using influence, it inspires people to do something even when they do not know why they are doing it.

THE MENTOR AS MUSE

In many cases, individuals do not realize they are on a path to leadership but suddenly wake up one day and go, *"Well, I did not know I would get here, but here I am. And now that I am here, I like it and want to do more. I want to give back."* Mentors affirm the potential, but it is up to the individual to perform and excel. But the path to professional growth often starts with the confidence of being encouraged. Mentoring is a natural and organic process that allows people to become someone they did not see in themselves.

These mentor/protégé relationships often stem from someone saying, "I think there's something here that you would be good at." Embracing the mentoring spirit to encourage personal innovation and developing leaders is another kind of innovation that sets firms apart. Mentoring — and the opportunities that come from that effort — often stem from private actions. When individuals develop expertise (the vertical bar in the "T" shape leader profiled in Chapter 9 - Agility) and apply innovative thinking, they are more thoughtful. Teaming with other experts, getting involved in professional and client organizations, and getting exposed to broader input, techniques, and experiences all lead to personal growth and leadership opportunities.

SEEKING AND GIVING FEEDBACK

Leaders need to recognize the impact of and include influence in their regular feedback loop with employees. Without it employees never know where they are. There is often a range of feedback from no feedback to casual/informal to formal 360-degree scored and charted data collection. 360s are an excellent process — providing insights into what can be learned up, down, and parallel to the individual. That comprehensive loop offers strong motivation for growth or change.

A leader's approach to influence is reflected in the firm's culture. A culture that accepts mistakes and values learning from them encourages teamwork and acknowledges successes and failures, demonstrating the significance of influence, agility, and honesty. Rather than provide overly positive feedback (e.g., *"You're so awesome. It is all good. I cannot think of anything you do to improve."*). The truth is always, *"There is always room for improvement."* So, frame feedback as what the individual can do better or how they can expand their skill set. The best influence systems encourage people to excel.

The best organizations survey all the employees about how they feel about various aspects of the culture and the company, including both technical and non-technical aspects of the workplace. When trends indicate decreased satisfaction there is an opportunity to initiate client-focused programs that engage staff to ideate and develop solutions

Proactive change brings positive results and helps create a culture of innovation. Framing the context regarding why and how to change the situation helps influence the leader. Accepting and implementing change falls back to leadership providing a mutually beneficial influential feedback loop.

INNOVATIVE INFLUENCE

Influence is another important trait of leaders who focus on innovation because of the long-term impact positive influence has on the organization:

- **Inspiring and Motivating Teams:** Developing the ability to inspire and motivate teams to think creatively, take risks, and innovate. Influence is crucial, as leaders who possess this trait persuade others to see their vision and embrace their ideas. An influential leader helps build a culture of innovation and empowers their team to develop innovative ideas and solutions.

- **Building Strong Relationships:** Relationships are crucial to success in professional service firms. A leader who has influence builds strong relationships with clients, stakeholders, and team members. They understand their needs and concerns through these relationships, gain trust and support, and develop partnerships that lead to innovation.

- **Navigating Complex Environments:** Professional service firms often operate in complex environments with multiple stakeholders with diverse interests and perspectives. Leaders who have influence navigate these environments effectively by building consensus, negotiating, mediating conflicts, and finding common ground. By doing so, they facilitate collaboration and drive innovation.

- **Overcoming Resistance to Change:** Innovation often requires change, which is difficult for many people. A leader's influence helps overcome resistance to change by persuading others to see the benefits of innovation and inspiring them to embrace innovative ideas and ways of working.

Influence enables leaders to inspire and motivate teams, and by doing so, drives innovation and helps organizations stay competitive in a rapidly evolving market.

SYNTHESIS

Influence and inspiration are closely related. A leader who has an impact inspires their team to think creatively, take risks, and innovate. To do this, they must communicate their vision and ideas compellingly and persuade others to see the potential of innovative ideas. At the same time, an inspiring leader also builds influence by gaining the trust and support of their team.

Similarly, integrity is essential for leaders who want to build influence and inspire their teams. Leaders who act with integrity, honesty, and transparency build trust with their team members and stakeholders. When people trust their leader, they are likely to follow their lead and embrace innovative ideas.

Influence, inspiration, and integrity work together to create a culture of innovation. A leader who is influential, inspiring, and has integrity creates an environment where team members feel empowered to take risks, share ideas, and collaborate. In such a culture, innovation flourishes, and the organization stays ahead of the curve in a rapidly changing market.

Influence, inspiration, and integrity impact the leader's reputation. A leader who is influential, inspiring, and has integrity is likely to be respected and admired by their team members, stakeholders, and peers, which helps build the leader's reputation as an innovative thinker, a trustworthy partner, and a respected leader in their field.

The Architecture of Vision

VIEWPOINT – **MARJANNE PEARSON**
Founder, TalentStar

Leadership is collaboration at its highest level — understanding when tough decisions must be made and making them — encouraging people to move forward from there.

— Marjanne Pearson

The Power of "Giving Leadership"

A few years ago, I heard the term 'giving leadership.' That is more important than what leadership means as a word. The concept is about the gift of leadership to others and not necessarily about taking leadership or the reins of leadership. Giving leadership is when you learn how to give agency to those who are doing the work because they want to do it, and to do it with you.

In the early days of my business career, I loved the books that Warren Bennis wrote about leadership — especially the story about the Wallenda factor. When you give leadership, you draw people onto the tightrope with you. Management is about figuring out how tall the posts need to be. How long does the wire need to be? How many people are you going to try and get up? How are you going to arrange the ladder? How are you going to make it happen? But leadership is convincing people that it is the right thing to do. Giving them the motivation, the opportunity to motivate themselves to do something.

Understanding Your Role as a Consultant

As a consultant — if you build a relationship with the people you are working with — it is a relationship of trust. You help your clients by introducing them to innovative ideas and ways of doing things

Influence

for their benefit. We based the Talentstar practice on the notion that we are here to help our clients do better, find their dreams, and create the right trajectory for sustainable success. We use a four-part relationship diagram to map the roles typically played with clients.

The first box is the 'Vendor.' Clients use vendors when they know what they want and how to do it, but they want to find someone to do it better, faster, and cheaper. Then there is the 'Consultant,' where the client knows what they want to do but is unsure how to do it and needs someone to help them figure out the best "how."

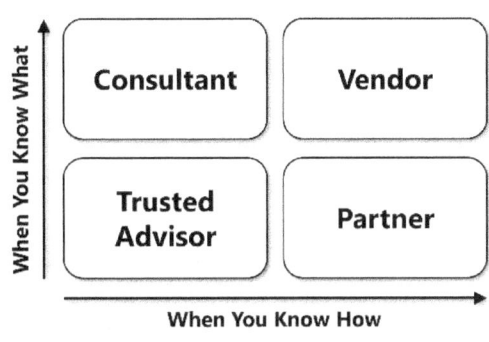

Figure 3 - Advisory Relationship Diagram™

The third box is the 'Partner.' The partner has skin in the game — both a financial and legal risk — and shares responsibility for determining the best "what" and delivering the outcome. Finally, there is a 'Trusted Advisor.' A trusted advisor is what a client needs when they are not confident about what they ought to do or how to do it and need someone they rely on ("trust") to help them make the right decisions from the beginning.

Why Trusted Advisors Matter

As a consultant, we want to be trusted advisors. We need to give the client the ammunition to convince others that it is the right

The Architecture of Vision

thing to do. Weld Coxe[17] would say that leadership is having the clarity of vision to understand what is in the organization's best interest and the traits and skills to assure the employees that it is the right decision and help them move forward.

I agree with the construct of innovation, inspiration, and integrity. But what needs to be added is the relationship piece. Leadership does not happen in a vacuum. I might produce all the inspirational and innovative ideas in the world. Still, as a leader, those ideas will not necessarily move forward if I do not have a relationship with whomever I am working with.

The Importance of Relationships in Leadership

Relationships are crucial to influencing change — which is what leadership is about. You could be a celebrity leader based on your ratings — or you might be an activist, a leader who figures out what needs to be done, how to pull the right people together, and why it matters. In his book Start with Why, Simon Sinek illustrated this with his Golden Circle.[18] That could be the innovation piece — where leadership creates opportunities for things to be done and understanding what could be as opposed to what can be.

In Nancy Duarte's book *Resonate*,[19] she explains the difference between 'what could be done' and 'what can be done.'

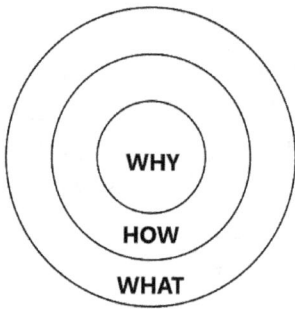

Figure 4 - Sinek's Golden Circle

---

[17] Web reference: https://talentstar.com/spotlight/weld-coxe-hon-aia-professional-services-visionary-and-thought-leader/

[18] Sinek, S., *Start with Why: How Great Leaders Inspire Everyone to Take Action*, Portfolio, 2009.

[19] Duarte, N., *Resonate: Present Visual Stories that Transform Audiences*,, John Wiley & Sons, 2010.

That is a core construct because successful leaders look at both. They are looking at what could be done and what can be done with the available resources, talent, financial funding, facilities, and tools. It is figuring out how to put together an idea in a way that allows people to create a better life and work environment.

So, inspiration is the impetus. Innovation is the creation of an opportunity. And integrity is why it matters and who benefits. That is particularly important right now, concentrating on the environment, sustainability and corporate governance, diversity, equity, and inclusion. We have had a lot of leadership and need to realize why it matters and who is affected fully. Now is our time to challenge and change that.

Leadership as a Collaborative Effort

None of us is as smart as all of us. One weakness of leaders is falling into the trap of a misinformed idea because someone expects the leader to solve a problem they still need to understand. We cannot be the 'deus ex machina.'[20] That's not how leadership works. Leaders need personal, emotional, or functional resources within a company. No one solves challenges by themselves. Leadership is collaboration at its highest level — understanding when tough decisions must be made and making them — and encouraging people to move forward.

When a firm is new, everyone wants to learn, and, at the same time, everyone is figuring it out. When you have an idea, you can put it forward at that stage, and people treat it respectfully. If it was a brilliant idea, it does not make a difference who you are within the

---

[20] An unexpected power or event saves a seemingly hopeless situation, especially as a contrived plot device in a play or novel. The term was first used in ancient Greek and Roman drama, where it meant the timely appearance of a god to unravel and resolve the plot.

organization. As firms mature, they tend to become more stratified and hierarchical.

I am delighted to see the firms where the hierarchical model has shifted. Phil Harrison, CEO at Perkins & Will, described it well as 'getting loose' — opening leadership to ideas, creativity, and innovation from within the company. Leaders tighten up when they feel as though they need control. That approach is more endemic in economic downturns (e.g., the pandemic) when suddenly people do not know what is going on, how to solve problems, or what they will do.

Leading Through Crisis: Lessons from the Pandemic

I find it remarkable how many companies have effected change since the pandemic. Remote working caused many firms to be more open in their communication. Everyone began to try harder. It is hard to communicate during challenging times, but everyone is trying harder this time. We saw an increased openness and willingness to share ideas, communicate, innovate, and provide feedback. As a result of our shared experience and resolve, we have had an opportunity to become better leaders and collaborators, with purpose, vision, and culture as our common thread.

Each firm's leadership development program will be different. We have one client — a small firm, fewer than twenty people — and they are now trying to figure out the next stage of evolution. We are having conversations about each of the leaders and potential leaders within the firm, what they could do, and what kinds of opportunities exist for leadership development through training or coaching.

We have another firm with a completely different organizational model. They have what they call an orca chart, not an org chart. They model a pod of whales. They have eliminated structural bosses and managers and instead have self-managed teams. You will not believe how well this works. They have young people taking the lead and succeeding.

I think there will be more companies like that — those who recognize that leadership potential exists but that people do not get the opportunity. These firms have leaders who do not have an ego or at least a very well-managed ego. They will have leaders who understand that staff would do it by themselves. These firms have leaders who look for people who make potent contributions at various levels.

Many companies are becoming more socially focused, providing needed services, and living their vision and values. There are still a lot of hierarchical organizations, but I see that shifting based on working with our younger clients. The Z-generation is intelligent, innovative, networked, and connected. They are not waiting for anybody.

Learning from the Best

The most relevant mentor for me is, of course, Weld Coxe. I first met Weld in 1976, shortly after he wrote his first book, *Managing Architectural & Engineer Practice*. I am still determining what I would do today if I had not met Weld.[21] Back in the early 1980s, I was at a crossroads. I considered attending law school; I might have done that without his wisdom and influence.

Instead, I joined The Coxe Group as a consultant, which led to everything that has come since. Others had a tremendous impact on my professional life. However, I had the good fortune of meeting Weld, learning so much from him, and meeting remarkable people like Nancy Egan and many others. I carry Weld's

---

[21] Coxe, W., *Managing Architectural and Engineering Practice*, Wiley, 1980.

wisdom with me every day and share it as he always did, and I will always be exceedingly grateful to him.

In any family, it is hard not to learn from different people. My dad was a natural leader. My mother was a professional singer who left her career but was always the Girl Scout leader or something like that. And I had an older sister who was as bossy as I am. Then, of course, there are all those teachers we had through the years. The woman who taught architectural history when I was in high school was one of the most inspirational teachers I have ever had. She loved her subject and loved helping us learn more.

Where do you get that kind of coaching, mentoring, and education? It is different for everyone, and yet it happens every day. And it is often unexpected. More often — when the mentor picks the protege, you are not out asking or raising your hand — they say, 'We see something in you that we think we help develop.' Interestingly, it helps both the mentor and the protégé grow. Then there are all our clients. I learn every time I do something with a client. I get as much out of the relationship as I hope they get from working with me.

The Misunderstanding of Marketing's Value

The relationship between leadership and marketing is more than just a connection. It is integral, whether you are talking about the execution or strategy part of marketing. For leaders, it is often the difference between a celebrity concerned with radiance or someone who wants to change the world for everyone.

As marketers, we want to improve things with leadership skills. From a leadership point of view, it is all about building relationships. It is all about ideas. And, as you said, it is about inspiration, innovation, and integrity. Instead of thinking just for us, we consider our companies, the world, and society. Leaders think about these extended venues, not just this little nucleus of me and my office. The key is how we feel about this in the larger context. Anyone in a marketing position in a leadership role, even an assistant. There are opportunities for everyone.

Unfortunately, in every recession, most senior marketers are usually the first to go because they are considered expensive. The disconnect is about something other than leadership. The disconnect is about value. And the disconnect is about business expansion. When you think of marketing as an overhead expense, you are much more likely to cut back, as opposed to thinking about business expansion and marketing as an investment.

What you make as an investment is an asset you cannot do without. It is challenging because many need to think about business or enterprise strategy. The value of marketing that people do not understand — because the emphasis is on sales — is that marketing helps the top line through expansion or the bottom line through visibility.

The Five Faces of Leadership

There is a book called *The Drama of Leadership* by Patricia Pitcher.[22] And she talks about four people in business: Artists, Craftsmen, Lunatics, and Fools. But she also says there is another one, which is the Technocrat. The technocrat is often the downfall when the visionary retires. When a technocrat takes the reins — someone who is solely focused on the financial side but does not understand the expansion side — unfortunately, they usually only focus on cutting costs.

The Responsibility of Marketers

Marketers must help employers understand the value they bring to the company to the highest level. They need to show how they are

---

[22] Pitcher, P., *The Drama of Leadership*, John Wiley & Sons, 1997.

helping the company become more successful and sustainable. Marketers cannot sit on their laurels. They need to communicate effectively what they do and why it matters. Unfortunately, most do not do it. That is one of the most significant flaws. Keep reinforcing it constantly because everybody else — from operations, finance, design, and engineering — does.

PROGRESSION | INFLUENCE: The Next Generation

Influence hides in words and actions. Be mindful. Influence is a constant drip that impacts colleagues.

AWARENESS: *Think about these statements on understanding the importance of* **Influence**.

1. Who has most influenced your life?
2. Who has most influenced your career?
3. What do you notice about leaders who practice positive influence?
4. What do you notice about leaders who practice negative influence?
5. Where are some areas that you have influenced others?

ACCEPTANCE: *Now, reflect on how you reacted when reading these statements. Reflect on what "acceptance" of your truth about what* **Influence** *means to you.*

1. Notice how open- or close-minded you are about others. When do you find yourself more open-minded regarding others, and when are you more closed?
2. Are you comfortable with expressing appreciation to others? If not, why not?
3. Are you satisfied with your current level of confidence? Are you comfortable speaking up with a differing opinion?
4. When you are not a team leader, how do you feel when things are not going as you wish? Do you reach out to the leader? How do you interact with other team members?

The Architecture of Vision

ACTION: *Follow these steps to incrementally put that awareness and acceptance into action to strengthen your ability to develop leadership with* **Influence.**

1. Read biographies of leaders who have demonstrated both positive and negative influencing traits.
2. Improve your speaking skills with a personal coach, Toastmasters, Improv Theater class, etc.
3. Watch at least one Ted Talk per week, and notice the communication style, word choice, and message organization.
4. Keep a log and refer to them when you are in a situation where you want to increase your influence.
5. Work with a protégé, formally or informally.
6. Read

Influence

SYNOPSIS

The characteristics of good leadership have influence as the core. Leadership is rooted in the ability to positively affect others' character, behavior, and development. Effective leaders value and integrate insights from newcomers or younger generations, leveraging these for organizational growth and cultural innovation. The best leaders serve as mentors, understanding that even informal moments can shape career trajectories and boost leadership capabilities in others. Constructive feedback, formal (like 360-degree reviews) and informal, plays a vital role in a leader's relationship with their team.

By offering opportunities and roles to younger employees, leaders cultivate an environment where innovation is prioritized and becomes a core part of the firm's culture. Leaders' informal influence, through comments or gestures, can result in significant changes in someone's career path. Recognizing and leveraging this influence can transform both individuals and the organization. By actively seeking feedback and integrating it into the company culture, leaders foster mutual understanding, a sense of belonging, and purpose. Effective leaders establish a culture that values learning from mistakes and teamwork and acknowledges both successes and failures.

Leaders must inspire and motivate their teams to embrace innovative thinking, fostering a culture of innovation. Cultivating strong relationships with stakeholders, clients, and team members is crucial. These relationships help leaders gauge needs and concerns and foster trust, which in turn supports innovation. Leaders must adeptly handle diverse interests and perspectives in multifaceted environments, promoting collaboration and innovation.

Since innovation often necessitates change, leaders must employ their influence to help teams see the advantages of innovative approaches, thereby overcoming resistance. In a constantly evolving marketplace, these leadership qualities are the linchpins for organizational success.

The Architecture of Vision

REFLECTIONS & INSIGHTS

Chapter 11 | **PURPOSE:** Creating A Culture

The kinds of nets we know how to weave determine the types of nets we cast. These nets, in turn, determine the kinds of fish we catch.
Elliot Eisner

FOCUS: Successful leaders focus on creating cultures where employees thrive.

Leaders often grapple with aligning a firm's vision with its operational culture. While many organizations define their values in terms like honesty or integrity, this can oversimplify the profound essence of purpose. Values represent the genuine relationship between employees, the organization, and the firm's brand promise.

Purpose, therefore, acts as a beacon for company actions, providing clarity to staff about the company's direction. When there's alignment between words and actions, firms flourish; however, discrepancies can lead to internal discord and hinder growth.

A significant challenge in leadership is ensuring that business practices align with generational shifts. Older leaders can sometimes be viewed as resistant to change, especially by younger generations seeking innovative approaches and transparency. Adopting objective metrics like OKRs and KPIs[23] can bridge this gap, emphasizing consistency and creativity.

---

[23] Objectives and Key Results — a clear, qualitative description of what you want to achieve, and specific, measurable outcomes that indicate progress — and Key Performance Indicators — metrics used to

Additionally, many professional service firms comprise specialists trained in a specific discipline. Rarely are they versed in business operations or finance, creating a potential shortfall in managing the business side of firms. Recognizing this, forward-thinking organizations hire experts for key operational roles, ensuring that the business runs efficiently without compromising the creative essence.

CREATING AN ENDURING PURPOSE

Defining a firm's purpose is vital for its legacy. In professional service sectors, a well-articulated purpose can set a company apart from competitors, ensuring its longevity and impact on society. This means establishing an impactful purpose for aspiring leaders, embedding it within the firm's operational fabric, and continually ensuring alignment between stated values and actual actions. Doing so ensures the company's success and creates an environment where employees feel a genuine sense of belonging and purpose.

The leader's purpose aligns with the vision and impacts culture. Purpose provides a perspective of creating a legacy — an enduring practice that continues after the leader's time. So many organizations define values in human-like terms, like integrity, honesty, or truth. That approach oversimplifies the purpose of purpose. Storybrand's Donald Miller advocates, *"Values are the key traits of the people who work at the company. Their purpose defines what must be done daily to keep the organization going toward its mission."*

It is common for firms and their leaders to discuss values in strategy development. However, their focus on an idealized culture does not necessarily distinguish the firm for its unique aspects. Every company thinks that it is special. Every firm has a culture that is unique to them.

---

evaluate the success of an organization, team, or individual in achieving objectives

What determines the great from the good is when those values are not just words on the wall or a website.

THE IMPORTANCE OF VALUES

Values are the relationships between employees and their interactions internally and externally. Each profession has a different model and a completely different culture. How each firm expresses its culture, internally and externally, is a good barometer for the brand. The exciting aspect of purpose and values is how they define an environment where people thrive because they belong (or not). In Maslow's hierarchy of needs,[24] the idea of belonging is critical. Employees will only love their company if they align with that company's culture.

When firms are struggling, it is usually what leaders say is different from what they do, or conversely, what they do is different from what they say. Defining purpose lets everybody know what is true. When words and actions align, it is positive. When there's dissonance, then that's when companies have significant problems. As a result, that lack of a defined purpose limits the ability to grow and become a leading firm in its niche.

Firms with a purpose provide more opportunities for people to be successful. People leave their managers. They do not leave the companies. It comes back to leadership. One of the essential components of leadership is alignment between what a leader says they are and how they behave. Values and purpose are critical to creating a sense of belonging for employees and building long-term sustainability for the organization.

The purpose is that blend of mission — what the company does every day to provide value — and vision — what the company aspires to be

---

[24] Web reference: https://en.wikipedia.org/wiki/Maslow%27s_hierarchy_of_needs

The Architecture of Vision

that offers greater value in the future. The firm and its leadership define its strategies for growth. It is the leader's responsibility to provide that clarity and consistency.

WALKING THE TALK

Our research found companies across a broad spectrum of the meaningful impact of defined values and purpose. The A/E/C industry is, by nature, highly creative. Many leaders come from creative design-oriented backgrounds and must be more grounded in traditional business management approaches. Today, a new generation in the workplace is entrepreneurial while simultaneously hungry for the consistency of best practices. The different generational perspectives challenge some leaders who resist change (i.e., the way we have always done it).

To younger staff, an older leader is seen as uncooperative because acknowledging the need for change reveals their weaknesses or implies that they do not know what they are doing. To counter that perception, an aware leader embraces metrics (e.g., objectives and key results (OKR) and key performance indicators (KPI)) to demonstrate how the fundamentals of good business practice that all service firms need to apply to their firm. From the standpoint of culture-building, this kind of transparency of business operational metrics helps overcome any perceived weakness while allowing the practitioners to do what they love — the creative side of the business.

EXPERTISE WHERE IT IS NEEDED

While exceptions exist, many people who enter professional services train in a specific discipline. Rarely does that discipline have a finance or operations component in the educational framework. For example, many schools of architecture require design labs and practice labs. Practice labs focus on translating design ideas into drawings and specifications rather than on running the business. This approach applies to engineering, construction management, and many other professional services with a knowledge-based educational practice focused on creative effort.

Innovative organizations recognize that flaw, and rather than assign a non-qualified person to be the head of finance or HR, they look outside for staff with appropriate training and experience. When fiscal responsibility solely focuses on net fees earned, it can clash with creative aspects of the practice and hinder investment in the firm's growth. This disconnect or dissonance is something a good leader helps resolve. A good leader talks about "why" finance is essential — but essential "in context," as opposed to the critical "end of the story."

Purpose is fundamental to leadership development in any organization, but it is crucial in a professional service firm. In this context, purpose refers to a clear and meaningful reason for the firm's existence beyond just making a profit. A well-defined purpose provides direction and motivation to the firm's leaders and employees, helping to guide decision-making and inspire a sense of belonging and pride in the organization.

In professional service firms, a clear sense of purpose is crucial to stay competitive, retain top talent, and differentiate from competitors by communicating unique value to clients. Moreover, purpose plays a critical role in shaping the firm's legacy. A purpose-driven organization will likely impact society and positively contribute to the greater good. A clear purpose helps to build a reputation for the firm as an ethical and socially responsible organization that values long-term sustainability over short-term gains. Such a legacy is a powerful asset for the firm, attracting new clients, employees, and partners with the same values and goals.

DEFINING PURPOSE

Purpose is vital to the legacy of a professional service firm because it helps to provide direction, motivation, and a sense of belonging to its

The Architecture of Vision

leaders and employees. It distinguishes the firm from competitors, contributes to its reputation as a socially responsible organization, and attracts new clients and talent who share the same values and goals.

Here are some steps that an aspiring leader can take to build purpose as a critical element of the business strategy for a professional service firm:

- **Define the Purpose:** This requires asking questions such as, "What problem does our firm solve for our clients?", "What are our core values?", "What impact do we want to make in the world?" and "What legacy do we want to leave behind?".

- **Communicate the Purpose:** Once the purpose is defined, it is essential to communicate it effectively to all stakeholders, including employees, clients, and partners, including creating a mission statement, incorporating the purpose into the firm's branding and messaging, and using internal communications channels to reinforce the purpose and its importance.

- **Align the Strategy:** Integrate the purpose into the firm's overall strategy and business plan, including identifying specific goals and initiatives that support the purpose and regularly reviewing progress to ensure alignment.

- **Embed the Purpose Into Operations:** Include words of purpose into the firm's procedures, policies, and practices, including recruitment, retainage, employee training programs, and performance evaluations.

- **Foster a Purpose-Driven Culture:** Reinforce the importance of the purpose and encourage employees to embrace it, including recognizing and rewarding employees who embody the purpose, creating opportunities for employees to contribute outside of their regular work, and fostering a sense of community and shared goals among employees.

Purpose

SYNTHESIS

Building purpose into the business strategy helps to create a sense of reason and meaning behind the firm's strategy, which guides the firm's decision-making and inspires its employees.

Purpose provides the foundation for inspiring and leading others, while inspiration and integrity are essential traits that help leaders bring that purpose to life. Purpose is the driving force behind innovative leadership. It is why the professional service firm exists and serves as the foundation for its values, vision, and mission. Purpose provides a clear direction for the firm and helps to motivate and inspire its leaders and employees.

Inspiration is a crucial trait of innovative leadership. It involves motivating and encouraging others to pursue the firm's purpose and vision. Inspirational leaders use their passion, enthusiasm, and positive energy to create a sense of excitement and commitment among their team members. They lead by example, demonstrate a deep commitment to the firm's purpose, and communicate a compelling vision that inspires others to act.

Integrity involves a solid commitment to ethical behavior, transparency, and honesty. Leaders with integrity demonstrate consistency between their words and actions, and they hold themselves and others accountable for their actions. They build trust with their team members and stakeholders by being transparent about the firm's goals, priorities, and challenges.

Purpose, inspiration, and integrity form a powerful combination that drives innovative leadership. Leaders who are passionate about their purpose, inspire their team members to pursue that purpose with enthusiasm and integrity, and create a culture of trust and accountability are likely to successfully achieve their firm's goals and make a lasting impact.

VIEWPOINT – **MARK VALENTI**, CTS
Retired President & CEO, The Sextant Group

> *Leadership is exhibiting the behaviors we want our teams to demonstrate — leading by example — and trusting them to do what you have hired them to do.*
> — Mark Valenti

Leading by Example

The best definition of a leader is to be a good example. For my teams, I always felt like what I did spoke more loudly than what I said. I tried to exhibit the kinds of behaviors that I wanted my groups to show. That has worked by and large. The other part of leadership is to trust your teams to do what you have hired them to do.

The Pitfalls of Micromanagement

I worked for a couple of guys who were micro-managers. They were constantly second-guessing and questioning to the point where their staff was paralyzed. I took that to heart. The Sextant Group was my third company.

In the first one, I was guilty of some micro-management style. One day, my team (we were only five then) pulled me aside and said, *'You know, this is a lot nicer place to work when you're not here.'* I was crushed, but that was a lesson I took to heart.

When I started my second company, I made it a point to hire good people and get out of their way. I only asked them to tell me what they needed to do their job and succeed. My job as the leader was to give them the tools and resources they needed to do their job correctly.

Purpose

When I formed my third company, The Sextant Group, I put 'Discovery | Innovation | Impact' on our business cards. Initially, we wanted the freedom to apply our technology skills to any business activity. We were innovative in the kinds of projects we took on or pursued. We became known for innovative solutions for some great clients. I see many people in the industry look to us and ask how The Sextant Group is doing things because they do it the right way.

The Cornerstone of Leadership

Integrity means to keep your word. If you say you are going to do something, do it. If you do it, acknowledge that, and do not run from it or hide from it. If you make a mistake, own up to it and make it right. When we had a problem — we are human, and all make mistakes — we called the client and owned the responsibility to make it right. And we did. Those clients became multiple project clients because they knew they could trust us beyond that first encounter.

A leader's integrity sets the tone for everything else the company does. It is one of those values that lets the employees believe in what they are doing and that they have value. Once a client gets to know you in the context of integrity, trust is established that supersedes everything else. When clients sense your integrity, everything else is more straightforward.

The Overlooked Trait in Leadership

One weakness some leaders face is not accepting their humanity. You must remind yourself that you are human, just like everybody else in your organization. Doing that makes it easier to accept the mistakes that come because I knew I made some mistakes along the way, too. The most important thing for me is recognizing that you are no better than anybody else. I knew many folks who worked for me were smarter than me. That was the reason I hired them. You could not do it yourself. The team needs to be more intelligent and better than you.

Leadership opportunities came as we grew the company. For example, we had a systems designer who we recognized had excellent client skills. Our clients took to him. So, we created a path for him from designer to project manager and from project manager to principal. He demonstrated the ability to grow along that pathway.

There will always be some people who struggle to progress in their careers because we cannot find a path to take them to the next level. There was nowhere else for them to go. One of the things that excited me about joining NV5 was that the size of that organization afforded key people a chance to take it to the next level and do something beyond what I could do for them at The Sextant Group.

Learning from the Best to Become the Best

I had a couple of influential mentors. One was a banker and an investor in my first recording studio business. His favorite saying was, 'Hard work brings good luck.' That has proven to be true. If you work hard and keep your eyes open, you can take advantage of an opportunity when it presents itself. If you are not working hard, you will miss that opportunity, or it will choose to ignore you because it recognizes you are not the one deserving.

Another mentor was the president and chief operating officer of a resort where I worked in college. He was a brilliant people person. I watched how he managed his team and engaged with everybody. He saw everybody at the same level. Everyone was equal in his eyes. I always remembered that. He had a considerable influence on me.

The Convergence of Leadership and Marketing

The role of marketing is to take your company's leadership traits and values and manifest them in the marketplace. Why is our organization different? Why is our organization better? Why is our organization the right advisor for you? Whatever that business relationship might be. It is marketing's responsibility to codify those traits and put the messaging out in a measurable fashion. Marketing is important. As president and CEO, I knew my marketing skills were my strength.

The Architecture of Vision

PROGRESSION – **PURPOSE**: Creating A Culture

Successful leaders focus on creating cultures where employees thrive.

AWARENESS: *Think about these statements on understanding the importance of* **Purpose.**

1. What do you like most about where you are in your career? (Think on many levels, including company, position, geographic location, opportunity, etc.)
2. What does success mean to you?
3. What do you like about your company's current culture?
4. What would you change if there were no constraints?
5. Is your company's culture allowing you to thrive?

ACCEPTANCE: *Now, reflect on how you reacted when reading these statements. Reflect on what "acceptance" of your truth about what* **Purpose** *to you.*

1. Review your company's mission statement and values. What do they mean formally, and what do they mean to you personally? Is there a difference?
2. Describe your first thoughts of the day when you think about work.
3. Is your level of satisfaction what you want it to be? What needs to happen to make it better?
4. What would motivate you to take extraordinary steps to participate in a company cultural shift?

Purpose

ACTION: *Follow these steps to incrementally put that awareness and acceptance into action to strengthen your ability to develop leadership with **Purpose**.*

1. Read Simon Sinek's book, *Start with Why*.
2. Discuss your positive and negative perceptions about your company's culture with a trusted advisor. Are you prepared to adapt to the culture over the long term, or do you prefer to leave?
3. Who are peers with whom you could have productive conversations about shifting cultural weaknesses? Do you have a team of like-minded professionals who want to be part of an organizational shift alongside you?
4. Read Warren Bennis' **On Becoming a Leader**. Bennis discusses the inner journey of leaders, which includes the discovering purpose.

The Architecture of Vision

SYNOPSIS

Great leaders ensure that a firm's values align with its operational practices. They avoid merely listing generic values like honesty or integrity and delve deeper into defining the company's purpose. Effective leaders embrace change and acknowledge generational perspectives, especially as younger individuals seek innovative practices and complete transparency. Recognizing potential shortfalls in operational knowledge, successful firms bring in experts for roles such as finance or HR, ensuring the smooth functioning of the company without affecting its creative essence.

A well-defined purpose is integral to a firm's legacy. By embedding purpose into the organization's fabric, leaders ensure alignment between declared values and actions, promoting the company's success and fostering a genuine sense of belonging among employees. Rather than just being words on a wall, values should represent the true relationships between employees and their internal and external interactions. When leaders ensure congruence between what is said and done, firms prosper. Based on research, companies that have clearly defined values and purposes show significant positive impacts. Effective leaders emphasize the importance of transparency in business operational metrics, even in industries that are primarily creative.

Leaders must be adept at articulating the firm's purpose and values, ensuring everyone understands the direction and the rationale behind decisions. A leader should embed the firm's purpose into its overall strategy, ensuring that actions align with the established mission and vision. Beyond just strategic insight, leaders should also ensure that the purpose is woven into everyday operations, from recruitment processes to employee training and evaluations.

A true leader fosters a purpose-driven culture, emphasizing the significance of the firm's purpose and inspiring employees to embrace

Purpose

and embody it. Leaders should always be receptive to learning, whether from generational shifts, industry trends, or their teams, ensuring they stay relevant and effective in their roles.

Purpose goes beyond profitability, offering direction, motivation, and a sense of belonging to leaders and employees. Effective leaders define, communicate, and embody this purpose, aligning it with the firm's strategy and operations and fostering a culture that thrives on these values.

The Architecture of Vision

REFLECTIONS & INSIGHTS

Chapter 12 | **PERSPECTIVE:** Leaving a Legacy

No person was ever honored for what he received. Honor has been the reward for what he gave.
Calvin Coolidge

FOCUS: Perspective is like moss on a stone wall; it grows slowly through the seasons and leaves a lasting impact as it transforms the wall's color and texture.

ORGANIZATIONS THAT DESIRE ENDURANCE and resilience often bank on two growth models: leadership development and expansion strategies, like mergers and acquisitions. The first emphasizes nurturing from within, providing a structured pathway for employees' evolution into future leaders through training, mentorship, and investment in the company.

The latter strategy, however, focuses on capitalizing on the strengths of external entities to drive growth. But with mergers and acquisitions, there is a risk: the original vision that once steered the company can become diluted, and integrating distinct corporate cultures can result in leadership vacuums.

Quality leadership is central to both models, particularly in reinforcing the company's brand reputation within its immediate client community and the wider global context. However, the leadership challenges vary. Firms growing through acquisition can face leadership gaps when leaders from the acquired company leave post-transition. Additionally, in their zeal to expand, firms sometimes risk diverging from their core competencies, straying into territories they aren't equipped for. This misalignment can stunt growth and erode client trust.

Moreover, as recent global events — like pandemics and economic recessions — have shown, adaptability in leadership is essential. Leaders are now more than ever required to pivot their strategies in the face of unforeseen challenges. This necessitates a robust market understanding, recognizing the balance between a team's capabilities and market needs. Successful leaders draw upon their experience, collaborate with others, stay transparent with their teams, and continue to learn and innovate, ensuring their organizations not only weather storms but also thrive in their aftermath.

BUILDING A LASTING LEGACY

The legacy of sustainable, resilient, and enduring organizations — ones, to borrow a phrase, that is *"built to last"* — evolve through a combination of leadership development and transition planning or mergers or acquisitions. The former provides a defined path for employees to grow and develop. The latter relies on increasing shareholder value through combining resources.

With leadership development, a conscious transition plan provides training, experience, and mentoring to develop an evolving generation of new leaders. Firm ownership and equity often play a part. Investing in the firm is seen as a commitment to the future.

With growth through acquisition, there is a new blended cultural model. Sometimes, the founder's vision — that initial entrepreneurial spirit — is lost. Leaders reflect on legacy versus momentum — doing something inspiring or making a change based on the long-term benefit to the firm and its clients. As an organization builds successful client relations and produces successful work, how growth manifests do not matter if the firm satisfies the client's needs.

Perspective

THE ENDURING BRAND

Whether expansion by internal organic development or growth through acquisition, leadership quality contributes to building brand strength for the organization recognized in the firm's client community and its regional, local, national, and international community, allowing the firm to continue to grow.

Many small, mid-, and larger firms have grown over many years using some combination of both models. Acquisition-based growth tends to be a more challenging approach to building a business in that it too often leads to a gap in leadership. The acquired firm's leadership stays for a transition period and then cashes out. That leaves a vacuum unless a formal transition plan for next-generation leaders is in place.

Many firms that have grown that way need to acknowledge that challenge. Sometimes, aspirations for growth must be tempered with reality. But clients look for demonstrated expertise. Buying a portfolio through acquisition is a way, but most clients see that the buyer needs to integrate the acquired firm into the buyer's culture. The age-old dilemma between specialists and generalists is a strategic choice most A/E/C leaders face daily.

That dilemma goes right to the importance of perspective, purpose, and alignment between words and actions. When there is no alignment, a firm can't grow. And you cannot fake it. Working on a renovation for a high school stadium bleacher does not qualify the firm to pursue (let alone win) a significant league practice stadium. Being a church member does not allow a skilled interior designer to design a new house of worship. Creativity and vitality are lovely, but the business of the practice is a balance between the staff's skills and the market needs that the leader must face head-on.

ADAPTING TO CHANGE

This challenge is particularly relevant in recessionary economic times or, as many have just experienced, during and after a pandemic. These changes in the status quo test a leader's ability to adapt and adjust. Perspective — drawing on personal experience and a long-horizon viewpoint — helps make decisions that keep the firm on the right path toward the future.

How leaders and their firms pivot in response to change is crucial to success. Influential leaders reach out to past clients during challenging times to learn how they handled similar challenges and explore mutually beneficial solutions. Focusing on improving conditions, whether resources, expense, or time, the effort to collaborate shows commitment to the relationship.

Challenging times reinforce the importance and benefit of focusing on the practice. Clarity of purpose and sharing perspective with employees are the hallmarks of strong leadership. The more self-aware a leader is — the more they accept who they are — the more willing they are to acknowledge that they do not know everything.

SHARING INSIGHTS & EXPERIENCES

Leaders leverage perspective to benefit the practice in several ways:

- **Share insights with the Team:** A leader's perspective drawn from experience is invaluable in identifying industry trends, challenges, and opportunities. Sharing these insights with the team helps the practice stay ahead of the curve and better serve its clients.

- **Mentor and Develop Team Members:** Leaders use their experience to mentor and develop team members, helping them to build their skills and knowledge, improving the quality of service the practice provides, and creating a more motivated and engaged team.

- **Develop Thought Leadership:** Leaders leverage their experience to develop thought leadership content such as whitepapers, case studies, and blogs, helping establish the practice as a trusted authority in the industry and attracting new clients.

- **Foster a Culture of Continuous Improvement:** Leaders use their experience to help the practice identify areas for improvement and develop strategies to address them, leading to increased efficiency, productivity, and profitability.

- **Embrace Innovation:** Leaders use their experience to identify areas where the practice innovates and adopts new technologies or processes, helping to stay competitive and attract new clients who value innovative solutions.

By sharing insights with their team, mentoring and developing team members, developing thought leadership, fostering a culture of continuous improvement, and embracing innovation, leaders help the practice achieve greater success and growth.

The Architecture of Vision

SYNTHESIS

A leader's perspective on innovation significantly impacts their style regarding inspiration and integrity. Leaders prioritizing innovation tend to be forward-thinking and visionary, inspiring their followers. They can often articulate a compelling vision for the future and inspire others to work toward that goal, which, in turn, helps motivate employees and creates a sense of excitement and enthusiasm within the organization.

Leaders who value innovation are often seen as more authentic and transparent, contributing to their overall integrity. They are willing to take risks and try new things, even if it means making mistakes or facing criticism. They build trust and credibility with their followers by being open about their failures and vulnerabilities.

Innovation requires leaders to be flexible and adaptable, contributing to a leader's perceived integrity. When faced with unexpected challenges or setbacks, leaders prioritizing innovation are likely to respond with agility and creativity, building trust and confidence among followers, who will appreciate the leader's ability to navigate complex situations.

Prioritizing innovation helps leaders to be more forward-thinking, authentic, and adaptable, leading to more success and satisfaction for both the leader and their followers.

Perspective

VIEWPOINT – **MIKE REILLY**, FSMPS
President, Reilly Communications

The leadership journey is so individual that it defies any attempt to make the experience universal.
— Mike Reilly

Leadership From the Ground Up

Leadership happens at all levels of an organization. That leadership must develop in an organization's junior to middle levels is critical to long-term survival. There's so much change and reinvention happening. Firms need new leaders from every part of the business. An exciting shift is opening leadership opportunities to people in their early career or mid-career. Companies need them more than ever before. The definition of leadership includes someone with something to offer to others at every level of the organization.

We live in a multi-generational world, but an apparent generational revolution is underway. There is a practical side to this trend that provides a two-way benefit. In terms of leadership, I often trade leadership roles seamlessly with my younger clients. I learned an incredible amount from them. I am also providing them with learning and an understanding of leadership.

The Evolving Landscape of Organizational Leadership

I am optimistic about where we are. It might be slow to develop because many boomers – like me - are hanging around. A greater appreciation and tangible support for younger people create the ladder, the opportunities, and the knowledge they need to make that step up. From my view — working with eight to ten organizations at any given time — they are all different in size and culture, but most say, 'We need more variety and diversity in our leadership here.'

The Architecture of Vision

The A/E/C business is highly innovative in its technical execution. But conversely, many firms lack innovation in terms of inspirational organizational development. Creativity is poured into projects, whether a bridge or a building, while leadership conventions remain functionally the same. What's lagging is the cultural innovation — internally and organizationally — because so much energy is directed toward the client. That saps latent inspiration opportunity out of the equation.

Redefining Organizational Priorities

Most of the focus is on risk avoidance. That is the culture of many construction, engineering, and architectural firms. That often translates to a cautious approach to organizational development and leadership. This mindset is changing, but we must convince them to equally apply creative and innovative efforts to the projects and make that same effort in leadership development. That would be a wonderful thing.

Inspiration is also a leadership issue. Firms need to help their staff develop communication skills and an understanding of all the various parts of the business, not just the delivery of a design or project. A holistic view is the foundation of an inspired team.

We can only reach our potential if we force ourselves to do something new. Ideally, every leadership exercise has a component of hands-on, self-created change. Do it. Create it. Own it. Leadership training and development must include challenging people to take on new initiatives – something outside their current day-to-day work context. Action begets change. Whether it is marketing or technical staff, the natural drift is back to the day-to-day, risk-averse, deadline-driven stuff once the training is complete.

Championing Positive Change and Breaking Patterns

When something is uncomfortable, it is much easier to run away from it than to run toward it and grow. That is my simple philosophy. It's especially true for marketing pros. Embrace the awkwardness, break the rules, and get noticed. Be the champion of positive change.

Instead of just suffering with the status quo, what would be one thing you can do to break the pattern? That change in agent role is the antidote to what we have been hearing about marketing not getting respect for decades. Well, get off your ass and change it. Make people say, *'Wow, look at that.'* It is not just better proposals or PowerPoints. Create a leadership Initiative. Don't wait for someone to assign it. Just do it.

In any organization, there are people ready for leadership. Good leaders seek them out and recognize the extraordinary and expansive thinkers prepared to take on more. It does not matter how young or old they are. Leaders are developed, not born. And each of us develops differently, with different objectives and commitment to the role. There are many leadership opportunities in A/E/C on the project side and in marketing, finance, and technology. You can express leadership in many ways, in your own way.

Adapting for Modern Challenges

Creating leadership opportunities is essential to a healthy company culture. Innovative companies continually invest in leadership development, but I've seen much haphazard training. Prescriptive, off-the-shelf programs too often fail to meet today's issues and opportunities. Look at the past few years and the pandemic we have just been through. See how the assumptions about people's emotional health and wellness have changed. And consider the generation differences in the workplace. How can any off-the-shelf approach to leadership training keep up with these developments? Training programs must be reimagined to align with the fundamental changes in what great leaders do now to meet the day's challenges.

Not everyone wants to be a principal or studio manager. And that is fine. There are other ways to lead, not just traditional leadership.

It may be through innovation on the project or by example, which is excellent. They may say, 'All I want to do is keep working on great projects.' That is okay. We will help you do that.

Lessons from Seasoned Leaders

A few mentors helped me with leadership in my business life. The best mentors were people who gave me the confidence to go out on my own. I learned so much from colleagues who had done it and helped me figure out how to do it. There is a huge leadership lesson in managing yourself as much as the clients or the finances.

For example, Janet Sanders[25] gave me the best advice about managing myself as a consultant. When I asked for her advice before starting my business, she said, 'I could tell you a bunch of stuff, but instead, I will tell you one important thing. When it feels like a no, say no.' At first, I had no idea what she was talking about. But today, that advice is something I think about all the time when opportunities come up. My go/no go process is to trust my instinct. When I get a call saying, 'Hey, we are looking for some help. Can I send you our RFP?' Or when I talk with a prospect and realize I can't help them (or don't trust them) These feel like a no. Thanks to Janet's advice, I say no or sometimes say, 'Let me suggest a couple of people who might be a better match for this.'

Overcoming Stereotypes and Mindsets

Marketing leadership, especially in the A/E/C industry, is about knowing the options and helping your team choose the right path forward. We must overcome the mindset and the stereotypes that marketing is overhead or disconnected from clients. Leadership is built on core strengths and skills, recognizing that everyone brings a distinct and valuable perspective. For marketers, the key is finding and developing your strengths, knowledge, and values — and applying them as a leader supporting your company's future.

---

[25] Janet Sanders, Ph.D., retired President of Clayton Consulting Group

From Skills to Strategic Problem-Solving

Marketers have a terrific opportunity to turn any lack of respect they encounter and turn it into an advantage by leading others in solving the strategic problems in the firm. If it works here, great. If not, take what you have learned on your journey somewhere else. My advice: Find something you are interested in that you're good at, and invest in becoming better, developing your skills, and becoming the marketing leader your firm needs. Each of us adds our distinctive values, strengths, and aspirations to serve our colleagues, clients, and personal development.

PROGRESSION – **PERSPECTIVE**: Leaving a Legacy

Perspective is like moss on a stone wall; it grows slowly through the seasons and leaves a lasting impact as it transforms the wall's color and texture.

AWARENESS: *Think about these statements on understanding the importance of* **Perspective.**

1. When was the last time you allowed yourself time to ponder, dream, think, and reflect? Remember the details: where were you, how long did you spend in this time of thought, and what were some insights you gained?

2. Think of a public figure or someone you admire for leaving a legacy. What do you notice about their communication and leadership styles? Look at both the positive and the negative.

3. Reflect on a recent crisis you encountered. What was your first response? How did it change over time? What did you learn about yourself because of the situation?

ACCEPTANCE: *Now, reflect on how you reacted when reading these statements. Reflect on what "acceptance" of your truth about what* **Perspective** *to you.*

1. Reflect on your career to date and what you anticipate in the future. What new skills do you want to learn, and what traits would you like to polish? What qualities have you honed so they are solid and helpful on your journey? (Use the eighteen attributes described in this book for this acceptance exercise.)

2. What trait has changed the most in your professional career? Are you satisfied with where you are now?

3. Review the traits that still elude you or ones you seem to avoid. Why are you resisting them?

ACTION: *Follow these steps to incrementally put that awareness and acceptance into action to strengthen your ability to develop leadership with* **Perspective.**

1. What legacy do you want to leave personally and professionally?

2. Write a Vision of the Future statement, a word picture of your life in five, 10, or 20 years. Be specific about your position, responsibilities, colleagues, accomplishments, and feelings of satisfaction and success.

3. Share your Vision of the Future with a trusted advisor or mentor. What insights do you gain from this discussion?

4. Read a biography of a public figure that spans a long-time career. What traits did they develop, and describe how they learned important life lessons.

5. Read Tom Kelley's ***The Ten Faces of Innovation: IDEO's Strategies for Defeating the Devil's Advocate and Driving Creativity Throughout Your Organization***. Kelley offers various perspectives on innovation and challenges to conventional thinking.

The Architecture of Vision

SYNOPSIS

Successful leadership in resilient organizations is characterized by a clear vision, adaptability, and the ability to navigate the intricate pathways of growth, be it through nurturing internal talent or through external strategies like mergers and acquisitions. A feature of strong leadership is the ability to maintain the original ethos and vision of the company, even amidst the complexities of integrating different corporate cultures. Adaptability further delineates effective leaders. They balance a team's capabilities and market demands, ensuring alignment with core competencies.

Effective leaders prioritize continuity and sustainability. They invest in leadership development, ensuring a conscious transition plan, which includes training, mentoring, and strategic investments, fostering an environment where employees see a clear growth path. Furthermore, when growth is pursued through acquisitions, these leaders ensure that the integration of cultures does not dilute the firm's founding vision.

They build an enduring brand reputation across local to global spectrums. These leaders stand out in challenging times by seeking collaborative solutions, staying transparent with their teams, and continuously adapting. They also recognize the importance of staying true to their firm's expertise and avoiding ventures into unfamiliar territories.

An individual aspiring to be a truly effective leader must hone several competencies, including utilizing personal experiences to make informed decisions and understand industry trends; embracing change and being agile in responses, especially during challenging times;, and recognizing personal strengths and limitations, ensuring that authenticity and transparency are maintained. In essence, the heart of leadership in enduring firms lies in balancing innovation with authenticity, inspiration with integrity, and vision with adaptability.

Perspective

REFLECTIONS & INSIGHTS

PART III | INTEGRITY – The Third Pillar

We acquire a particular quality by constantly acting in a particular way.
Aristotle

FOCUS: Integrity establishes trust with clients and employees, fosters a culture of ethical behavior, and enhances the reputation and long-term success of the firm.

INTEGRITY IS A CORNERSTONE OF EFFECTIVE LEADERSHIP, often assumed but not always exhibited. Leaders face challenges when this inherent trust in their integrity is undermined. To lead with true integrity, one must speak the truth and align one's actions with one's words. Leaders are also responsible for holding themselves and their teams accountable for upholding the organization's values.

This accountability extends to making realistic promises to clients and being transparent when challenges arise. Failures in these areas can strain client relationships, tarnish the organization's reputation, and create internal conflicts. The essence is to say you have integrity and demonstrate it in every decision and action.

In the professional service industry, understanding client needs is vital. The relationships between primary and subcontracting firms further highlight the need for transparency and honesty, as misalignments can lead to financial disputes and a lack of trust. Negative actions or decisions, especially those violating the integrity of commitment, have long-lasting impacts on the organization's image and internal and external relationships.

Integrity should guide every aspect of an organization, from its leadership to its daily operations. A leader's character influences the organization's culture, client relationships, and reputation. Acting with integrity attracts business, fosters trust, and cultivates long-term relationships. It's not merely about having integrity as a value but consistently living and leading by it.

CONSISTENT AND TRANSPARENT INTEGRITY

Integrity is one of those aspects of leadership everyone says is essential. Meeting anyone in business who does not think they have integrity is rare. So, it is crucial. We trust our leaders are honest. Because of that, defining the traits associated with integrity is a challenge because integrity in our leaders is assumed. The challenge comes when that assumption is proved wrong. Acting with integrity is the foundation of a strong leader's philosophy. They say what they believe and do what they say.

Additionally, influential leaders hold themselves and others accountable for their actions. They do not tolerate unethical behavior or actions that go against the organization's values and principles. When an issue arises, influential leaders take swift and appropriate action to address it and prevent it from happening again.

Integrity means being honest, transparent, and accountable and acting in the best interest of clients, colleagues, and the organization. Leaders who strive to create a culture of integrity and hold themselves and others accountable for upholding these values build strong client relationships, improve team collaboration, and enhance the reputation and success of their organization.

PURPOSEFUL ACTION

The integrity of purpose is the *'why'* of professional service. The integrity of vision is the goals and benefits of professional service. Together, they form the framework for solid client relationships. The leader must walk that talk.

Successful professional service firms are responsive to clients' needs. It is easy to over-promise and under-deliver. Integrity frames the promise, not with caveats, but with reality. Be honest. Be open. Say, *"From what is understood, this is what we can accomplish."* Unfortunately, in response to the highly competitive marketplace and not so much about delivery. Many leaders over-promise, leading to conflict in staff and client relationships.

Integrity is acknowledging reality (e.g., not having enough resources) and proposing a process to get appropriate resources promptly (e.g., a solution to the need). Clients respond positively to that approach. There is a significant difference between saying that you do it — and knowing that you can — versus over-promising because work is needed or not wanting to let the client down.

Professional services firms work with multiple clients and strive to meet all deliverable schedules. When schedule conflicts occur, integrity demands that an open, honest conversation happens regarding "need by" dates to meet client expectations without causing hardship to another client's deliverable schedule. Open communication is the foundation of trust.

Strong leaders start client conversations with an understanding that the services desired must align with the ability to perform — at a quality, timely, and cost-appropriate level. Setting unrealistic expectations is the root of most client conflicts.

GETTING REAL

In Mahan Khalsa's insightful book on building robust B2B relationships, *Let's Get Real or Let's Not Play*, he says, "People don't care how much you know until they know how much you care." That is the foundational part of his conversational model developed to understand the basis of client needs.[26]

Framing conversations from the clients' perspective provides the basis for a shared understanding of solving their key issues. Bringing integrity into the conversation leads to acknowledging that sometimes you might not be the right firm to solve it. Framing the context of what you can do well provides the basis for understanding and appreciating the value of the service offering. It supports the client's ability to see their financial investment as an incentive.

IT TAKES A TEAM

A level of mutual support is critical in professional service relationships. Multidisciplinary teams are commonplace in the A/E/C industry. The industry relies on supporting and teaming relationships to deliver complex projects that span services only sometimes provided by a single firm. The 'prime' 'sub' inter-relationships rely on the integrity of commitment.

For example, when a prime uses a sub-consultant's qualifications to present capabilities and win work but then switches to a cheaper alternative firm when negotiating the client contract, it is the antithesis of integrity. Finding ways to have candid conversations about value brought and value delivered early helps all parties better understand expectations from the client's perspective.

Integrity is about financial accuracy as well. The conversation on mutual commitment extends to the service fee collection process.

---

[26] Khalsa, M., *Let's Get Real or Let's Not Play: Transforming the Buyer/Seller Relationship*, Portfolio, 2008.

Financial fluidity is one of the challenges of all businesses. The prime/sub relationship regarding accounts payable and receivable is often the source of conflict. Applying leadership to the process sets clear expectations early and ensures everyone on the project team is treated fairly and equitably.

AVOIDING NEGATIVE IMPACT

When the integrity of commitment is violated, it colors all future interactions. Business decisions are made for assorted reasons, but when trust is broken, rebuilding takes time. There are ways to improve a broken relationship by showing a willingness to overlook things that happened years ago because circumstances and people have changed. However, institutional memory is long and challenging to overcome — even more, a reason to conduct all aspects of business with integrity.

Another aspect of integrity comes in interdisciplinary relationships. The service and client teams often need help with design, schedule, and cost. Remember that while commitment to the client is primary, supporting the position of all members of the service team is equally important. There are ways to communicate a disagreement, but not in front of the client. And that is an integrity issue, too. Praise in public and critique and correct in private. Taking that approach increases the value perceived by the client or anyone on the team. When leaders tolerate poor or conflicting behaviors within a team, it reflects on the firm's culture. Everyone must act with integrity in every way, every day.

When a leader sees behavior patterns that negatively impact client and affiliate relationships, inaction can affect the company's culture. Tolerating bad behavior shows the leader does not want to deal with the conflict. Worse, it is because the person exhibiting the bad behavior brought in the work.

It always comes back to integrity. Leaders do the right thing because it is the right thing to do. Dealing with someone who acts with less than complete integrity requires a leader's strong hand because allowing harmful behavior negatively impacts the organization's culture and client relationships.

RAISING THE BAR

Integrity sets the bar for acceptable behavior. The organization's (and its leader's) approach to integrity defines expectations and impacts every aspect of culture and client relationships. An organization that allows the opposite — any element of deceptive, predatory, or illegal behaviors — is doomed to fail. When behaviors do not follow cultural values, it becomes clear why the leader's character is important. Integrity is a fundamental quality essential to leadership in a professional service firm.

- **Inspire Trust and Confidence.** As a business providing expert advice and guidance, clients must trust and believe in the firm's leadership to deliver effectively. By demonstrating integrity in words and actions, leaders earn their clients' and the firm's employees' trust and confidence.

- **Set a Positive Example for Your Team.** Personal integrity sets the tone for the organization's culture by creating a positive and ethical culture that staff and team emulate.

- **Enhance the Practice's Reputation.** A powerful reputation is crucial to the success of any professional service firm. The firm's brand identity and image are enhanced, and the practice attracts more business by consistently exhibiting integrity.

- **Build Long-Term Relationships.** Trust and integrity are vital components of any successful long-term relationship. Demonstrating integrity in all client interactions builds solid and lasting relationships that benefit the firm and its clients.

Integrity inspires trust and confidence, sets a positive example for your team, enhances your reputation, and helps to build long-term relationships.

We identified six traits of leaders with Integrity — **Trust, Impact, Values, Courage, Harmony,** and **Character**— that we explore in the following chapters. Each trait's aspects and related behaviors build on an individual's strengths and contribute to personal growth.

SYNTHESIS

Integrity-based leadership development is critical to the success of expected inspirational and innovative leadership. Leaders who prioritize integrity in their personal and professional lives create a culture of trust and accountability within their organizations. Integrity drives innovation and inspires their teams to reach their full potential.

In professional service firms, success is measured by the ability to deliver high-quality services that meet clients' needs profitably. Leaders must have the courage to make tough decisions and take calculated risks. Service requires integrity and authenticity that inspires trust and confidence in their teams, clients, and stakeholders.

Leaders who need more integrity or don't prioritize it in their decision-making process undermine their credibility and erode trust, making it difficult to establish and maintain long-term relationships with clients and colleagues. They may also create a culture of fear and distrust within their organizations, which stifles creativity, innovation, and growth.

In contrast, leaders prioritizing integrity-based leadership development create a culture of trust, respect, and collaboration that inspires their teams to perform at their best. They lead by example, modeling the behaviors they expect from their teams and holding themselves accountable for their actions and decisions, fostering an environment where innovation, creativity, and collaboration thrive, leading to improved client satisfaction and increased business success.

By prioritizing integrity, leaders build trust, accountability, and collaboration that inspires their teams to achieve their full potential and deliver high-quality services that meet clients' needs.

Integrity

SYNOPSIS

Leadership integrity isn't just an assumed quality; it must be actively demonstrated. Effective leaders align their words with their actions and are accountable to themselves and their teams. The leader's character plays a pivotal role in shaping the organization's culture, reputation, and client relationships. In the professional service industry, clear and honest communication is vital, particularly between primary and subcontracting firms. Leaders must avoid over-promising and instead be transparent about what can realistically be achieved. Leaders must establish clear expectations and hold both themselves and their teams responsible for upholding organizational values. They swiftly address and correct issues, fostering an environment of trust.

Leaders ensure that their vision and purpose align with client needs. They set realistic expectations and communicate openly about potential challenges and solutions. By doing so, they build a foundation of trust. In industries like A/E/C, multidisciplinary teams collaborate on complex projects. The interplay between primary firms and subcontractors is underscored by the integrity of commitment, emphasizing the importance of mutual support and accurate communication. Effective leaders are proactive in addressing issues that can damage trust. They understand the long-term implications of broken promises and strive to maintain a consistent commitment to their teams, clients, and business affiliates.

Understanding and addressing the client's needs from their perspective is crucial. A leader must be able to frame conversations in a way that acknowledges the firm's capabilities while highlighting the value of their service offering.

Leaders should be equipped to address conflicts, especially when they involve financial disputes or strained relationships between primary and subcontracting firms. They ensure fairness in financial transactions and set clear expectations from the outset.

Leaders must have personal integrity and cultivate it within their organizations. They inspire trust and confidence, set positive examples, and foster cultures prioritizing ethics and accountability. This, in turn, bolsters the firm's reputation and facilitates long-lasting client relationships.

Chapter 13 | **TRUST:** Speaking the Truth

It turns out that trust is, in fact, earned in the smallest of moments. It is earned not through heroic deeds or even highly visible actions but through paying attention, listening, and gestures of genuine care and connection.
Brene Brown

FOCUS: Suspicious eyes are always on the leader, and trustworthy words and behaviors are critical.

LEADERS OFTEN FACE THE CHALLENGE of establishing trust and credibility, particularly in professional service firms where integrity is paramount. Trust is the foundation of any successful leader-client and leader-team relationship. Building this trust requires leaders to prioritize honesty, be transparent, and lead by example.

When leaders uphold these principles, they foster a culture where employees feel valued and empowered, leading to proactive problem-solving and improved decision-making. Furthermore, by nurturing this trust-based environment, leaders can ensure a positive and productive work atmosphere, leading to repeat business and growth opportunities.

However, trust is fragile, and once broken, it is notoriously challenging to rebuild. In today's interconnected and social media-driven world, perceptions can be swayed rapidly, making the consistent demonstration of integrity crucial.

Leaders must be vigilant in their actions, ensuring they always act honestly and hold their teams accountable. Taking steps like effective communication, setting clear expectations, delivering on promises, and emphasizing continuous improvement can help leaders build and maintain a trust-based culture in their organizations, ensuring long-term success.

> *Leading by example and transparency are essential to building trust. Do what you say and expect others to do the same. Hold people accountable for their actions.*
> — **Kevin Power,** PE, President, KPE & EngTech

THE IMPORTANCE OF TRUST

Honesty in leadership cannot be overstated, especially in professional service firms where integrity is a fundamental trait that clients expect. Leaders who prioritize truth-telling and transparency build credibility with their teams, clients, and stakeholders, which is essential for long-term success.

One of the primary reasons trust is vital in leadership is because it fosters a culture of openness and honesty. When employees feel that their leaders are truthful, they are likely to speak up about issues affecting the company, allowing leaders to address these concerns proactively, which leads to better decision-making and improves the company's bottom line.

In contrast, when leaders compromise their integrity and encourage employees to lie or deceive, it has significant consequences for the organization. Such actions erode trust and result in a loss of internal and external credibility. Employees may become disengaged and disenchanted, leading to high turnover rates, decreased morale, and hostile work culture. Clients may also lose faith in the company, resulting in the loss of business and reputation.

MAKING TRUST A PRIORITY

Leaders who prioritize trust and honesty also demonstrate their commitment to ethical behavior. This commitment is crucial in professional service firms where clients rely on their advisors to act with integrity and maintain confidentiality. When leaders model honorable behavior, it sets the tone for the entire organization, encouraging employees to follow suit.

Trust and honesty are critical traits for a leader in a professional service firm. Leaders who prioritize truth-telling and transparency build credibility with their teams, clients, and stakeholders, leading to improved decision-making, a positive work culture, and sustained success. Conversely, leaders who compromise their integrity risk losing trust and credibility, significantly affecting the organization's long-term viability.

Trust is another essential trait of a leader. The high importance of integrity in an organization becomes part of its core values and flourishes within the firm, communicating a message of high integrity throughout the organization. However, once trust is broken, it is hard to rebuild, and it colors the perception of the person's trustworthiness, even if 90% of what they do is good.

How a person behaves is critical to building trust. It is a process that requires consistency over time. Perception is reality. Integrity is vital in business in our social media-driven world. It is essential to focus on truth and building trust, which are pivotal to an organization's and its leader's perceived value.

BUILDING TRUST

Trust builds over time through behaviors that demonstrate truth and honesty. A broken trust is challenging to repair. Even a slight breach damages the perception of a leader's trustworthiness. High-integrity firms flourish, and their brand value is directly proportional to their integrity. Leaders with integrity create a culture of trust within their organizations, which leads to success and growth for the firm. Clients need to trust service providers, and service providers need to trust their clients. A lack of trust leads to unethical behavior.

In the professional service sector, clients expect their service providers to be trustworthy and to act in their best interests. Clients entrust sensitive information, confidential data, and critical projects to their hiring firms. Clients must be confident that their consultants will act in their best interests. A breach of trust has profound consequences, including legal and financial repercussions.

BUILDING A TRUST-BASED CULTURE

Trust is essential in building solid relationships with clients. Professional service firms rely on repeat business from satisfied clients, and trust is a critical component of building and maintaining those relationships. When clients trust their service provider, they are likely to recommend the firm to others, which leads to new business opportunities.

Trust builds a positive and productive work environment. When employees trust their leaders, they will likely feel motivated, engaged, and committed to their work. Trust also encourages open communication, which is critical in professional service firms where collaboration and teamwork are essential.

Building trust is essential for any professional service firm, and it starts with just a few steps by the firm's leadership:

- **Lead by Example:** Strong leaders model behavior wanted in their employees by being transparent, honest, and ethical in all their dealings, internally and with clients.
- **Communicate Effectively:** Communicate regularly and honestly, providing timely updates on projects, potential issues, and any changes in the firm's strategy.

- **Set Clear Expectations:** Outline expectations of the team and what the team expects from their leader and set the expectations for success.

- **Deliver on Promises:** Commit to delivering quality work on time and within budget. The leader ensures that their team is held accountable for meeting these expectations.

- **Foster a Culture of Accountability:** When employees take ownership of their work and are responsible for their actions — achieved by setting clear goals, providing regular feedback, and celebrating successes — the leader, the firm, and their clients all benefit.

- **Listen to Feedback:** Seek feedback from employees and clients and use this feedback to improve the firm's processes and services.

- **Emphasize Continuous Improvement:** The leader encourages their team to learn new skills, stay updated with industry trends, and seek new growth opportunities.

Taking these steps builds a culture of trust for a professional service firm's leader, employees, and clients, which leads to stronger relationships with clients, higher client satisfaction, and more success for the firm.

The Architecture of Vision

SYNTHESIS

Trust-based leadership is crucial for inspiring and innovative leadership. When leaders foster a culture of trust, they create an environment where employees feel valued, respected, and empowered.

Trust-based leadership encourages open communication and collaboration, vital components of innovation. When employees feel that their opinions are valued and that they communicate openly with their leaders and colleagues, they are likely to share their ideas and work together to develop innovative solutions.

A leader who clients trust also inspires innovation by fostering relationships built on mutual respect and collaboration. Clients are likely to share their challenges and work collaboratively with a trusted advisor, which leads to more innovative solutions.

Trust-based leadership is essential for inspiring and innovative leadership. By fostering a culture of trust and collaboration, leaders encourage employees to be more creative and innovative and build stronger relationships with clients, leading to more innovative solutions.

VIEWPOINT – **NANCY USREY**, FSMPS, CPSM
Associate Vice President, HNTB

It is hard to be all things to all people. It is challenging to be down-to-earth and approachable and still have your view high enough to see where you are going.

— Nancy Usrey

The Essence of Leadership

When I think of leadership, I think of leadership as a combination of direction and charisma. It is hard to follow somebody that you do not want to follow. So, while you need to like the leader as a professional, you may like them differently than a friend. With a good leader, followers find ways to respect or admire them — a reason to want to follow them.

A good leader engenders that kind of respect from the people around them. The leader sees what needs to be done and whatever it takes to get it done. Sometimes they do it themselves. Most of the time, they find the smartest people around them — or the ones with the most passion — and pull them together to create a team that moves forward and accomplishes the goal.

My role today is to work with diverse groups of people around the country focused on winning work. We identify the geographic division. We recognize a project that we want to go after. We place the right people and prepare the team. My job is to collaborate with the assembled team to meet the project requirements.

I bring a broader experience and help guide, encourage, and teach them the best practices for winning the pursuit. So, from that perspective, my role is not visionary but more charismatic. I act reactively to an existing opportunity, but my work is equally important because I help the team focus on how to go about winning the job. My role is to help develop threads of thoughts and messaging that roll through that proposal and unite the team behind that understanding.

Overcoming Resistance

Charisma comes from jumping into a group of people you do not work with daily and being recognized for what you bring. There have been many situations where somebody did not appreciate my being there. They did not think I was needed. Or they did not believe I represented someone they did not want to be involved with.

My role as a leader is to overcome those objections with ideas and approaches grounded in my experience. I aim to make people comfortable at all levels — from a geographic division president, the technical team, the marketing coordinator, and everyone in between — and show that I have the experience and bring the thought leadership to help them succeed.

The three pillars — Inspiration, Innovation, and Integrity — all align. You must inspire people to follow directions. You must inspire people to follow your ideas of innovation. A good leader must articulate a goal to give people a better outcome than they have had, or they will get tired of following you.

That does not mean that you must reinvent the wheel every time. That means you can hold patents or transform the organization's work. Being a leader means that you must continually improve. If you run a business, you must be open to all the factors around you. You may decide to stay in a particular market. That is good and well, but everything evolves. A good leader knows you must innovate to stay ahead of the game. Otherwise, you are just a follower. A good leader is always a step forward.

On integrity, if people can't trust you to do what you say you will do, you had better have a solid reason to break the rules. If you do not keep your word or if you talk about people behind their backs, that behavior undermines everything you are. People are going to need to trust you. They will not come to you with ideas or thoughts, want you on their team, or want you to lead.

One of the biggest leadership challenges in a large company is employee perception. Employees must feel like the people above them need to be there — how decisions are made must be clarified.

Sometimes, leaders need to take time to think about what they are saying. Or they say one thing, and they do something else. They do not think about the optics of what they are doing or saying. Influential leaders must stop to think about what they say and do and how it appears to others who report to them. Related to integrity, a leader must always be careful about perception.

Versatility in Leadership

I think about the concept of servant leadership. A servant leader is only sometimes taking charge but someone 'in the pack' working with a team, pushing everyone toward a goal. You can be a leader that way, too. There is the CEO or department head leader, but there is also the one person who pulls a team together and keeps them moving optimistically toward their goal.

As a leader, you see what the people above you need to succeed and those below you need to succeed. Your interpretation of leadership changes depending on where you are in the matrix. Servant leaders may need more experience or knowledge but are ready to learn. They are there to help. They ask questions when they make a mistake. They own it and find out what to do differently next time. People gravitate to people with that approach. They want to work with them. And that makes them as

The Architecture of Vision

much a leader in the place where they are as someone running the entire team.

It is hard to separate yourself from everyone else, but you must hold yourself to a higher level as a leader. That goes to the integrity issue related to words and concepts. It is hard to say, but if you get too close to people, it is hard to lead them. Some leaders have a narrow vision. They focus on solving a problem or only on making a change.

If they are not careful — if they do not get input from 360-degree reviews — they often do something without recognizing the consequences of that action. At the same time, do not paralyze yourself to get all the views. So, there must be a balance. A strong leader makes decisions quickly, combining input and trusting their gut. Good leaders recognize what is working and what is not and adjust to reach their goals. Good leaders are open-minded to innovative ideas and take the time to self-develop. We know that it takes diverse thought to grow a firm. So, leaders must be open-minded.

Fostering Leadership at Every Level

A professional service firm must be able to grow to open up leadership positions. So, from the outset, identifying the vision is critical. Then, when you find someone with a passion for the vision, you encourage them to follow their passion, which leads to a leadership role. For example, a young vice president in our firm had an idea for a growth line. He put together a business plan that showed how to staff it and where the market would come from, and he sold the idea.

Management agreed to allow him to start this business online, with regular check-ins on progress. After about 18 months, they realized there needed to be more market to warrant the new service. The young leader told me, "They could have easily made me feel like I had failed. They could have fired me because I had lost some money for the company. But they did not. They pulled me in, and we talked about what we had learned and what we would do differently. Ultimately, it was probably the best learning experience I ever had." Good leadership is about trusting people. Giving people a chance to lead on their own, knowing each accomplishment turns into a better path for them or the company.

The Role of Mentorship in Leadership Development

Anyone in leadership needs to see where people excel and help them to grow into a place where they do even better. Or it could be about giving people the opportunity to do something different. Allowing people to follow their path, seeing a chance, and supporting it provides opportunities for new leadership roles to be established.

The mentors who have had the most significant impact on me have always encouraged me to do something new. They have presented an idea and brought me to help. They immediately treated me as a team member, so I was contributing. Mentors do not have to be formal. They are as simple as someone who gives you a wake-up call to think differently and then provides support, opportunity, and encouragement.

There are distinct levels of mentor influence. The little things often become big things when you look back. The old saying is true: People need to remember what you say. They remember how you make them feel. When I stop and think back about how I got where I am, the people who made me think differently about something and motivated me to do something new or different are the ones I value.

Taking An Interdisciplinary Approach

Good leaders acknowledge that marketing differs from what many people think. Once they realize it is not just promotion — sending out brochures or developing resumes and project descriptions — it changes the firm's trajectory. The marketing effort related to pursuits is its discipline. Marketing spans leadership (the why and whom we serve), project management and workflow (the how and when of what we do), and the work breakdown and fee structure (the bottom-line benefit to the firm).

There is a total disconnect when marketing, leadership, and operations work separately. When we integrate marketing into the workflow, everybody recognizes the value. Similarly, marketing teams need to understand project management principles, how to develop a work plan for their effort, and how to integrate that with the rest of the group. They must appreciate scheduling and budgeting.

It all comes back to the bottom line — on every project and to the firm. That is where marketing and leadership come together. Whether human resources, technical delivery, management, or marketing, the quality comes from an integrated team focusing on satisfying the client. That is always the final product. Good leaders know there's power with everyone at the table.

PROGRESSION – **TRUST**: Speaking the Truth

Suspicious eyes are always on the leader, and trustworthy words and behaviors are critical.

AWARENESS: *Think about these statements on understanding the importance of* ***Trust.***

1. What is the harshest thing you have ever said to another person?
2. What is one challenge that you are facing in your life right now?
3. What is one thing that makes you feel insecure?
4. What is the most meaningful change you would like to make in your life right now?

ACCEPTANCE: *Now, reflect on how you reacted when reading these statements. Reflect on what "acceptance" of your truth about what* ***Trust*** *means to you.*

1. Has someone you trusted with personal information ever violated that trust? What happened?
2. What is the silliest mistake you have ever made?
3. Do you have a dream that you have given up on? Why?
4. Have you ever judged someone only to discover you were wrong?

The Architecture of Vision

ACTION: *Follow these steps to incrementally put that awareness and acceptance into action to strengthen your ability to develop leadership with* **Trust.**

1. What is your biggest fear? Research that fear with books or online resources to learn more about it, and then determine what action items you take to resolve this fear in the future.

2. With a trusted advisor or mentor, discuss a time when you covered up a mistake instead of owning up to it. What were the consequences of this action? What are you willing to do about it now?

3. What is a problematic situation that you are now facing? Make a list of actions you take to resolve the problem, including positive and negative responses. Write down who would be affected by all the different options and what could be some consequences if you chose that option. Share your insights with a trusted advisor or mentor.

4. Read a biography of a public figure who had legal challenges, spent time in prison, or had to completely change their life plan when they faced incredible challenges and fears. How did they face their fears and overcome the problem? What are your takeaways from this story?

5. Read Stephen M. R. Covey's **The Speed of Trust: The One Thing That Changes Everything.** Covey breaks down the elements of trust and its central role in leadership.

SYNOPSIS

In professional service firms, the bedrock of effective leadership lies in trust. Distinctive hallmarks of excellent leadership are evident when leaders prioritize honesty and transparency and lead by example. Leaders who uphold these tenets foster a culture of empowerment, leading to improved decision-making, proactive problem-solving, and a thriving work environment. An authentic leader espouses these values and consistently acts upon them, creating a reliable bond with team members and clients.

However, this trust is delicate. In our modern, hyper-connected era, even minor breaches in trust can significantly impact a leader's reputation, emphasizing the continuous need for integrity. Leaders must consistently act honestly, ensure their teams are accountable, and respond to feedback. Key competencies for leaders to cultivate include clear communication, setting and managing expectations, delivering on promises, and emphasizing continuous improvement.

When integrated into their leadership approach, these competencies sustain organizational success and foster a conducive environment for innovation. In such an atmosphere, employees feel valued, open communication is promoted, and clients are more inclined to collaborate, leading to groundbreaking solutions.

The Architecture of Vision

REFLECTIONS & INSIGHTS

Chapter 14 | IMPACT: Leading with Intention

Leadership is about making others better as a result of your presence and making sure that impact lasts in your absence.
Sheryl Sandberg

FOCUS: Leaders focus effort where it matters most.

LEADERS IN PROFESSIONAL SERVICE FIRMS face multifaceted challenges as they navigate the demands of a constantly evolving business landscape. First, they need to understand the critical role impact plays in leadership. Focusing on impact ensures long-term success by aligning the firm's strategies with its mission, but it also builds a powerful reputation, attracts top talent, and promotes client loyalty.

The importance of clear communication cannot be overstated; leaders must effectively communicate the practice's mission and values, foster an inclusive culture, and lead with empathy. These communication techniques ensure employees and clients feel valued and understood, establishing trust and mutual respect.

Moreover, continuous feedback mechanisms are vital for any leader aiming for success in the professional services industry. Leaders must cultivate an environment where employees feel comfortable providing feedback through surveys, focus groups, or one-on-one meetings. This feedback is crucial for improving internal processes and ensuring employee satisfaction.

Likewise, understanding the client's perspective is paramount. By actively seeking and implementing client feedback, leaders can enhance service delivery, strengthen client relationships, and adapt to changing market demands. Whether it's through satisfaction surveys, advisory boards, or regular client relationship meetings, gathering this feedback enables leaders to refine their strategies and ensure the practice delivers maximum value.

DEFINING IMPACT

Impact defines a leader's effectiveness in a professional service firm because it helps ensure that the practice achieves its goals and makes a positive difference in the lives of its employees, clients, and the wider community.

A leader who focuses on impact is likely to develop and implement strategies that help the practice achieve its goals and be successful in the long term. By prioritizing impact, leaders ensure that the practice provides value to its clients and employees and positively contributes to the community, ensuring its success.

Focusing on impact helps build a powerful reputation as a trusted and effective provider of services. When clients and employees see that the practice positively impacts their lives and the wider community, they will likely recommend it to others and continue working with it.

Making an impact also helps attract and retain top talent. When employees see that the practice is making a positive difference in the world, they are likely to feel motivated and engaged in their work and want to stay with the firm for the long term.

By focusing on impact, leaders ensure that the practice is providing high-quality services that meet the needs of its clients, measured by increasing client satisfaction. This loyalty, in turn, helps attract new clients and grow the practice.

Impact

STEPS TOWARD INTENTIONAL IMPACT

Leaders use influence and intention to benefit the practice, its employees, and its clients by following these steps:

- **Clearly Define the Practice's Mission and Values:** Leaders clearly understand their practice's mission and values and communicate these to their employees and clients, helping to ensure that everyone is aligned and working toward the same goals.

- **Build Strong Relationships:** Leaders build strong relationships with their employees and clients and work to understand their needs and goals, helping to foster trust and loyalty and create a culture of collaboration and mutual respect.

- **Develop a Clear Strategy:** Leaders embrace strategies aligned with the practice's mission and values and communicate this to their employees and clients, ensuring everyone works toward the same goals and uses resources effectively.

- **Empower Employees:** Giving employees the autonomy and resources they need to be successful — including ongoing training and development and recognition of achievements — fosters a culture of innovation and creativity.

- **Create a Client-Centric Culture:** A client-centric culture — where the needs and goals of clients are always top of mind — comes from regularly seeking feedback and continuing to use this information to improve the practice's offerings and services.

- **Continuously Monitor and Adjust:** Soliciting feedback from employees and clients and continually monitoring changes in the market and competitive landscape — including that of client clients and the community of practice — helps ensure that the practice remains agile and responsive to evolving needs and opportunities.

THE VALUE OF COMMUNICATION

Leadership is all about communication. Communicating effectively with employees and clients — regularly sharing updates on the practice's progress and soliciting feedback — sets the stage for being more responsive to employee and client concerns and addressing them promptly and effectively.

Fostering a culture of diversity, equity, and inclusion — where everyone feels valued and respected, regardless of their background or identity — includes regularly reviewing and improving hiring practices and creating opportunities for underrepresented groups to advance within the practice.

Leading with empathy — as shown in Chapter 3 — by taking the time to understand and address their employees' and clients' unique challenges and concerns, including being open and transparent about the practice's decision-making processes, shows empathy and understanding when tough decisions must be made.

By using influence and intention in these ways, leaders of professional service firms create a culture of collaboration, innovation, and mutual respect that benefits everyone involved. The impact of this leadership trait leads to increased employee engagement, client satisfaction, and overall success for the practice.

SURVEY SAYS...

Eliciting employee feedback to learn about areas where the practice can be improved positively impacts the firm.

- **Conduct Regular Employee Surveys:** Surveys are a practical way to gather employee feedback about various aspects of the practice. Internal surveys cover topics such as job satisfaction, work environment, leadership, and opportunities for growth and development. When administered anonymously, they encourage honest feedback.

- **Hold Focus Groups or Town Hall Meetings:** Providing a forum for employees to share their opinions and ideas about the practice in a group setting is an effective way to foster collaboration and generate innovative ideas for improving the practice.

- **Implement an Open-Door Policy:** Leaders who create an open-door approach — where employees are encouraged to share their feedback, concerns, and ideas with them — build trust and strengthen the relationship between employees and leadership.

- **Use Suggestion Boxes or Feedback Forms:** Providing employees with easy and anonymous ways to share their feedback and ideas is a valuable way to gather input from employees who might feel uncomfortable sharing their opinions in a group setting.

- **One-On-One Meetings:** Leaders who hold regular one-on-one meetings with employees — to discuss their feedback and ideas in a more personalized setting — help build stronger relationships and provide a more nuanced understanding of the needs and concerns of individuals.

- **Monitor Online Reviews and Social Media:** Tracking online reviews and social media provides insight into how clients and the wider community view the practice, which provides valuable feedback on where the firm can improve its service delivery or communication methods.

By implementing these feedback-gathering strategies, leaders better understand their employee's needs and concerns and identify areas where the practice can be improved to have a significant and positive impact.

LISTENING TO THE VOICE OF THE CLIENT

Similarly, soliciting feedback from clients and potential clients about areas of the practice that have been improved can positively impact the perceived value of the services provided.

- **Satisfaction Surveys:** Surveys that gather client feedback about their experience with the practice are sent after completing a phase, a project, or a service engagement, covering topics such as communication, responsiveness, quality of work, and overall satisfaction.

- **Use Website Feedback Forms:** Forms on the practice's website provide clients an easy and anonymous way to share their feedback and ideas about the practice.

- **Online Reviews and Social Media:** Tracking online reviews and social media through Google Alerts or other software provides valuable feedback about areas for the practice to improve service delivery or communication and insights into how clients and the community perceive the practice.

- **Advisory Boards or Panels:** Establishing a regular forum for input from clients, potential clients, and affiliate consultants provides a structured opportunity to solicit outside opinions and ideas in a group setting and is an effective way to foster collaboration and generate innovative ideas for improving the practice.

- **Client Relationship Meetings**: Leaders who hold regular one-on-one meetings with clients — to discuss their feedback and ideas in a more personalized setting — help build stronger relationships with the practice and provide a better understanding of the needs and concerns of both the client and the market.

By implementing these feedback-gathering strategies, leaders better understand their client's needs and concerns and develop strategies that positively impact the services' value in the client's eyes.

The Architecture of Vision

SYNTHESIS

The leader's focus on impactful communication, collaboration, and connection with employees and clients directly impacts their ability to be inspirational and innovative. Effective communication is essential for inspiring and motivating employees and clients. Leaders who communicate clearly and authentically create a sense of trust and openness that allow employees and clients to feel valued and understood, fostering a culture of innovation where employees feel comfortable sharing their ideas and collaborating to find novel solutions.

Collaboration is also essential for driving innovation and finding new ways to deliver client value. Leaders who encourage collaboration and foster a culture of teamwork inspire employees to work together to solve complex problems and find new growth opportunities, which leads to more innovative and creative solutions that help the practice to stand out in the marketplace.

Building strong connections with clients creates a sense of loyalty and commitment to the practice. Leaders take the time to get to know their clients personally — and focus the relationship on creating a shared purpose and commitment to innovation and excellence — inspiring advocacy for the practice.

By prioritizing these factors, leaders create a resilient, adaptive practice that focuses on delivering exceptional value to clients.

Impact

VIEWPOINT – REBECCA JONES, MBA
Chair, SafeworkCM

Many people are termed 'leaders,' but few represent principled and purposeful leadership.
— Rebecca Jones

A Leader with Purpose

I define leadership as someone who has a purpose. Within that purpose, a leader understands the desired outcome and brings together a select group of people to achieve it. I describe outstanding leadership as service. I think of myself as a servant leader. The A/E/C profession depends on groups of people in disparate locations, all acting on behalf of the company and serving a client. To keep them doing what they do best, I help them. It goes back to having a clear purpose, understanding what outcomes you want, and getting a group of disparate individuals to move with you toward that outcome.

I am going to let you in on a secret. I have read two books and countless articles on what a CEO is supposed to be. I agreed with some of it, and some did not. I am lucky to have a strong president responsible for day-to-day operations, business development, and quality control. My job as CEO is to serve the company and the firm's leaders by ensuring our brand is vital.

My job as the head of the company is to be very visible and to ensure communication with the outside world is one voice. I make sure that people know that our culture is still strong, our ability to serve our clients is still strong, and that we are taking care of our employees. I share that message with our clients and potential clients. I promote the company by carrying the standard of the brand. And, while I have the brand standard, the president and I must agree for it to work, so we share leadership as a collective effort.

Inspiration: The Hallmark of Effective Leadership

One of the most important jobs a CEO does is to be inspiring. What makes a leader? Is it because they are technically competent? Sometimes? Is it because they are charismatic individuals? Sometimes? Or is it because they inspire the greatness that lives in everybody? The leader's job is to be inspirational to those they are working with regardless of position in the firm's hierarchy because leaders are everywhere.

One innovation principle is to listen for what is needed, not just what is wanted. Then, step beyond that and develop the idea of what is required that the client may not even know. It is essential to innovate internally, too. There may be a better way to do simple things, like a better way to present. We have done much about improving presentations in the past two years. At first, when no one could present to clients in person, we had a series of horrific calls where you could see how not to do presentations.

Innovating from Within

One of our team had the idea to develop an in-house studio with our banner using green screen technology. We even had makeup artists coming in. That was fun. Innovation means points of light. It is the point where somebody has a better idea of how to do something. The innovation point of light is a critical part of leadership, but those points come from anybody in the organization. Innovation does not necessarily come from leaders. It comes from somebody with a great idea. A great leader sees that point of light and does something with it.

The idea of our studio did not come from me. It did not come from our president. It came from someone saying, 'I was just on this

Zoom presentation, and it was awful. Don't you think we would like to do something about that?' And, boom, the idea caught fire. We used it for a presentation at a national conference and turned it into something more like a TV program. We had never done it before, and it set us apart in that situation. We stood out as leaders in adapting to the new virtual meeting environment based on the feedback we got.

When these points of light come up, it is fantastic what catches fire. These innovative ideas do nothing but good for us. Good leadership must be open to that thinking, and ideas can come from somewhere other than the top of the food chain.

The Pillar of Integrity

Integrity is an interesting word. We discussed this a lot while drafting our mission and vision statements. How would you define integrity? Are we honest? Yes? Do we keep our word? Yes. Our words are our bond. Do we do the best we can? Yes. If that is the definition of integrity, then we, as a company, have integrity.

Does the leadership have integrity? Do we break laws? No. Are we honorable people? That depends on your definition of honorable. Are we ferocious competitors? You bet we are. Do we play to win? You bet we do. Are we kind? Yes! Do we take care of our employees appropriately to the best of our ability? Yes. If we promise something, do we keep that promise? Yes, we do. Those definitions of integrity are understood from the top of the organization. If your definitions of integrity do not align with ours, you do not get to work with us.

The Listening Gap

One of the weaknesses of strong leaders is often listening. It would help if you listened to give feedback, but that is often hard to do because of what you want to jump in and respond to. People with strong opinions are often seen as strong leaders, but they often stumble over simply listening to another person in the group. If that person happens to be younger or older or of a different gender, it presents a bias and a challenge, and often, we are completely unaware that we are doing that. All leaders improve if they focus on improving their ability to listen.

We aim to instill a culture recognizing leadership opportunities for new hires and every employee. With our support, we want everyone to know they can grow in any direction. We look for opportunities for them. That means that if you work hard and care for your clients and the company, we allow you to grow as much as you would like. We will do our best to figure out what that is with you. And that goes back to listening. One of our company's leadership jobs is to look for opportunities for those working with us and find out where they would like to go.

The Role of Mentors and Peers

It is interesting how mentors appear in your life. I have had people that have watched me. I have had the folks that mentored me. I have had employees that have helped me. It is amazing how they show up. They do not have to be older. They do not have to be women. They do not have to be men. They appear.

So, I have been fortunate to have several mentors along the way. I had one. I call her my reverse mentor. She told me I did not have a future in construction management because I was not an engineer or a man. Her perspective, which I never believed, led to me starting my firm with the support of the men we reported to.

As much as mentors are essential, my women peers are those who say something, think about it, and give you good advice, which is as vital as having or being a mentor.

Impact

PROGRESSION – IMPACT: Leading with Intention

Leaders focus effort where it matters most.

AWARENESS: *Think about these statements on understanding the importance of* ***Impact.***

1. Start with knowing what you want. Why do you get out of bed each morning?
2. What is your purpose, and what makes you feel alive?
3. Look at your calendar and bank statement. Where do you spend your time and money?
4. From the list above, what are you willing to let go of to increase something else?
5. Do you focus on goals so much that you must remember to enjoy the journey? Explain in your journal.

ACCEPTANCE: *Now, reflect on how you reacted when reading these statements. Reflect on what "acceptance" of your truth about what* ***Impact*** *means to you.*

1. What did you notice about how you spend your time and money? Is there anything you would like to change?
2. As a leader, much of your time focuses on your employees and clients. When you reflect on the Awareness questions, do you notice areas where you might want to experiment with expanding your empathy and communication skills to learn about the intentions of others? Explain.
3. How comfortable do you accept that leaders are more focused on people than operations or technical tasks? Explain.

The Architecture of Vision

ACTION: *Follow these steps to incrementally put that awareness and acceptance into action to strengthen your ability to develop leadership with* **Impact.**

1. Schedule meetings with colleagues and ask them the Awareness questions (without criticism or judgment). What do you notice about your conversations and discussions?
2. Get in the habit of asking "why" with colleagues and clients to uncover more profound thoughts and insights.
3. Research tactics (online resources, Ted Talks, social media influencers) on active listening. For one day, focus on listening to understand instead of how to respond. Notice insights that you gained. Add another day of active listening until it becomes more habitual and comfortable.
4. Do something of which you are proud. Share with a trusted advisor or mentor.
5. Let go of something that you noticed in Awareness
6. Read Stanley McChrystal's **Team of Teams.** McChrystal shows how restructured teams can create a significant impact in complex environments.

Impact

SYNOPSIS

Leaders prioritize the long-term impact to align firm strategies with its mission, boosting reputation, attracting top-tier talent, and fostering client loyalty. Emphasizing the importance of articulating the firm's mission and values, fostering inclusivity, and leading with empathy. This approach assures both employees and clients feel appreciated, thus establishing trust. Leaders encourage feedback from both employees (via surveys, focus groups, or individual meetings) and clients (through satisfaction surveys, advisory boards, etc.) to adapt to changes and improve processes.

Defining and communicating the firm's mission and values ensures alignment and mutual understanding of objectives. Building strong relationships and engaging deeply with both employees and clients and understanding their needs fosters a sense of loyalty.

Devising and communicating strategies that resonate with the firm's mission empowers employees and leads to a culture of innovation and commitment. Leaders fine-tune the services offered by consistently seeking feedback from clients and staff. Further, continuous assessment of feedback and market dynamics ensures agility and relevance in changing landscapes.

Leaders should consistently update stakeholders on the firm's progress, listen actively, and address concerns. Adopting practices that value everyone, irrespective of their background promotes diversity, equity, and inclusion. By leading with empathy, leaders can understand and resonate with the unique challenges employees and clients face.

A collaborative environment breeds innovation, where sharing and iterating on ideas is encouraged. Building strong client connections involves getting to know clients personally and focusing on building a mutual commitment to innovation and excellence.

The Architecture of Vision

REFLECTIONS & INSIGHTS

Chapter 15 | **VALUES**: Acting with Humility

Good values are like a magnet – they attract good people.
John Wooden

FOCUS: A leader lives at the intersection of personal and business values — humility allows both to proceed smoothly.

LEADERS FACE THE CHALLENGE OF ALIGNING personal and organizational values to ensure integrity, authenticity, and brand consistency. Many organizations have value statements that are meant to represent their cultural ethos. However, these can often be perceived as mere generalizations, failing to capture the true essence of the company or its individuals.

A misalignment between a leader's and the company's values can damage the organization's reputation, harming the brand image and diminishing trust internally and externally. Furthermore, a leader's behavior, both publicly and internally, is scrutinized as the embodiment of these values. When inconsistencies arise, it raises doubts about the leader's integrity and the genuineness of the organization's culture.

The importance of values transcends just the leader; they are the foundation upon which company culture, reputation, and brand are built. For a leader to be successful, they must recognize the power of intention and act with consistency, humility, and alignment with the company's values.

Values need to be actively communicated, lived, and reinforced, ensuring that the entire organization 'walks the talk.' Feedback, such

ns, and a strong understanding of
The Architecture of Vision

as client surveys, is essential in assessing alignment and understanding brand perception. For professional service firms, the values held by the leader and reflected in the firm's statements play a crucial role in employee engagement, client loyalty, reputation, and branding. Hence, defining these values should be thorough, involving market research, internal discussions, and a strong understanding of industry standards to ensure they resonate authentically with both employees and clients.

AN HONEST REFLECTION

Values reflect personality and character. As a leadership trait — specifically within the aspects of integrity — values define the leader. Everyone has values, and many organizations have value statements. Those statements represent the client-facing cultural values that the firm — and everyone in the firm — imbue. Unfortunately, these value statements are too often generalizations and platitudes and do not reflect those of the culture or the individual.

Is it essential for a leader to embody your company's values? Yes! A leader must ensure that their values are consistent with company values as manifested in their actions, internally and externally. If there is an inconsistency, there is a huge disconnect. Where the behaviors of those at the top do not reflect the company's values with the community — when those inconsistencies are notable — it raises questions of integrity and, by reflection, of the authenticity of the company's culture. That harms the company's brand image.

THE POWER OF INTENTION

When leaders believe in their values and act with intention based on them consistently and with humility, it is evident to all they lead. A leader recognizes they are not on a pedestal but are the public face of the values their company represents in their community. Humility aligned with those values is critical for leadership success. Leaders

Values

must also be open to change if they consistently act with the company's values.

Many firms post their value statement on the wall. Employees need to remember that they are there and what those values mean. Values never overtly communicated within and outside the firm have little, if any, impact. If values are essential — and they are — a leader's values and those of the firm must be consistent with the services offered and how they are delivered.

The leader's role is to communicate the importance of values and the importance that everyone — not just the leader — walks the talk those values represent. Values are one of those aspects of leadership that must be reinforced regularly. If, for whatever reason, those values no longer define how the firm (or the leader) sees themselves, it is critical to address the differences and restate the value definition.

It is hard to imagine a value going out of style or importance, but it is crucial to evaluate regularly if these values genuinely represent what the firm stands for. It is related to understanding that the firm's brand is how it is perceived by the client base, by its clients (if the firm is a sub-consultant or subcontractor), and within the community. If those firm values do not reflect how the firm is perceived, then it is time to revisit them.

VALUES HAVE IMPACT

Chapter 14 - Impact notes that client surveys are an excellent way to check value and brand alignment. If the question is not asked, the answer is never known. Many firms avoid client surveys, reasoning that they are likely to hear negative aspects than positive ones. However, as tricky as they are to hear, negative feedback provides insights to address needed change. Knowing a negative comment allows you to improve, even if only incrementally.

The Architecture of Vision

It behooves the leader to define values. A value statement establishes the quality of service a firm provides and its guiding principles. Both are important in the context of leadership and culture. The firm's brand reflects its brand identity — how the firm defines itself — and, more importantly, its brand image — how it is perceived in the market by its clients, its client's clients, and its community.

A leader's brand is equally reflected in the practice's image and should be values-driven. The words a leader speaks, the behaviors they exhibit, how the firm delivers services, and how they treat employees are all reflected in the brand. The leader manages that perception in the workplace and with clients. When identity and image align — the calculus behind brand equity — it benefits both the firm and the leader. The reverse is also true. When not aligned, both are lessened.

BRAND REFLECTIONS

Brand alignment and consistency are crucial for a leader to be successful. Value is a key term here because when it is not communicated — or communicated in a way that the staff or clients perceive as insincere or inaccurate — it undermines the credibility of the whole firm.

Professional service businesses are sometimes led by a technical person who does not necessarily understand the value of marketing and business development — how to bring work in the door. When firms limit shareholder status to those with the right degree or professional license, they restrict the ability to take advantage of all the other equally important functional and operational parts of the business, including human resources, finance, and technology support.

Firms that value marketing — and find ways to identify, support, train, teach, and coach the technical staff to understand better the role they fill in the marketing continuum — have great success. When the technical staff is responsible for proactive outreach and relationship development, storytelling, service innovation research, and identifying

Values

new opportunities, they are more effective in their internal and external interactions as team leaders or seller-doers.

THE VALUE OF VALUES

The values of a professional service firm leader and the firm's value statements significantly impact both employees and clients. Here are some ways:

- **Employee Engagement:** A leader's values and the firm's value statements set the tone for the company culture. Suppose the values align with employees' values. In that case, they are likely to feel engaged and motivated to contribute to the company's success, leading to increased productivity, higher job satisfaction, and lower turnover rates.

- **Client Loyalty:** A firm's values also impact how clients perceive the company. If the values align with the client's values, they are likely to develop a sense of loyalty to the firm, leading to repeat business, positive reviews, and referrals.

- **Reputation:** A leader's values and the firm's value statements impact the company's standing in the industry. If the values align with industry standards and ethical principles, the company is likely to be viewed as trustworthy and respected.

- **Branding:** Values are also essential to a firm's branding strategy. If the values are well-defined and communicated effectively, they help differentiate the firm from its competitors and attract clients who share the same values.

- **Employee Retention:** Employees are likely to stay if they feel that the company's values align with theirs, leading to a more stable and committed workforce, benefiting the firm's bottom line.

Ensuring these values align with the company's mission and culture, a firm creates a positive and productive work environment while building a committed staff and a loyal client base.

DEFINING VALUES

Defining values is essential for any professional service firm and critical to aligning these values with the benefits that the firm's clients perceive. Here are some ways:

- **Conduct Market Research:** Surveys, focus groups, and other data collection methods identify key factors clients consider when choosing a service provider.

- **Analyze Client Feedback:** Client reviews, social media comments, and other feedback forms identify common themes and concerns and identify the values most important to clients.

- **Identify Distinct Strengths:** Identifying singular strengths and expertise, highlighting features, benefits, and proven results, offers distinct messages to competitors and helps define important values and market differentiators.

- **Conduct Internal Discussions:** Collaboratively conduct internal discussions with employees to identify the core values the company does or wants to embody, including brainstorming sessions, team-building exercises, and other team-focused activities.

- **Review Industry Standards:** Understanding and adhering to industry-accepted guidelines and rules of professional practice help align values with established standards and

Values

demonstrate commitment to professionalism and high ethical behavior.

By conducting market research, analyzing client feedback, identifying unique strengths, conducting internal discussions, and reviewing industry standards, leaders define values authentically that help differentiate the firm in the market.

The Architecture of Vision

SYNTHESIS

In the context of integrity, firm and leadership values are critical for any professional service practice. These values help establish a culture of trust and ethical behavior, which is essential for building solid relationships with clients and stakeholders. At the same time, the need for leaders to be inspirational and innovative is also vital in today's fast-paced and competitive business environment.

Inspirational leadership empowers employees to achieve their full potential and work toward a shared vision. A leader who embodies the values of integrity is likelier to inspire trust and respect from their team, which leads to a more engaged and motivated workforce, essential for driving innovation and achieving success.

Innovation is finding new and creative ways to solve problems and meet clients' evolving needs. Leaders who prioritize integrity are likelier to foster a culture of open communication where employees feel comfortable sharing latest ideas and taking calculated risks, which leads to a more innovative and agile organization that responds better to changing market conditions.

Integrity is about doing the right thing, even when it is not the easiest or most profitable option. Leaders who prioritize integrity are likely to make ethical decisions that align with the company's values and mission, inspiring employees to do the same and creating a culture of ethical behavior essential for building trust with clients.

Clients are likely to work with a professional service practice they trust and respect. Leaders who prioritize integrity build strong relationships with clients by demonstrating their commitment to ethical behavior and delivering high-quality services, leading to increased loyalty and repeat business, which is essential for the long-term success of any professional service practice.

Values

VIEWPOINT – **RON WORTH**, CAE, FSMPS, ASSOC. AIA
Retired CEO, IAAO & SMPS

Leadership is about trying different things at different levels through innovation, inspiring people to get things done, and having the integrity to trust your people to do the right thing.
— **Ron Worth**

The Cornerstone of Leadership

Leaders have a vision. No one expects the leader to have all the answers. Great leaders surround themselves with people smarter than they are and then collaborate with them on the vision, goals, and direction of where they want to go. The best leaders get out of the way and let others do their jobs. That has been the most successful strategy for me. Leaders remove obstacles and find resources — money, staff, or support from stakeholders at a higher level — to enable the vision.

Adapting in Crisis: The Skunkworks Initiative

I had five years at the International Association of Assessing Officers (IAAO) to build a new team. I was hired to revamp and rebuild the Association's programs, domestically and internationally. They needed staff with skill sets to shift to virtual education, which still needed to be done then. I began by surrounding myself with capable people, but I only realized how talented they were once we had the pandemic.

So, we were shocked over the first few weeks of the pandemic because no one knew what to do. I said, 'Let's adjust to where we're at right now.' We started talking about a strategy. What do we need to do? We had already lost so much revenue because of canceling in-person programs.

Everyone was in panic mode. The board wanted to cut the staff, which only compounded the problem. We would be left with people without the skillsets to implement technologies. Instead, I reduced our salaries by 20% and focused on making our programming virtual. So, we set up a kind of 'skunkworks' initiative.

We asked the team how to turn our conference into a virtual meeting. How do we turn the education we offer, domestically and internationally, into a virtual mode? The Skunkworks team was terrific. They came through, and the education we delivered built back close to the revenue we had lost. As a not-for-profit (501.c.6), we used some Federal PPP programs to help fund the initiative. As a result, more than 1,200 people came to our first virtual conference. More than half were first-time attendees because, in the past, they could not afford the travel expenses.

We reduced the price by 50% but knew the program was still valuable. Our members need continuing education credits. I allowed our people to develop the solution while providing the required support. It was different from me being an innovative leader.

The Value of the Inspirational Leader

For me, inspiration has always been the most critical aspect of leadership. Those who know me know I am full of ideas. If you say we have a problem, I devise thirty ways to solve it. They may not all be the answer. When there is a challenge — like the pandemic — you do not just say, *'There's nothing we can do.'* As much as I would love to hide under a rock and wait until it is over, you cannot do that.

Values

As a leader, you support everyone who works for you — their lives, families, and livelihoods — not just the executive team. Plus, in our case, our membership depended on us. The inspiration is to produce different ways to do it. You allow your people to be innovative. We do not have to reinvent the world, but there are things we need to do now. How do we adapt what others have done to work for us? So again, they went out and did that, used the first inspiration and my belief in them, and took the innovation to the next step.

A leader with integrity has faith and trust in their people to move forward with the organization's goals. The leader serves as the bellwether to champion their cause. Leaders need to be behind them to be trusted and believed in, so they know you will do whatever you need to help them.

The Importance of Listening

Leadership is about trying different things at different levels through innovation, inspiring people to get things done, and having the integrity to trust your people to do the right thing.

One of the most significant weaknesses of leaders is thinking they have all the answers. I do not have all the answers. It shows when leaders do not listen to the people they serve. It is a function of egotism. It is a big issue in the A/E/C industry. I believe in professional development. So, what we do well, we do. What we cannot, we outsource.

The Integration of Marketing

When I got into marketing, it was a life-changing event. Marketing integrates into everything you do. It shows the value to the people you serve. That is the question marketing needs to ask about the people you serve: 'What's in it for them?' We must not be looking at what is in it for us. Leadership must always look at what is in it for the people we serve. And marketing does that explicitly and well. Marketing is every employee and permeates everything we do.

Integrating marketing into our educational programs highlighted the quality of our programs domestically and internationally. We made a huge difference by showing value, using social media, and upgrading our tools and resources.

Values

PROGRESSION – **VALUES**: Acting with Humility

A leader's ego sits at the intersection of personal and business values; humility allows both to proceed smoothly.

AWARENESS: *Consider these statements on understanding the importance of* ***Values.***

1. Is humility a strength or weakness? Explain.
2. What are examples of ways you express your humility?
3. Describe situations when you felt you had to stand up for yourself. What was the outcome, and how did you think about your level of assertiveness?
4. List your top five personal values. Then, review your company's values. Are they similar? Or different? How have you felt when your personal and company values were not aligned?

ACCEPTANCE: *Now, reflect on how you reacted when reading these statements. Reflect on what "acceptance" of your truth about what* ***Values*** *mean to you.*

1. Are you satisfied with your level of humility? Explain.
2. How comfortable are you with being open to hearing criticism from others?
3. How did you react to a conflict resulting from differing personal and professional values? Explain.

The Architecture of Vision

ACTION: *Follow these steps to incrementally put that awareness and acceptance into action to strengthen your ability to develop leadership with* **Values.**

1. Let others speak before you express your opinions about a business situation. Use active listening and prompting statements to draw out their feelings and values.
2. Study mindfulness and accept the reality of moments, positive and negative.
3. Meditate regularly.
4. Say thank you the next time you experience criticism and ask the other person how you could avoid the situation.
5. Ask for help when you need it.
6. For one day, notice how often you talk about yourself without consideration for the other person. Use your journal to reflect on what you have seen when you are always the center of your intention.
7. Read Patrick Lencioni's **The Five Dysfunctions of a Team: A Leadership Fable.** Lencioni's fable emphasizes the foundational values necessary for team cohesion and success.

Values

SYNOPSIS

Leadership, especially in professional service firms, is not just about skills or strategy; it's about values. The essence of leadership lies in aligning personal values with those of the organization. When a leader's actions reflect the organization's core values, they exude authenticity and integrity. However, a misalignment can damage the organization's brand and diminish trust.

For a leader to be truly effective, they must consistently act with intention, humility, and alignment with company values. It's essential to recognize that value statements, often displayed in firms, should go beyond generalities and genuinely reflect the culture and the individuals within it.

Effective leaders understand the power of brand consistency. They talk about values and ensure that the entire organization embodies them. Feedback mechanisms, such as client surveys, are crucial in gauging the alignment between the company's values and public perception.

Firms that actively define and live their values witness higher employee engagement, increased client loyalty, and a stronger reputation. When there's a mismatch between the firm's values and public perception, effective leaders take proactive steps to address the discrepancies. They understand that values directly impact client relationships, employee satisfaction, and the overall brand image.

Individuals need more than technical expertise or managerial skills to be an effective leader in today's business environment. They must be deeply rooted in values that resonate with employees and clients. Regular evaluation of these values to ensure they align with the organization's mission and culture is critical. Effective leaders also engage in market research, internal discussions, and a thorough understanding of industry standards. They encourage a culture of open communication, which fosters innovation and creativity. Prioritizing

The Architecture of Vision

integrity, these leaders make ethical decisions even when they might not be the most lucrative or popular, setting a precedent for the entire organization. The competencies required for effective leadership extend beyond knowledge or skill; they delve deep into character, authenticity, and a genuine commitment to the organization's core values.

Values

REFLECTIONS & INSIGHTS

Chapter 16 | COURAGE: Effort & Mindfulness

The courage to be vulnerable is not about winning or losing; it's about the courage to show up when you can't predict or control the outcome.
Brene Brown

FOCUS: Courage is the trait that leaders use to navigate smooth and stormy waters and requires accepting risk and failure so the goal is accomplished.

LEADERS FACE AN ARRAY OF CHALLENGES, especially during times of change or adversity. These challenges range from the need to voice harsh truths and realign strategies to the daunting step of laying off employees during economic downturns. Furthermore, leaders must often introduce new, unproven services to clients, which involves taking risks and promoting a culture of innovation.

To do all this effectively, courage is indispensable. Courage is not just about confronting issues; it's also about embracing failure as a pathway to learning, understanding client needs to identify market opportunities, and having the tenacity to push beyond conventional methods.

Courage acts as a cornerstone for effective leadership. By setting clear values, leaders provide direction for their organizations. They demonstrate courage by taking calculated risks, leading by example, by fostering a culture of transparency, and adapting to ever-evolving market demands.

The Architecture of Vision

Cultivating courage encompasses embracing vulnerability, promoting a vision, endorsing risk-taking, ensuring collaboration, and investing in personal growth. The rewards of such courage are manifold: enhanced resilience, better decision-making, a sterling reputation, heightened innovation, and a motivated workforce. The courage to lead is pivotal for confronting challenges head-on and charting a successful path forward.

THE ESSENTIAL NATURE OF COURAGE

Courage is essential for leaders in professional service firms, particularly in times of difficulty and change. Leaders must have the courage to speak brutal truths and acknowledge needed changes, even if they are unpleasant or uncomfortable. The traits of a courageous leader include having the courage to realign strategy, lay off or furlough employees during a recession, and face complex challenges head-on. Leaders must recognize the realities of their business and have the courage to speak up and address issues that arise.

In addition to speaking difficult truths, leaders must also have the courage to take risks, including pursuing new services and solutions, even if they are untested or unfamiliar. It takes courage to sell new services to new clients and to take the time and effort to build a successful track record. Leaders must also have the courage to motivate their teams to assume these risks and overcome the challenges of pursuing new opportunities.

Leaders must engage with their clients and understand their needs and challenges to take these risks. By identifying gaps in the market and opportunities to provide value, leaders pursue new services and solutions that meet their clients' needs. Courage requires thinking beyond traditional practices and considering their clients' broader operational and strategic business aspects.

Finally, leaders must have the courage to fail. Failure is inevitable in taking risks and pursuing new opportunities, but it is also a valuable

Courage

learning experience. Leaders must be courageous to embrace failure, learn from it, and keep pushing forward. By acknowledging the possibility of failure and mitigating its impact, leaders build resilience and foster a culture of innovation and growth within their organizations.

STRENGTH IN THE FACE OF FAILURE

It takes courage to speak difficult truths, take risks, engage with clients, and embrace failure. By embodying these principles, leaders build resilient organizations that thrive in times of change and uncertainty.

Leaders use various methods to demonstrate courage and establish the foundation for the practice to succeed:

- **Define and Communicate Clear Values:** Defining and communicating values establishes a foundation for the practice and ensures that everyone is working toward the same goals.

- **Take Calculated Risks:** Risk helps the practice by engaging in strategic investments or pursuing new business opportunities where risk leads to significant rewards.

- **Lead by Example:** Leaders demonstrate the courage they expect from their employees, including taking on complex tasks, making tough decisions, or standing up for what is right even when it is unpopular.

- **Foster a Culture of Openness and Honesty:** An open and honest culture where employees feel comfortable sharing their ideas and opinions helps find areas for improvement and drive innovation.

- **Continuously Adapt and Evolve:** Meeting changing market conditions and client needs requires the courage to abandon old ways of doing things and embrace original and innovative approaches.

Influential leaders show the courage to establish a solid foundation and framework for their practice to succeed.

FINDING COURAGE

Developing courage takes time, effort, and intentionality, including several steps to include in personal development:

- **Embrace Vulnerability:** Acknowledge fears, insecurities, and limitations, be open to feedback, admit mistakes, and be transparent about decision-making processes.

- **Set a Clear Direction:** Setting and communicating a clear vision for the firm helps create a sense of purpose and direction and inspires team members to take risks and innovate.

- **Encourage Risk-Taking:** Creating a culture that values risk-taking and experimentation supplies opportunities for team members to take on challenging projects, make decisions, and learn from failures.

- **Foster Collaboration**: Leaders understand they do not have all the answers and are willing to seek input and ideas from others by creating a collaborative work environment where team members feel comfortable sharing their opinions and ideas.

- **Lead by Example:** By modeling courageous behavior, influential leaders take calculated risks, stand up for their beliefs, and make tough decisions when necessary.

- **Invest in Personal Development:** Ongoing personal growth and development comes from the investment in personal and professional development by attending conferences, taking courses, and seeking out mentorship and coaching.

THE COURAGE TO LEAD

Developing courage as an inherent trait benefits both the leader and the firm. Some of these benefits include:

- **Increased Resilience:** Leaders who show courage are better equipped to manage challenges, setbacks, and failures. They will likely bounce back from demanding situations and find solutions to problems.

- **Improved Decision-Making:** Leaders willing to take risks and make tough decisions based on their convictions lead their firm in the right direction. Courageous leaders are fearless in challenging the status quo and making unconventional decisions that help the firm eventually.

- **Enhanced Reputation:** Leaders who show courage inspire their team and clients, earning their respect and admiration. A leader who stands up for their principles and values has a reputation as trustworthy and ethical, attracting more clients and talent to the firm.

- **Increased Innovation:** Courageous leaders will likely encourage experimentation and innovation within their firm. They are not afraid to try new things and are willing to take risks to stay ahead of the competition.

- **Improved Employee Engagement:** Employees are likely to be engaged and committed to a leader who shows courage. When leaders are transparent and authentic, it creates a sense of trust and loyalty among team members, leading to a more productive and positive work environment.

SYNTHESIS

An inspirational and courageous leader of a professional service firm plays a crucial role in driving inspiration and innovation within the practice. When a leader proves courage and inspires their team, it creates an environment that fosters creativity, risk-taking, and experimentation.

By showing courage, the leader sets an example for their team. They encourage their team to think beyond conventional ideas and embrace new and innovative approaches to problem-solving, which, in turn, fosters a culture of innovation where team members are encouraged to share their thoughts, experiment, and take risks without fear of failure.

Moreover, an inspirational and courageous leader helps to create a positive work environment that motivates and energizes the team. A leader who genuinely cares about their team fosters loyalty, commitment, engagement, productivity, and job satisfaction among team members.

VIEWPOINT – **SAMANTHA SANNELLA**
Sr. Managing Director, Cushman & Wakefield

The best leaders are people who inspire others. That is the simple thing.
— Samantha Sannella

The Art of Inspirational Leadership

The best leaders are people who inspire others. That is the simple thing. My approach has always been to hire people smarter than me. My job is to encourage them to do their best. When you do that, you have a successful team.

The Triad of Success

Inspiration is important. You are not motivated to do your best if you do not work at an inspiring workplace. Inspiration is critical. Innovation is constantly wanting to do better. I tell my staff, 'You must improve on everything you do. You do not just rinse and repeat. Even if it is a slight change, improve something. Number one, it makes you more competitive. Number two, it is self-motivating.' And it is critical for leaders to operate at the highest degree of integrity, now more than ever. It is not easy to teach people virtue, but it comes down to working, acting, and speaking in the client's best interest.

Acknowledging Weaknesses

The biggest weakness for most leaders is being afraid to admit what they do not know. Owning that is something you get, or you will figure it out or hire somebody who knows it. When you pretend to know something you do not know, intelligent people see through it. Unfortunately, a lot of leaders do that. Right away, you lose respect. And once you lose respect for somebody, you do not want to do business with them. It comes back to integrity. The most significant challenge most leaders must overcome is recognizing their shortcomings.

Navigating Scale

We do an excellent job of promoting inclusiveness, diversity, and innovation. We are an exceptionally large firm of 60,000-plus people. As a company, we are constantly striving to be the best. Because we are that large, it is like steering a ship. Changes take a long time. Smaller firms often turn faster and more responsive. We support leadership development initiatives and invest, knowing we will see positive results.

The Role of Mentorship

I have had great mentors. One taught me the importance of work ethic — putting in the time needed to finish the job. He had so much integrity, and I appreciated his knowledge and willingness to share. He valued thought leadership. He often said, 'If you don't publish it, it doesn't exist.' That stuck with me. Researching, creating, and sharing inspiring and innovative content is an important lesson he taught me.

The Underestimated Value of Marketing

Marketing is undervalued at most firms. It is a shame because marketing makes an enormous difference. I include them in projects, especially in change management and communications. I do not understand why, when we teach people to value design, they do not equally love that leg of the stool, especially in publishing thought leadership. Marketing is about telling the story in a way that inspires.

Generational Dynamics

We continually incorporate the generational aspect into our workplace strategy. My team ranges from millennials to boomers. Honestly, it is a challenge. They all respond to things differently. Younger people need more handholding, feedback, and emotional support. GenX are the most resourceful entrepreneurial people. They are not team-oriented, but if you give them anything to do, they'll figure out how to do it. The Boomers put the most detail into their work. So, there are differences in management and work styles that leaders need to consider.

The Architecture of Vision

PROGRESSION – **COURAGE**: Effort & Mindfulness

Courage is the trait that leaders use to navigate smooth and stormy waters and requires accepting risk and failure so the goal is accomplished.

AWARENESS: Think about these statements on building an understanding of the importance of **Courage**.

1. What are you most afraid of? Explain.
2. Recall a time when you surprised yourself with your courage.
3. How are you mindful? Explain.
4. Do you consider yourself a risk-taker? Explain.
5. Describe your approach to resolving conflict.
6. Describe when you have felt disappointed in yourself for avoiding a demanding situation.

ACCEPTANCE: *Now, reflect on how you reacted when reading these statements. Reflect on what "acceptance" of your truth about what* **Courage** *means to you.*

1. What do you most admire about yourself?
2. How do you feel when you miss reaching a goal?
3. What is your usual response When a person or situation challenges you? What would you change about your typical response if you could?
4. Describe a time when you felt courageous. How do you feel when you reflect on that situation? Avoid criticizing yourself and thinking about what else you could have done. Sit with your courageous feelings for at least five minutes.

ACTION: *Follow these steps to incrementally put that awareness and acceptance into action to strengthen your ability to develop leadership with* **Courage***.*

1. Research social media influences who focus on overcoming fears, including Judi Holler, Jen Sincero, Gabby Bernstein, Brene Brown, etc.
2. Share motivational and inspirational quotes on social media or with your friends and family.
3. Repeat affirmations daily, such as when dressing, driving/commuting, during work breaks, or before bed.
4. Exercise regularly.
5. Practice breathing exercises at least once a day.
6. Read Brene Brown's **Dare to Lead: Brave Work. Tough Conversations. Whole Hearts.** Brown's exploration of vulnerability provides insights into the courage required for authentic leadership.

The Architecture of Vision

SYNOPSIS

Leaders must have courage, especially in professional service firms facing challenging times. Noteworthy leaders are characterized by their ability to confront uncomfortable truths, realign strategies, and take decisive actions, such as layoffs during recessions. They possess the courage to introduce new, untested services, understanding client needs deeply and thinking beyond traditional practices. These leaders embrace failures not as setbacks but as opportunities to learn and innovate.

Effective leaders actively set and communicate clear organizational values, ensuring alignment in vision and direction. Through courage, they take calculated risks, adapt to evolving market needs, and exemplify the values they preach, establishing a strong foundational framework for their firms. Their courage enables them to foster cultures of transparency, openness, and honesty, promoting innovation and adaptability. The outcomes of such leadership are manifold: organizations become more resilient, decision-making is enhanced, reputation is bolstered, innovation is heightened, and employee engagement and trust are deepened.

An individual must engage in intentional personal development to become an influential leader. This involves embracing vulnerability, which means acknowledging fears and being open to feedback. They inspire and motivate their teams towards risk-taking and innovative thinking by setting a clear vision. Effective leaders prioritize collaboration, recognizing the importance of collective insight and expertise. By leading by example, they cultivate an atmosphere where courage is admired and emulated. Moreover, continuous investment in personal and professional growth through education and mentorship ensures they remain at the forefront of leadership excellence.

Courage

REFLECTIONS & INSIGHTS

The Architecture of Vision

Chapter 17 | HARMONY: Alignment & Resonance

Only when diverse perspectives are included, respected, and valued can we start to get a full picture of the world.
Brene Brown

FOCUS: Leaders artistically balance people, resources, opportunities, and challenges.

Leaders are constantly navigating the complexities of various harmonies in the workplace - generational, gender, geographic, discipline, and technological. These distinctions necessitate fostering an environment where conversations flourish, maximize teamwork, and establish a positive culture. However, leaders grapple with numerous challenges, including conflicting deadlines, unexpected setbacks, new opportunities, and myriad distractions.

Pursuing personal harmony becomes a cornerstone for leaders, allowing them to maintain serenity amidst the chaos, think innovatively, and guide their organizations effectively through life's ebbs and flows. The Buddhist practice of finding the middle way becomes crucial, helping leaders balance their leadership journey, regardless of where they are on their developmental spectrum - from a novice to a visionary leader.

Leaders need to integrate personal harmony into their leadership style to instill a harmonious environment. This involves practicing mindfulness, effectively communicating expectations, building genuine relationships with team members, and fostering a culture of respect and inclusivity.

By doing so, they can achieve heightened employee engagement, improved teamwork, bolstered trust and loyalty, reduced turnover, and a positive reputation. Moreover, this harmony extends beyond the organization, enhancing client communication, fostering trust, facilitating collaborative problem-solving, and bolstering the firm's reputation. Thus, establishing and promoting harmony is indispensable for leaders aiming for long-term success in professional service firms.

THE ESSENCE OF PERSONAL HARMONY

Finding ways to develop and promote harmony is crucial to leadership development. Harmony involves being mindful, being centered, and being aware. The aim of harmony is the ability to weather any storm, live in serenity, and convey understanding based on a mindful approach to life. Harmony is a little like courage in the earlier chapter, where leaders learn to face difficulties knowing that the organization's foundation works together effectively during times of challenge.

Distinct types of harmony exist in the workplace, such as generational harmony, gender harmony, geographic harmony, discipline harmony, and technological harmony. Every kind of harmony brings together different people, allowing conversations, teamwork, and culture to thrive.

Achieving harmony is challenging since there are always conflicting deadlines, unexpected challenges, new opportunities, and other distractions. Leaders who step away from the chaos take the time to help themselves stimulate innovative ideas and build an organization that deals with the ebbs and flows of life. Finding the middle way, a Buddhist practice, helps leaders find the balance they need to lead their organization.

Harmony

MILESTONES & MARKERS

Setting goals is critical to finding harmony. Influential leaders have a clear vision of their organization's direction, as discussed in Chapter 1 - Vision. For a practice where everyone understands they have a place as a leader, finding harmony is critical to achieving the firm's strategic goals.

How harmony resonates with leaders depends on where they are on a personal development spectrum.[27] The novice may see their role from an egoist perspective and focus on "I" or "me," and harmony is only personal. The more experienced leader expands their worldview to focus on others, frames input on "you," and frames harmony as serving others.

The enlightened leader sees their efforts as crucial to the collective, and with a focus on "we" effort, communicates the benefits of harmony organization-wide. A visionary leader sees their efforts extending to their clients, their client's clients, and their community, and focus on "us" in applying methods to ensure harmony is a crucial quality of the service-client relationship. We explore this concept again in the **AFTERWORD** chapter.

Harmony is critical to the long-term success of professional service firms. Leaders consumed with solving problems may be unable to create a harmonious environment. A harmonious organization needs leaders who find balance and focus on the goals they have set. Leaders must find the middle ground, which is the path to success.

---

[27] Wilber, K., A Theory of Everything: An Integral Vision for Business, Politics, Science, and Spirituality, Shambala, 2000.

The Architecture of Vision

FINDING HARMONY WITHIN

Building a balanced approach to one's leadership style is crucial in creating a positive and effective work environment. There are several steps a leader or developing leader take to build harmony in their style:

- **Practice Mindfulness and self-awareness:** Leaders find their strengths and weaknesses by becoming more self-aware and working to improve themselves. Mindfulness practices like meditation and breathing exercises help leaders stay calm and centered, which leads to a more harmonious workplace.

- **Communicate Effectively:** Effective leaders communicate expectations clearly and listen actively to their team members. Encouraging open dialogue and feedback builds trust and fosters a more collaborative work environment.

- **Build Relationships:** Effective leaders take the time to get to know their team members personally and show genuine interest in their lives and work, which helps build trust and create a more cohesive team.

- **Foster a Culture of Respect and Inclusivity:** Strong leaders foster a culture of respect and inclusivity by promoting diversity and inclusion, teamwork, and constructive conflict resolution.

By implementing these steps, a leader or developing leader creates a positive and effective work environment that helps the team and the organization.

WHY HARMONY IS KEY

Leaders receive many benefits from building a harmonious approach to their leadership style, including:

- **Improved Employee Engagement and Productivity**: When employees feel valued, heard, and respected, they are likely to be engaged in their work and productive. A harmonious leadership style helps to create an environment where employees feel supported and motivated.

- **Better Teamwork and Collaboration:** A harmonious leadership style encourages teamwork and cooperation, which leads to better outcomes for the organization. Employees who feel part of a team will likely work together effectively and achieve shared goals.

- **Enhanced Trust and Loyalty:** Employees who feel their leader has their best interests at heart will likely be committed to the organization and work hard to achieve its goals.

- **Reduced Turnover:** A harmonious leadership style helps reduce turnover by creating a positive work environment where employees feel supported and valued. Employees who are happy at work are less likely to seek employment elsewhere.

- **Improved Reputation:** A leader known for their harmonious leadership style enhances the organization's reputation. A positive reputation helps to attract top talent, clients, and investors and helps to improve the overall success of the organization.

The benefits of modeling harmony within a firm extend to leaders, staff, and clients, resulting in:

- **Improved Communication:** Harmony translates into more empathetic, active listeners who are open to feedback, which leads to improved communication between the firm and its clients, resulting in better understanding and alignment on project goals and expectations.

The Architecture of Vision

- **Increased Trust:** Harmony fosters a culture of trust within their teams, which also extends to the client relationship, as clients will feel more confident in the firm's ability to deliver on promises and meet their needs.
- **Enhanced Problem-Solving:** Harmony leads to resolving conflicts and finding solutions that work for everyone involved, resulting in better client problem-solving and a more collaborative approach to project execution.
- **Positive Reputation:** Harmony has an impact on the brand image. Harmony supports a positive reputation that the firm is easy to work with, respectful, and values its clients' needs, increasing business opportunities and building long-term client relationships.

Harmony

SYNTHESIS

When an inspirational leader embodies harmonious behavior, it inspires others to follow suit. They become role models for their team members and encourage them to adopt similar traits, supporting a positive work culture that fosters innovation and creativity.

Harmonious leaders value collaboration and teamwork. They create environments where everyone's contributions are valued and everyone has an opportunity to speak, which fosters a sense of community and leads to more innovative ideas and solutions.

Leaders who manifest cooperative behavior tend to be more empathetic toward their team members. They take the time to understand their employees' needs, concerns, and challenges and work with them to find solutions, creating a sense of trust and respect, which inspires team members to be more innovative and take risks.

When leaders value harmonious behavior, they create an environment where team members feel safe to take risks, share their ideas, and experiment with original approaches, leading to breakthroughs and innovative solutions that help the organization.

An inspirational leader who manifests harmony positively affects the need for inspirational and innovative leadership by inspiring others, fostering collaboration, demonstrating empathy, and encouraging creativity.

The Architecture of Vision

VIEWPOINT – **STEVE OSBORN**, PE, SE
President, CE Solutions

Leadership is lonely. It requires a clear vision, foundational principles, core values, discipline, commitment, passion, perseverance, humility, and grace.

— **Steve Osborn**

The Cornerstone of Effective Leadership

The best leaders lead by example. They show the ability to bring people together toward a unified vision. Vision is a big part of what we do in our company. Since I started this business, I have had a vision for the company. As I brought new people on board, I communicated that vision to ensure we were on the same page. Then, we all participate as we continue to grow through that process.

We revisit the vision every few years. Leadership comes down to having a vision, developing a strategy, executing that strategy, and being surrounded by core values. Those values are the foundational principles that lead us to move forward. They define who we bring into the company and who we do business with.

From Employee to Entrepreneur: A Leadership Journey

I did not come out of school thinking I would ever start my own business. I worked for three different multi-disciplinary civil engineering firms in the first 20 years of my career. Through those experiences — working with and watching how those firms were led — I never felt I was a good fit in any of them. I started thinking about the company I would like to work with. I have always been a student of leadership and self-development. I am always looking for successful people to try to understand how they got where they are. I read a lot about mentoring and being mentored by successful people.

I had this idea about a company that would build a culture conducive to lifelong learning and opportunity, creating a place nobody ever wanted to leave — with strong leadership, guidance, and the willingness to listen to the people.

Creating Culture

It helps if you are careful about who you bring into the company. A big part of our strategy is our hiring process. The key is finding people who are like-minded people — who share similar ideals and similar values — to make it easy to grow. We are very protective of our culture. That has been critical to our success. It refers to our foundational principles of solid relationships, mutual respect, integrity, and ethical practice. Those values are built around the concept of care — care for us, care for our clients, and care for the communities where we work. The results are successful outcomes and lasting relationships. Those goals are reflected in the three arcs in our logo.

We create lifelong opportunities for our employees. We develop lifelong relationships with the people we do business with. Did I envision all this? No, but it evolved. I could not get comfortable where I was. Something was missing. So, I wanted to create it. I started this experiment 23 years ago. It is going well.

Inspiration is a big part of the equation for any leader. At an early age, I was inspired by a college professor who spoke about civil engineering. That stuck with me. He also said we are a serving profession. We need to be engaged in society to contribute and make a difference.

I will give kudos to Tim Barrick, too. He was instrumental in helping me think through this and giving me the confidence to start my own business. He has been supportive. I am trying to pay it forward, inspiring the next generation in our profession. I am active in professional circles through professional association work, SMPS, ACEC, and ASC. I volunteer on four different boards.

Innovation is a challenge. We are always looking for new and different ways to serve our clients. We are investing in new methods to be seen as a leader in our industry, not just a follower. We constantly challenge ourselves, looking for new and creative ways to bring value to our clients.

Integrity is one of our core foundational principles. You define integrity in a lot of different ways. One is to do what you say you are going to do. Follow through. Refrain from saying what you need to say to get the job. Keep promises and honor commitments. That goes a long way. One of our clients said, *'People tend to over-promise and under-deliver, but your firm is the opposite of that. You under-promise and over-deliver.'* That is what we constantly try to do.

It is easy for leaders to over-commit themselves. I am guilty of that. There is so much we want to try to do. There is so much that needs to be done. But there is only so much time in the day. It is a matter of finding balance. I am still working on it. Stay true to what is essential. Focus on what is important. That includes family, friends, and community, not just business. It is easy to get consumed by the company. From an entrepreneurial standpoint, there is an adrenaline rush when things finally come together. But keep sight of what is essential. Be available to focus on your well-being.

Balancing Commitment and Well-Being

When we created our 15-year strategic vision, it included leadership transition. We are a small firm, under twenty people, so everyone was involved in the dialogue, and no one was surprised, wondering, 'Hey, wait, why not me?' We still include all the senior people in engineering, project management, and marketing in all critical decisions. That is one of the benefits of being small. I have systematically delegated more leadership and responsibility to my designate, and we have added three new associates. Hence, a leadership continuum and a natural succession plan are in place. I know the firm will be in competent hands.

I have been lucky to have had several people as mentors. I have mentioned Tim Barrick and Craig Galati, who I know have also contributed to this book. Tim was one of the first people I met in SMPS when I joined in 1993. We immediately hit it off. To say he has influenced our business is an understatement. He has been an advocate and supporter. He loves helping other people and helping firms grow. I met Craig Galati at another SMPS national conference. We hit it off right away, talking and sharing ideas. I learned a lot from his experiences. He helped with our first visioning session in 2005.

Gaining by Giving Back

I saw a principal from one of my first employers a few years ago. He was the impetus for many of our core principles. I informed him about our firm's recent developments and how he had influenced me. He was surprised because he did not consider himself a mentor. Yet, he was. I could go on.

I continued to learn from the people I met through SMPS and other organizations. I have learned from my younger people, too. A mentor does not have to be older than you. I am where I am today with those people's shared wisdom. They are always a source of how we apply innovative ideas and innovation to our business.

The Vital Role of Marketing

I founded our business on marketing principles. Business and marketing are intertwined. Unfortunately, many leaders in professional service firms need to respect marketing and business development and the people who do it. Because while many of the leaders of professional service firms are technical people, they still need formal training in business and marketing. So, they do not find value in those skills. Instead, it is the technical professionals who rule.

I am generalizing, but there are a lot of firms doing that. Those who do promote marketing and business development staff in leadership positions see a lot of value. Marketing professionals are excellent at business strategy that technical professionals are not. Unfortunately, most university architecture, engineering, and construction programs hardly touch on business and marketing as part of the specialized curriculum. Suppose we want to elevate that level of our firms when we are out looking to hire. In that case, we need to look for marketing professionals with some understanding and knowledge of professional services.

PROGRESSION – **HARMONY**: Alignment & Resonance

Leaders artistically balance people, resources, opportunities, and challenges.

AWARENESS: *Think about these statements on building an understanding of the importance of* **Harmony**.

1. List ten times when you went out of your way to help a friend or colleague.
2. List ten times when someone else went out of their way to help you.
3. Do you prefer to work on a team or alone? Why?
4. What excites you about a new project or task?
5. Think of the people you work with. What do you admire about them, and what do you find annoying?
6. What is the hardest thing about your job?

ACCEPTANCE: *Now, reflect on how you reacted when reading these statements. Reflect on what "acceptance" of your truth about what* **Harmony** *means to you.*

1. How easy is it for you to ask for help? How would you change this?
2. When you see someone struggling, what is your response? Do you help or wait for them to ask? Explain the current situation and note how you handled this.
3. Consider a recent situation when you and your team faced a challenge. How willing were you to make sacrifices for the success of the team? What did you agree to do, and what would you not do? What was the outcome, and how do you feel about it?

The Architecture of Vision

ACTION: *Follow these steps to incrementally put that awareness and acceptance into action to strengthen your ability to develop leadership with* **Harmony**.

1. Learn the names of all colleagues, including those in distinct roles or locations.
2. Say please and thank you regularly in person and by email.
3. Write thank you notes often. Set a goal to send out a specific number each week.
4. Avoid gossip. Walk away from situations when others are gossiping.
5. Leave your door open and be willing to accept interruptions whenever possible.
6. Volunteer for a charity or organization.
7. Socialize with colleagues outside of work.
8. Read Peter Senge's **The Fifth Discipline: The Art & Practice of the Learning Organization**. Senge's systems thinking approach emphasizes the need for harmony within organizations.

Harmony

SYNOPSIS

Personal harmony is emphasized in leadership as a pivotal component for success, especially within professional service firms. This concept of harmony focuses on being mindful, centered, and aware, allowing leaders to navigate the myriad harmonies within a workplace, such as generational, gender, geographic, and technological. The objective is cultivating an environment where conversations thrive, teamwork is prioritized, and an enriching culture emerges. Yet, the journey is fraught with challenges like conflicting deadlines, unforeseen obstacles, and new opportunities. Leaders, therefore, must detach from the turmoil, explore innovative solutions, and guide their organizations with resilience and equanimity. The Buddhist principle of finding the middle way becomes instrumental in helping leaders maintain balance, whether they're novices or visionaries.

Leadership's essence lies not only in addressing immediate challenges but also in setting milestones and markers. Effective leadership means having clear goals and a vision setting a harmonious tone for achieving strategic objectives. Harmony's resonance varies based on a leader's developmental stage. For instance, while novice leaders focus on personal harmony, visionary leaders emphasize harmony in service-client relationships. Crucially, harmony's significance transcends the immediate workspace. It is foundational for the long-term viability of professional firms; demanding leaders strike a balance and concentrate on their set objectives.

To truly embody harmonious leadership, one must foster personal harmony within. Leaders must adopt a multifaceted approach: practicing mindfulness to remain centered, communicating effectively, forging genuine relationships, and establishing a culture of respect and inclusivity. The resultant benefits are manifold. A harmonious leadership style augments employee engagement, teamwork, and trust, reduces attrition rates, and elevates the organization's reputation.

The Architecture of Vision

Beyond the internal team, the ripple effects of harmony extend to client relationships, enhancing communication, instilling trust, fostering collaborative problem-solving, and positively impacting the brand's reputation. In essence, for those aiming to be truly effective leaders, understanding and implementing the principles of harmony is non-negotiable.

Harmony

REFLECTIONS & INSIGHTS

Chapter 18 | CHARACTER: The Responsible Person

Leadership is hard to define and good leadership even harder. But if you can get people to follow you to the ends of the earth, you are a great leader.
Indra Nooyi

FOCUS: Character is the magnet that keeps the leader's compass pointing north.

LEADERSHIP IN PROFESSIONAL SERVICE FIRMS requires a manifestation of character rooted in integrity. This character is essential for personal representation and how clients and colleagues perceive the leader. However, maintaining and exemplifying such character consistently presents challenges.

As professionals climb the ladder, they must cultivate their character, embodying trustworthiness and ensuring alignment with the firm's values. Failure to do so, especially in overlooking or rationalizing low-character behaviors, can severely undermine an organization's culture and brand value.

Therefore, young professionals aspiring to leadership roles must invest time in studying, reflecting on, and upholding strong character standards. Mentorship is invaluable in this development, as experienced leaders guide newcomers in understanding and embodying the firm's leadership values.

The development of character isn't a one-time task but an ongoing commitment, demanding regular introspection and growth. An

The Architecture of Vision

individual's character influences decision-making, fosters trust and respect, and enhances overall leadership effectiveness. For firms, leaders with solid character not only motivate their internal teams but also amplify the organization's reputation, trustworthiness, and service quality in the eyes of clients. Such leadership ultimately results in long-term client relationships, a strengthened brand reputation, and a competitive advantage in the marketplace. Thus, emphasizing and nurturing character remains paramount for personal growth and organizational success.

THE MANIFESTATION OF INTEGRITY

Character reflects a person's trustworthiness and ability to inspire and promote innovation. Character is the embodiment of walking the talk, and it is crucial to recognize how colleagues and clients perceive one. Young professionals looking to become leaders develop their character by studying it, thinking about it, and establishing standards of conduct and behavior. Mentoring is crucial to character development; spending time thinking about it, learning it, and recognizing it is essential.

Strong leaders promptly identify and address low-character behavior, as overlooking bad behavior or rationalizing it is detrimental to the organization. Like values, strong organizations have rules about the behaviors they tolerate and those they do not. Accountability and responsibility related to character play an essential role in ensuring that the organization's culture aligns with its leadership values.

SETTING A BAR

While it is not easy to have great character, it is critical to live within the standards of the character set both personally and organizationally. The impact of negative behavior by employees is wide-ranging. Clients have a long memory. How organizations address negative character behavior reflects the brand value of the firm. Character is a leadership issue not rectified by simply saying, "Oops."

Character is the walking the talk of leadership. A leader's character is self-realized and how they are perceived by the people who work with and for them and their client base.

Leadership is crucial to the organization's success in a professional service firm. A leader's character plays a significant role in creating a positive organizational culture that attracts and retains top talent and clients. Leaders with solid character inspire their teams to work toward a common goal and go the extra mile to achieve it. They lead by example and set the standard for behavior and conduct, establishing non-negotiables and ensuring alignment with the values and principles of the firm.

MAKING SPACE FOR GROWTH

Developing character takes time and effort, and it is a lifelong process. Young professionals seeking to become leaders need mentorship to better understand character as a leadership trait. Mentors guide them in studying, thinking, recognizing the importance of character and establishing standards of conduct and behaviors they are unwilling to negotiate.

Organizations establish rules that define acceptable and unacceptable behaviors to reflect the organization's values. Holding individuals accountable and responsible for their actions reinforces those standards. Strong organizations do not tolerate low-character behavior. Leaders promptly identify and address bad behavior to prevent it from potentially damaging the organization's reputation and culture.

Leaders with solid character set the standard for behavior and conduct, inspire their teams, and create a positive organizational culture that attracts and retains top talent and clients. Developing character is a lifelong process, and young professionals looking to become leaders should seek mentorship to understand the importance of character as a leadership trait.

BUILDING CHARACTER

As a developing leader, building character is essential to personal practice. Here are some steps you can take to develop character:

- **Define Values:** Take time to reflect on the most important values. Identify motivations and beliefs, which help establish a clear sense of direction and purpose — essential for building character.

- **Act with Integrity:** One of the most critical aspects of building character is acting with integrity, which means being honest, transparent, and consistent in all actions, even when difficult. It also means staying true to values, even when faced with adversity.

- **Practice Self-Awareness:** Take the time to reflect on actions and decisions and be honest about strengths and weaknesses, identifying areas for improvement and growth.

- **Be Accountable:** Take responsibility for actions and decisions and be responsible for any mistakes, which helps personal growth and develops resilience.

- **Develop Empathy:** Empathy helps build understanding and connection with others. Practice listening actively and try to see things from other people's perspectives, which develops stronger relationships and builds trust with others.

- **Seek Feedback:** Ask others for input on actions and behavior and be open to constructive criticism. Identify blind spots and areas for improvement and the development of self-awareness.

- **Continuously Learn and Grow:** Commit to consistent learning and growth as a leader. Attend workshops and training sessions, read books and articles, and seek out mentors and role models who help develop skills and build character.

THE BENEFITS OF CHARACTER

Developing strong character traits as a leader brings several benefits, including:

- **Improved Decision-Making:** Leaders with solid character traits are better equipped to make ethical and responsible decisions, positively impacting the firm's reputation and client relationships.

- **Increased Trust and Respect:** By demonstrating integrity, honesty, and accountability, leaders earn the trust and respect of their team members, clients, and other stakeholders, building strong relationships and a positive reputation for the firm.

- **Enhanced Leadership Skills:** Developing character traits like empathy, humility, and emotional intelligence helps leaders become more effective communicators and collaborators, which improves team morale, productivity, and engagement.

- **Reduced Risk of Ethical Breaches:** When leaders embody strong character traits, they are less likely to engage in unethical or illegal behavior, which mitigates the risk of legal and reputational harm to the firm.

- **Personal Growth and Fulfillment:** Engaging in practices that build character helps leaders develop a stronger sense of purpose and pride in their work, which translates into greater motivation and commitment to the firm's success.

CHARACTER AND VALUE

The benefits that clients experience when the leaders understand the value of character add brand strength to the firm and strengthen the entire organization:

- **Increased Trust:** Clients trust firms whose leaders have a strong character. When leaders prioritize ethical behavior, transparency, and honesty, they build client trust.

- **Improved Client Service:** Focusing on character leads to better client service. When leaders prioritize empathy, active listening, and communication, it creates an environment where clients feel heard, understood, and valued.

- **Long-Term Relationships:** Clients are likely to continue working with a firm where the leaders prioritize character. Building strong client relationships is essential for long-term success, and leaders prioritizing character are likely to create those lasting connections.

- **Enhanced Reputation:** A firm with leaders who prioritize character builds a formidable reputation in the industry, leading to more referrals and new business opportunities.

- **Competitive Advantage:** In a crowded market, firms with leaders who prioritize character stand out. Clients are increasingly looking for firms prioritizing ethics and values, and focusing on character gives those firms a stronger competitive advantage.

Character is the last — but not least — in our study on effective leadership traits. Taken together, the eighteen traits that define inspirational, innovative, and high integrity leadership provides a framework for continuous development along your leadership journey.

Character

SYNTHESIS

Leaders who embody character have a positive impact on organizational goals in several ways:

- **Inspiring and Motivating Employees**: Consistently demonstrating high integrity and ethical behavior inspires and motivates employees to emulate those qualities, increasing employee engagement, job satisfaction, and productivity.

- **Fostering Innovation:** Prioritizing honesty, transparency, and accountability creates a culture that supports innovation. Employees are likely to take risks and suggest innovative ideas when they trust their leaders will support and reward them.

- **Building Trust with Stakeholders:** Acting honestly builds trust with clients, investors, and employees. This trust leads to increased loyalty and positive word-of-mouth recommendations.

- **Managing Risk:** Leaders who prioritize ethical behavior and character help organizations avoid legal and reputational risks. Leaders create a compliance and risk management culture by modeling ethical behavior and setting clear employee expectations.

A leader with integrity and strong character helps create an organizational culture that supports innovation, risk management, and stakeholder trust, all of which contribute to achieving organizational goals.

The Architecture of Vision

VIEWPOINT – **TIM BARRICK**, FSMPS
Principal/Chief Marketing Officer, RATIO

A true leader inspires followers to accept their goals as their own.

— Tim Barrick

The Essence of Authentic Leadership

Leadership is having the people who follow you accept your vision and ideas as their own. To me, that's authentic leadership.

I have always been a player/coach, inspiring our people who, because they have all been practitioners, are only sometimes motivated to go out and do business development and bring business into the future. Inspiration has always been a part of what I had to do to teach people to become seller-doers.

Pioneering with Purpose

From an innovation standpoint, we believe in thought leadership. We have innovative tools to research or communicate a vision with our clients.

Integrity is everything to me. For us to be successful has always meant that our clients had to trust me with information and that I would use it to benefit myself and them. Our clients know that the first time we betray that trust, we will never get information from them again. And so, integrity has always been important to me. My father said that integrity is the only thing a man has that is his own. I have carried that belief my entire life.

The Cornerstone of Authentic Relationships

Leaders need to learn empathy. Some people have it naturally. Some people gain it over time. Empathy is my most valuable tool in leadership. I always try to understand when I am in a situation where I have people reporting to me or looking to me for leadership, to practice with empathy.

We have deliberately built a flat organization. We are now close to two hundred people. The flatness of our organization gives our people paths to step up and lead. We have about six standing committees, such as Culture and Education. Anyone can step up and lead a committee. That provides leadership opportunities. Those leadership skills translate into growing as a professional and growing the firm.

We also have leadership training. We have a full-time educator who manages and works with the Education Committee. She has developed leadership training programs and a development coach system. I have five people assigned to me that I coach annually.

Learning from the Masters

My own experience with mentoring came when I joined Meyer Gibson in 1980. Bill Pilgrim was one of the structural engineers who did much work for our firm. I got to know Bill, and he became a mentor to me from a business standpoint. As a young marketing person, Bill showed me around. He knew everybody in the community. Bill was a gentleman. He was a solid professional. Bill inspired me to be like him.

Overcoming Industry Bias

Some firms still value marketing less than they value their technical staff. Professional arrogance still exists in the industry due to training and licensure. Many licensed professionals feel superior to everybody else. I have been fortunate to have never worked for anyone who felt that way. Marketing's role is not to feed the firm but to assist those who want to eat.

The Architecture of Vision

I have witnessed marketing grow from a single person to a team of individuals to an in-house agency. The more we study and understand the practice's business, the more valuable we become. The quickest way into the boardroom is by coming to the table with solutions, not problems.

Character

PROGRESSION – **CHARACTER**: The Responsible Person

Character is the magnet that keeps the leader's compass pointing north.

AWARENESS: *Think about these statements on understanding the importance of* **Character.**

1. How accountable are you? Explain in detail. Provide examples.
2. How do you deal with others you do not think are being accountable? Provide examples.
3. Describe someone you know who an example of a person with high character is. Provide details and examples.
4. How do you respond when someone else is not as accountable or responsible as you wish? What is your response, either in words or actions?
5. Develop a personal character statement framed by words and actions demonstrating exceptional character, accountability, and responsibility.

ACCEPTANCE: *Now, reflect on how you reacted when reading these statements. Reflect on what "acceptance" of your truth about what* **Character** *means to you.*

1. How satisfied are you with your level of accountability and responsibility at work?
2. If you had to admit that you are not 100% accountable and responsible, what would be your current percentage? Are you satisfied with that number?
3. Are you chronically late, disorganized, or allow yourself to get away with behaviors that annoy you about other people? Notice how you feel and record your thoughts in your journal.

The Architecture of Vision

ACTION: *Follow these steps to incrementally put that awareness and acceptance into action to strengthen your ability to develop leadership with* **Character.**

1. Revisit the values you described in Values, Awareness #4. Create a visual reminder of those values and post them so you see them daily (in the bathroom, office, car, etc.)

2. Set some standards of excellence related to your accountability and responsibility. For example, set a time to respond to texts, phone calls, or emails. In your journal, track when you meet those expectations and when you do not.

3. Practice self-discipline (food, exercise, shopping, TV, social media, etc.) for one day, then one week.

4. Build your accountability by doing what you say you will do. Track promises made and kept for a month.

5. Tell the truth, with love, when necessary.

6. Read Max DePree's **Leadership is an Art.** DePree's reflections on leadership dive deep into the essence of character and its role in leading effectively.

Character

SYNOPSIS

Leadership in professional service firms hinges upon the vital trait of character. Character embodies trustworthiness, integrity, and a deep alignment with the firm's values. It represents the essence of "walking the talk." This is evident in a leader's self-perception and how clients, colleagues, and subordinates perceive them.

Character becomes the yardstick by which leaders are judged, making it a determining factor in their ability to inspire, innovate, and solidify their personal brand within the organization. While inherent to some degree, character requires ongoing cultivation, introspection, and mentorship, especially for budding leaders.

Leaders with robust character possess the ability to influence both the internal and external dynamics of a firm significantly. Internally, such leaders motivate their teams, fostering a culture prioritizing ethical conduct and innovation. The tangible outcomes include higher team morale, increased productivity, and a greater sense of purpose.

Externally, character-driven leadership amplifies the firm's reputation, translating into enduring client relationships, amplified trust, and a competitive edge. Overlooking or merely rationalizing instances of low-character behavior can tarnish the firm's image, emphasizing the need for consistent accountability.

For individuals aspiring to lead, the journey to imbuing character is multifaceted. It begins with defining personal values that offer a clear direction. Acting with unwavering integrity is paramount even in the face of challenges. Self-awareness demands regular reflection, acknowledging strengths and weaknesses alike.

Taking accountability for one's actions and decisions is non-negotiable. Empathy strengthens bonds and trust within teams, while actively seeking feedback aids in self-improvement. Continuous learning, coupled with the guidance of mentors, facilitates character development. The rewards of this endeavor are manifold, encompassing improved decision-making, increased trust, and personal fulfillment. Ultimately, a leader's character becomes an invaluable asset, driving both personal and organizational growth.

Character

REFLECTIONS & INSIGHTS

The Architecture of Vision

AFTERWORD | Your Leadership Journey

Leadership is not about being in charge.
Leadership is about taking care of those
in your charge.
Ken Wilber

FOCUS: Leadership development is vital for the long-term success of the individual and the firm. Leadership development enhances performance, drives innovation, builds a robust organizational culture, and attracts and retains top talent.

AS YOU HAVE READ, there are many important aspects to developing leaders grounded in inspiration, innovation, and integrity. Leaders who have confidence in themselves make mistakes and change their minds when necessary. Leaders have a clear vision for the practice that is authentic and inspirational to others — employees, stakeholders, and clients.

Leadership is not management. Leadership is about inspiring others to achieve a greater goal. Leadership is about building structure in an organization and supporting all the roles — design, management, marketing, finance, human resources, etc. — that contribute to the professional service process, inspiring staff, clients, and the community with innovative service and solutions delivered with the highest integrity.

Influential leaders have a foundational understanding of the three pillars of leadership — Inspiration, Innovation, and Integrity — and the inter-related eighteen traits rather than relying on personality and technical abilities. We found that the most influential leaders inspire others by establishing something outside themselves for people to follow. They create innovative solutions to meet client needs and serve — internally and externally — with the highest levels of integrity.

FOUR QUADRANTS OF DEVELOPMENT

We adapted and applied our four-quadrant model for leadership development — an integral framework for understanding human development and experience — from Wilber's book, *A Theory of Everything*.[28] See Figure 5.

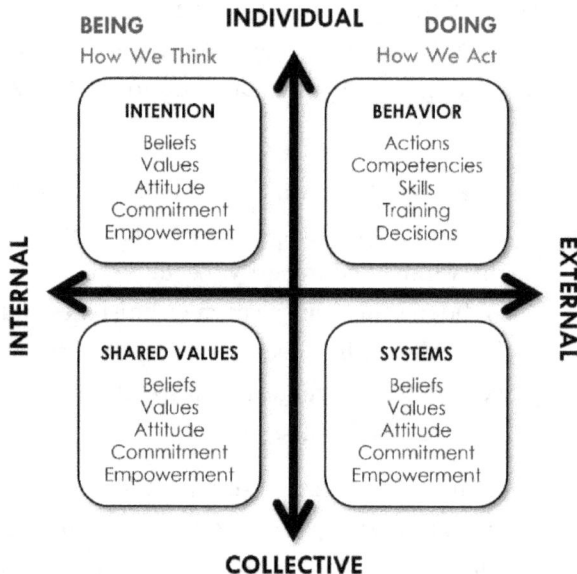

Figure 5 - Four Quadrant Model of Development

Wilber is an American philosopher, author, and integral theorist who has significantly contributed to philosophy, psychology, and spirituality. He is recognized as one of the most influential American philosophers of our time, and his work continues to inspire and inform

---

[28] Wilber, K., *A Theory of Everything: An Integral Vision for Business, Politics, Science, and Spirituality*, Shambala, 2000.,

Afterword

people from all walks of life. Wilber's work is based on the idea that human knowledge and consciousness continually evolve.

FOUR QUADRANTS OF LEADERSHIP

This model represents the various aspects of leadership interactions and their interconnections. The vertical axes represent the range of individual and collective perspectives, and the horizontal axes represent the range of internal and external aspects of experience.

Each quadrant frames development in terms of Being (how we think) and Doing (how we act):

- **Internal/Individual** (Upper-Left Quadrant)**:** This quadrant represents the inner, subjective experiences of the individual, characterized by a focus on "I" or "me," which includes our thoughts, emotions, and personal values. "Being" in this quadrant refers to our self-awareness and self-reflection. "Doing" in this quadrant relates to our personal choices, intentions, and behaviors. In leadership development, this quadrant defines the leader's self-awareness, emotional intelligence, and personal values.

- **Internal/Collective** (Lower Left Quadrant)**:** This quadrant represents the community or society's shared cultural values and beliefs, characterized by a focus on "we" or "our," including religion, ethics, and social norms. "Being" in this quadrant refers to our identification with cultural or social groups. "Doing" in this quadrant reflects participating in social rituals, traditions, and practices. In leadership development, this quadrant defines the leader's abilities to communicate, delegate, motivate, and manage tasks.

- **External/Individual** (Upper-Right Quadrant)**:** This quadrant represents the observable behaviors and actions of an individual, particularly in interactions with others ("you"). It includes things like body language, facial expressions, and physical movements. "Being" in this quadrant refers to our physical presence and how we appear in the world. "Doing" in this quadrant relates to our actions, habits, and routines. In leadership development, this quadrant reflects the leader's ability to build and maintain relationships, foster collaboration, and create a positive organizational culture.

- **External/Collective** (Lower-Right Quadrant): This quadrant represents the external systems and structures of society, such as institutions, organizations, and governments, related to a more global ("us") perspective. "Being" in this quadrant refers to our place in the larger social and economic systems. "Doing" in this quadrant relates to our roles and responsibilities within those systems. In leadership development, this quadrant reflects the leader's ability to navigate complex systems, anticipate and respond to change, and create positive social impact.

Referencing the framework helps developing leaders improve their ability to lead teams by:

- **Developing Self-Awareness:** The Internal/Individual quadrant emphasizes the importance of self-awareness and self-reflection. Developing leaders use this quadrant to understand their values and beliefs and how they impact their leadership style. A better understanding of oneself helps a leader be more authentic, build stronger relationships with team members, and communicate more effectively.

- **Understanding Team Dynamics:** The Internal/Collective quadrant emphasizes the importance of shared values and cultural norms. A developing leader uses this quadrant to understand their team's cultural norms and shared values and how these impact team dynamics. Understanding the

Afterword

internal/collective builds a more robust team culture, fosters a sense of belonging among team members, and develops shared goals and objectives.

- **Observing and Adapting Behaviors:** The External/Individual quadrant emphasizes observable behaviors and actions. A developing leader uses this quadrant to observe their behavior and the behavior of team members and identify improvement opportunities. Understanding the external/individual allows leaders to be more aware of their behaviors and adapt their communication style, leadership approach, and decision-making processes to meet their teams' needs better.

- **Addressing Systemic Issues:** The External/Collective quadrant emphasizes the importance of social and economic systems. A developing leader uses this quadrant to understand the significant systemic issues impacting their team and organization and work to address them. By being aware of the larger external/collective context in which they operate, leaders identify opportunities for innovation and growth and develop strategies to overcome systemic barriers to success.

This framework helps developing leaders in professional service firms improve team leadership skills by enhancing self-awareness, aligning with organizational values, analyzing team behavior, and understanding the broader context, which results in improved team performance, engagement, and business outcomes.

ASSESSMENT & DEVELOPMENT TOOLKIT

Our goal for this book was to provide valuable insights into the traits and qualities necessary to develop inspirational, innovative, high-integrity leaders in professional service firms.

The Architecture of Vision

To take these learnings to the next step, we have developed a simple assessment program to allow leaders and developing leaders to access their relative place on the development continuum across the three pillars and the related traits reviewed herein.

INTEGRAL LEADERSHIP ASSESSMENT (ILA)

The ILA provides a holistic evaluation of leadership development, covering seven stages and considering various dimensions, including personal, relational, and organizational aspects. You can also apply it to technical and support functions throughout the practice to provide the context for a professional development plan. This assessment offers a 360-degree feedback approach, measuring specific leadership behaviors and providing feedback from various sources.

This assessment model provides clear markers for your potential personal and professional growth.

Integral Leadership Assessment (ILA)

You cannot have exterior development without interior development to hold it in place.

Ken Wilber

The Integral Leadership Assessment (ILA) is a simple tool designed to help leaders and aspiring leaders in professional service firms evaluate their leadership skill levels, identify areas of strength and development, and guide their growth across seven stages of leadership development.

Based on the 4-Quadrant framework, the ILA provides a well-rounded view of an individual's leadership capabilities, offering personal and professional growth insights.

Instructions: Reflect on your place in your organization, your experiences, and behaviors, and answer the following twenty-one questions using the scoring scale below:

Scoring: For each question, give yourself a score of 1-7, with:

- "1" – Strongly Disagree
- "2" – Disagree
- "3" – Somewhat Disagree
- "4" – Neither Agree Nor Disagree (Neutral)
- "5" – Somewhat Agree
- "6" – Agree
- "7" – Strongly Agree

Rate yourself using the following statements. Total the results and see your Integral Leadership level in the **Interpreting the Result** section.

The Architecture of Vision

INTEGRAL LEADERSHIP ASSESSMENT	SCORE (1-7)
1. I rely on my title or position to get things done.	
2. People follow me because they must, not because they want to.	
3. I need help motivating and inspiring my team.	
4. I have positive relationships with my team members.	
5. I listen to my team member's concerns and ideas.	
6. I create a safe and supportive environment for my team.	
7. I set clear goals and expectations for my team.	
8. I hold myself and my team accountable for achieving results.	
9. I celebrate successes and learn from failures.	
10. I invest time and resources in developing my team members.	
11. I provide feedback and coaching to help my team grow.	
12. I empower my team to take on new challenges and responsibilities.	

Integral Leadership Assessment

13.	I have a clear vision and purpose for my team.
14.	I inspire and motivate others to achieve their full potential.
15.	I have a positive impact on my organization and community.
16.	I have a growth mindset and continuously seek to improve myself.
17.	I take risks and embrace challenges to learn and grow.
18.	I prioritize self-care and well-being to sustain my efforts.
19.	I have a sense of purpose and meaning beyond myself and my organization.
20.	I contribute to the greater good because that aligns with my values.
21.	I inspire others to join me in positively impacting the world.
	TOTAL

The Architecture of Vision

INTERPRETING THE RESULTS

Based on your total score, your current Leadership level can be defined as follows:

Score = 21 – 41: Level 1 - Reflective

- You rely on your title or position to get things done, and people follow you because they must, not because they want to.

Score = 42 – 62: Level 2 – Interpersonal

- You have positive relationships with your team members but may need to help motivate and inspire them.

Score = 63 – 83: Level 3 – Managerial

- You set clear goals and expectations for your team and hold yourself and your team accountable for achieving results.

Score = 84 – 104: Level 4 – Technical

- You invest time and resources in developing your team members, but you may need to work on empowering them to take on new challenges and responsibilities.

Score = 105 – 125: Level 5 – Strategic

- You have a clear vision and purpose for your team, and you inspire and motivate others to achieve their full potential. You have a positive impact on your organization and community.

Score = 126 – 146: Level 6 – Collaborative

- You have a growth mindset and continuously seek to improve yourself and your team, but you may need to prioritize self-care and well-being to sustain your leadership.

Integral Leadership Assessment

Score = 147 – 168: Level 7 – Visionary

- You have a sense of purpose and meaning beyond yourself and your organization, but you may need to work on inspiring others to join you in positively impacting the world.

Note: This assessment tool is not a scientifically validated instrument, but it provides a general sense of where an individual may fall on the seven levels of the Integral Leadership assessment scale.

THE BENEFITS OF AN INTEGRAL ASSESSMENT

Using the 4-Quadrant framework and the 7 Levels of Integral Leadership development assessment — framed by the Holistic Leadership Assessment — helps leaders and developing leaders improve their behaviors and their ability to be inspirational, innovative, and work with high integrity. The benefits of applying this framework include the following:

1. **Understanding the Stages of Development:** The model identifies seven stages of development, each characterized by different worldviews and value systems. A developing leader uses this model to understand better their stage of development and that of their team members. By doing so, they can tailor their leadership approach to meet the needs of each individual and help them move to higher stages of development.

2. **Embracing Diversity:** Wilber's model recognizes the importance of diversity in driving innovation and progress. A developing leader uses this model to create a culture of inclusion and embrace diversity in all its forms, including thought, culture, background, and experience. By doing so, they foster an environment that encourages creativity and innovation.

The Architecture of Vision

3. **Practicing Self-Reflection:** This model emphasizes the importance of self-reflection in personal growth and development. A developing leader uses this model to cultivate a practice of self-reflection, taking time to reflect on their values, beliefs, and biases. Doing so makes them more self-aware and better equipped to lead with integrity.

4. **Fostering a Learning Culture:** This model recognizes the importance of ongoing learning and development in personal growth and organizational success. A developing leader uses this model to promote a culture of continuous learning within their team by providing opportunities for training and development, encouraging experimentation and innovation, and creating a safe space for learning from failures.

5. **Emphasizing Ethical Leadership:** The model emphasizes the importance of ethical leadership in creating a sustainable and thriving organization. A developing leader can use this assessment to underscore the importance of ethical behavior within their team, setting clear ethical standards, modeling ethical behavior, and holding team members accountable for their actions.

By applying this framework and assessment model, leaders of professional service firms improve their behaviors and ability to be inspirational, innovative, and work with high integrity, resulting in higher engagement levels, enhanced team performance, and better business outcomes.

REFLECTING ON THE SCORING

Your scores for each question will help you identify areas where you may need to focus your attention and development efforts. For example, suppose you score low in the Collective Exterior (LR) quadrant for Level 3: Managerial. In that case, you must improve the

Integral Leadership Assessment

systems and processes supporting your team's productivity and efficiency.

It is important to note that leadership development is a continuous process, and there is always room for growth and improvement. By regularly assessing your leadership skills and identifying areas for development, you become a more effective and impactful leader.

Besides self-reflection, seeking feedback from team members, colleagues, or mentors can provide valuable insights into how others perceive your leadership and identify blind spots or areas for improvement you may have missed. This framework provides a holistic view of leadership development — a leader's observable behaviors and skills — and their inner experience, relationships, and impact on the organization.

By focusing on all these dimensions, leaders become more well-rounded, effective, and better equipped to lead teams or organizations toward success. Using the framework, leaders gain a more comprehensive and integrated view of their leadership development and identify areas for growth and improvement in each quadrant.

Creating Your Development Framework

Developing inspirational, innovative, and high-integrity leaders requires a comprehensive development program incorporating multiple dimensions of leadership growth. Here are some key elements you may consider in creating your own holistic development program:

1. **Competencies:** The first step in developing leaders is identifying the critical competencies required for success. These competencies include strategic thinking, communication skills, emotional intelligence, adaptability, and ethical decision-making. A competency-based approach helps leaders identify their strengths and areas for development and create a personalized development plan.

2. **Assessment:** Next, identify the current leadership competencies using the Holistic and Integral Leadership Assessment tools. Include 360-degree feedback and performance evaluations. This assessment provides valuable insights into their strengths and areas for development and helps them create a targeted development plan.

3. **Development Plan:** Based on the results of the two leadership assessments, create a personalized leadership development plan that includes specific goals, action steps, and timelines. Align the program with the organization's strategic goals and focus on developing the most critical competencies for success.

4. **Training:** To develop the competencies identified in the leadership development plan, create a range of training and development activities, such as workshops, coaching, mentoring, and on-the-job learning. Design these activities to build strategic thinking, communication, emotional intelligence, and ethical decision-making skills and knowledge.

5. **Support:** Developing leaders requires ongoing organizational support, including access to coaching and mentoring, creating opportunities for leaders to collaborate and share best practices, and providing resources and tools to support leadership development.

6. **Evaluation:** To measure the program's effectiveness, leaders undergo a follow-up assessment to evaluate progress and identify areas for further development that help leaders and the organization assess the program's impact and adjust as needed. Evaluation should be an ongoing process that informs continuous improvement and refinement of leadership development initiatives.

7. **Culture:** Developing leaders requires a culture that supports and values leadership development. Organizations that create a strong culture encourage continuous learning, feedback, and growth across the entire practice, providing opportunities for leaders to participate in training and development programs, recognizing and rewarding leadership excellence, and creating a supportive and collaborative work environment.

8. **Diversity and Inclusion:** Developing leaders prioritize diversity and inclusion by supporting a company culture that values and leverages all employees' unique perspectives and experiences. Leaders trained to recognize and address unconscious biases are more effective and allow the organization to actively seek out and promote diverse talent.

9. **Technology:** Technology plays a critical role in leadership development. Effective programs leverage technology to provide on-demand training and development resources, facilitate virtual coaching and mentoring, and track progress and performance.

Creating a Leadership Development Framework

10. **Continuous Improvement:** Developing leaders is an ongoing process that requires continuous improvement. Organizations should regularly evaluate their leadership development programs and adjust as needed to ensure they are effective and aligned with their strategic goals.

Organizations develop inspirational, innovative, and high-integrity leaders equipped to succeed in professional services by using a comprehensive framework that incorporates these elements. Organizations prioritizing leadership development create a culture that values and supports leadership excellence and drives success in all professional services.

The Architecture of Vision

ENDNOTES | Additional References

"Write a new ending for yourself, for the people you're meant to serve and support, and for your culture."
Brene Brown

BEYOND OUR LOOK AT THE THREE PILLARS
Framework for leadership development, many other excellent frameworks exist. Here are a few of the most popular:

- **Situational Leadership:** This framework, developed by Paul Hersey and Ken Blanchard, suggests that effective leadership depends on adapting one's leadership style to the situation. The framework identifies four different leadership styles (directing, coaching, supporting, and delegating) and suggests that leaders should adjust their style based on the competence and commitment of their followers.

- **Transformational Leadership:** This framework, developed by James MacGregor Burns and later expanded upon by Bernard Bass, suggests that influential leaders inspire and motivate their followers to achieve their full potential. Transformational leaders articulate a compelling vision, build strong relationships with their followers, and empower them to take ownership of their work.

- **Authentic Leadership:** This framework, developed by Bill George, suggests that effective leadership depends on being true to oneself and one's values. Authentic leaders are self-aware, transparent, and willing to take risks.

The Architecture of Vision

- **Servant Leadership**: This framework, developed by Robert Greenleaf, suggests that influential leaders prioritize their followers' needs over their own. Servant leaders have humility, empathy, and commitment to serving others.

The best leadership development framework for each person or firm depends on the organization's or individual's specific needs and goals seeking to develop their leadership skills.

DEVELOPMENT RESOURCES

There are also many leadership development resources specific to professional service firms in the architecture, engineering, and construction (A/E/C) industry, including:

- **The ACEC Leadership Institute:** The American Council of Engineering Companies (ACEC) offers a leadership development program specifically tailored to the needs of A/E/C professionals. The program includes workshops, webinars, and coaching sessions on strategic planning, team building, and communication.

- **The AIA Leadership Institute:** The American Institute of Architects (AIA) offers a leadership development program for architects and other A/E/C professionals. The program includes workshops, seminars, online business strategy, project management, and leadership skills courses.

- **The Construction Leadership Council:** The Construction Leadership Council (CLC) is a group of young professionals in the construction industry committed to developing their leadership skills. The CLC offers networking events, mentorship opportunities, and leadership development programs.

- **The Design Futures Council:** The Design Futures Council **(DFC)** is a think tank focused on the future of the A/E/C

Endnotes

industry. The DFC offers leadership development programs, research reports, and other innovation, sustainability, and leadership resources.

- **The Society for Marketing Professional Services (SMPS):** The Society for Marketing Professional Services (SMPS) is a professional association for marketers in the A/E/C industry. SMPS offers leadership development programs, webinars, and other resources focused on business development, branding, and leadership.

ADDITIONAL RESOURCES

Numerous websites provide motivational information and resources for leadership development. Some of these websites include:

- **Center for Creative Leadership** – ccl.org
- **Entrepreneur** – entrepreneur.com
- **Fast Company** – fastcompany.com
- **Forbes** – forbes.com
- **Great Leadership** – greatleadershipbydan.com
- **Harvard Business Review** (HBR) – hbr.org
- **Inc.** – inc.com
- **Leadership First** – leadershipfirst.net
- **LinkedIn Leadership** – linkedin.com/showcase/skills-leadership-development
- **McKinsey & Company Insights** – mckinsey.com/insights
- **MIT Sloan Management Review** – sloanreview.mit.edu
- **Simon Sinek** – simonsinek.com
- **TED Talks** – ted.com

The Architecture of Vision

These websites offer a variety of motivational content, including articles, podcasts, videos, and interviews, which can help individuals develop and enhance their leadership skills. Remember that untapped resources are constantly emerging, so exploring and staying updated on the latest thought leadership is always a clever idea.

Before starting your leadership journey, research additional resources and consult with colleagues and industry experts to determine which frameworks, programs, and resources best suit your needs.

FINAL THOUGHTS

We framed our book on the idea that individuals and organizations can proactively develop strong leadership by studying the traits and characteristics of inspirational, innovative, and high-integrity leaders. By applying a learning framework based on awareness, acceptance, and action, these teachings can manifest in stronger and more successful leaders throughout your professional practice.

- **Awareness:** Take personal agency to further your and your firm's leadership development. Someone wise once said that the ten most important two-letter words were, *"If it is to be, it is up to me."*
- **Acceptance**: This book has many references to the idea of "Lead by Example." Taking on the mantle of the leader — whether for a project, a team, or the organization — is accepting responsibility for achieving the vision behind the challenge and setting an example for all involved in the solution.
- **Action:** Commitment to personal development is hard, but it does not have to be lonely. Work with your team to build a leadership-focused organization using 'The Architecture of Vision" framework.' The result will be the creation of a truly enduring professional practice.

We would love your feedback and to hear your stories. Please connect with us.

BIBLIOGRAPHY | Recommended Reading

Not all readers are leaders, but all leaders are readers.
Harry S. Truman

WE ARE READERS AS WELL AS WRITERS. Over the years, we have collected many useful resources for professional practice leadership, strategy, and inspiration. We recommend these to you as further study on your leadership journey.

Alexander, J. & M. Hordes, **S-Business:** Reinventing the Services Organization, New York, NY: SelectBooks, 2003.

Arbinger Institute, **Leadership and Self-Deception**, Berrett-Koehler Publishers, 2015.

Bass, B. M., & Riggio, R. E., **Transformational Leadership** (2nd ed.). Psychology Press, 2006.

Bennis, W., **On Becoming a Leader**, Perseus Press, 1994.

Beckwith, H., **Selling the Invisible:** *A Field Guide to Modern Marketing*, Grand Central Publishing, 2012.

Brown, B., **Dare to Lead:** *Brave Work. Tough Conversations. Whole Hearts.* Random House, 2018.

Burrus, D. & J. Mann, **Flash Foresight:** *How to See the Invisible and Do the Impossible*, HarperBusiness, 2011.

Collins, J. & J. Porras, **Built to Last: Successful Habits of Visionary Companies**, HarperBusiness, 1997.

Covey, Stephen M. R. **The Speed of Trust:** *The One Thing That Changes Everything*, Simon & Schuster, 2006.

Covey, S. R., **The 7 Habits of Highly Effective People**, Simon & Schuster, 1990.

Daniell, M., **Strategy:** A Step-by-Step Approach to the Development and Presentation of World Class Business Strategy, Palgrave Macmillan, 2004.

DePree, M., **Leadership is an Art**, Dell, 1989.

DePree, M., **Leadership Jazz**, Dell, 1993.

Goldsmith, M., **What Got You Here Won't Get You There** – How Successful People Become Even More Successful!, Hachette Books, 2007

Goleman, D., **What Makes a Leader?** Harvard Business Review's 10 Must Reads on Leadership; Harvard Business Review Press, 2006.

Hamel, G., **Leading the Revolution**, Harvard Business Press, 2000.

Harari, O., **The Leadership Secrets of Colin Powell**, McGraw-Hill, 2002.

Hiebeler, R., T. Kelly & C. Kelly, **Best Practices**, Touchstone Books, 2000.

Hunter, J., **The Servant**: A Simple Story About the True Essence of Leadership, Prima Publishing, 1998.

Kanchier, C., **Dare to Change Your Job and Your Life**, Jist Works, 2000.

Johansson, Franz, **The Medici Effect**: Breakthrough Insights at the Intersection of Ideas, Concepts, and Cultures, Harvard Business Review Press, 2004.

Kanter, R., **Evolve:** Succeeding in the Digital Culture of Tomorrow, Harvard Business Press, 2001.

Kelley, T. and D. Kelly, **The Art of Innovation:** Lessons in Creativity from IDEO, Doubleday, 2001.

Bibliography

Kelley, T. and J. Lippman, **The Ten Faces of Innovation**: *IDEO's Strategies for Defeating the Devil's Advocate and Driving Creativity Throughout Your Organization*, Doubleday, 2005.

Kim, W.C. and R. Mauborgne, **Blue Ocean Strategy:** *How to Create Uncontested Market Space and Make the Competition Irrelevant*, Harvard Business Review Press, 2015.

Kouzes, J. M., & Posner, B. Z., **The Leadership Challenge:** *How to Make Extraordinary Things Happen in Organizations*, Wiley, 2017 (6th ed.).

Lencioni, P., **The Five Dysfunctions of a Team:** *A Leadership Fable.* Jossey-Bass, 2002.

Maister, D., C. Green & R. Galford, **The Trusted Advisor**, Touchtone Books, 2001.

Malandro, L., **Fearless Leadership**: *How to Overcome Behavioral Blindspots and Transform Your Organization*, McGraw-Hill Education, 2009.

Maxwell, John C., **Good Leaders Ask Great Questions**, John Murray Press, 2016.

McChrystal, S., **Team of Teams**, Portfolio, 2015.

Monahan, M., **Strength of Character and Grace:** *Develop the Courage to be Brilliant*, Vittorio, 2010.

Newport, C., **Deep Work:** *Rules for Focused Success in a Distracted World,* Grand Central Publishing; 2016.

Northouse, P. G., **Leadership:** *Theory and Practice*, SAGE Publications, 2018 (8th ed.).

Paulson, D., **Competitive Business, Caring Business**, Paraview Press, 2002.

Peters, T. **Thriving on Chaos:** *Handbook for a Management Revolution*, Alfred A. Knopf, 1987.

Peters, T., **The Pursuit of WOW!**, Vintage Books, 1994.

Peters, T., **The Circle of Innovation,** Vintage Books, 1999.

Pine, J. & J. Gilmore, **The Experience Economy**, Harvard Business School Press, 1999.

Prosen, B., **Kiss Theory Goodbye:** *Five Proven Ways to Get Extraordinary Results in Any Company*, Gold Pen Publishing, 2006.

Rath, T., **Strengths Finder 2.0**, Gallup Press, 2007.

Sanborn, Mark, **You Don't Need a Title to Be a Leader:** *How Anyone, Anywhere, Can Make a Positive Difference*, Crown Currency, 2006.

Schmidt, B., T. G. Papone & A. Campbell, **On the Up and Up:** *Achieving Breakthrough Performance Through Insight*, Hyperion, 2004.

Senge, P., **The Fifth Discipline:** *The Art & Practice of the Learning Organization*, Currency/Doubleday, 1994.

Sinek, S., **Start with Why:** *How Great Leaders Inspire Everyone to Take Action.* Portfolio, 2009.

Wacker, W., J. Taylor & H. Means, **The Visionary's Handbook:** *Nine Paradoxes That Will Shape the Future of Your Business*, HarperBusiness, 2000.

Whitely, R., **The Corporate Shaman:** *A Business Fable*, Harper Collins, 2002.

Wilber, K., **A Theory of Everything:** *An Integral Vision for Business, Politics, Science and Spirituality*, Shambala, 2001.

Willink, J. & L. Babin, **Extreme Leadership:** *How US Navy Seals Lead and Win*, Macmillan Publishers, 2015.

Bibliography

Young, V., **Secret Thoughts of Successful Women**, Crown Publishing Group, 2011.

Zeithaml, V., A. Parasuraman & L. Berry, **Delivering Quality Service**, Free Press, 1990.

Zenger, J. & J. Folkman, **The Extraordinary Leader**, McGraw-Hill Trade, 2019 (3rd ed.).

Zenger, J., J. Folkman, R. Sherwin, & B. Steel, How to be Exceptional: **Drive Leadership Success by Magnifying Your Strengths**, McGraw-Hill Education, 2012.

ABOUT OUR CONTRIBUTORS

No one of us is as smart as all of us.
Anonymous

 **WE ARE FORTUNATE TO HAVE WORKED WITH MANY GREAT LEADERS** and volunteered in service to our profession with many more. When we began the journey that led to this book, we reached out to many of them. We were thrilled when they replied positively and shared the insights included herein.

Our contributors were respondents to our initial research survey in late 2019 and interviews in 2020. They provided valuable insights into the nature, challenges, and strengths that great leaders face in serving their professional service community of employees, stakeholders, and clients.

Our contributors' input provides reference points for the framework of personal leadership development. As many noted, each person's path is unique. Leadership experiences are unique to everyone. We bring diverse backgrounds, experiences, and perspectives to the leadership equation. The value of the stories in the book is the sharing of broader insights and their interpretation and impact. The synthesis between these ideas makes these leaders' learnings so valuable.

We note that our survey and interviews were conducted in 2020 and early 2021, and many of our contributors reference the impact of the COVID-19 pandemic on their practice. The following are brief bios of each of our contributors:

The Architecture of Vision

Tim Barrick, FSMPS, Principal/Chief Marketing Officer, RATIO, Indianapolis, IN

> Barrick leads the marketing and business development efforts at RATIO Architects — a national architectural design practice with a diverse portfolio. An active member of SMPS, Tim served as President of the Indiana Chapter in 1992 and National President in 1997. He is an SMPS Fellow, Distinguished Life Member, and 2017 Weld Coxe Marketing Achievement Award recipient. Barrick studied Construction Technology at IUPUI.

Amanda Bogner, PE, BEMP, President, Energy Studio, Omaha, NE

> Bogner leads Energy Studio — a consulting firm helping architects, engineers, developers, and building owners maximize efficiency and minimize costs through applied energy modeling. Achieving her goals is based on cultivating relationships with clients who share similar visions and desire to join us in achieving these goals. Bogner is a registered Mechanical Engineer and is LEED® Accredited by the US Green Building Council. Bogner received a BS in Architectural Engineering from The University of Kansas.

Linda Crouse, Principal/Chair of the Board, BAR Architects, San Francisco, CA

> Crouse leads BAR — a diverse architectural design practice serving many clients, from custom homes to state-of-the-art corporate campuses, wineries, or new communities. BAR brings passion, professionalism, integrity, and an ongoing desire for its clients to enjoy the process as much as they do. As a principal of the firm, she is responsible for all marketing-related functions, including strategic planning, client development, and public relations. She received a Bachelor of Arts in Urban Planning and Sociology from Rutgers College, Rutgers University, New Brunswick, NJ.

About Our Contributors

Michael Davis, Founder/Chief Executive Officer, DAVIS, Phoenix, AZ

Davis leads *DAVIS* — an Architecture, Interior, and Urban Design firm specializing in exceptional commercial and residential mixed-use properties. They create inspired architecture for everyday life for the nation's best corporations and developers. They have designed 75 million square feet of successful business, residential and social environments with a $20 billion value.

Craig Galati, FAIA, FSMPS, Principal/President, LGA Architecture, Las Vegas, NV

Galati leads LGA — a design firm that consults in architecture, sociology, and sustainability. Galati is a Las Vegas Metro Chamber of Commerce Government Affairs Committee member and the Board of Directors for The MOB Museum. Galati is a former President of SMPS Las Vegas a past SMPS National President, and the 2023 Weld Coxe Marketing Achievement Award recipient. He is a former President of both AIA Las Vegas and AIA Nevada. Galati holds a BArch from the University of Idaho. Galati is the author of several books, including *The Reluctant Leader*.

Kathleen Held, CPSM, President/Chief Executive Officer, Cini-Little International, Germantown, MD

Held leads Cini-Little International — the people who help create, improve, and enhance the kitchens and serveries in the places you eat. She leads the firm's marketing efforts, overseeing a team of marketing professionals and championing client development and marketing for the firm's nine worldwide offices. She is responsible for developing strategic marketing programs, strengthening name recognition, and developing and maintaining relationships in the global marketplace. Held received a BS in History/Art History from Frostburg State University.

Christine Hill, President, AOI, Omaha, NE

Hill leads AOI, a general contractor, Herman Miller furniture dealer, and DIRTT distribution partner, helping organizations build, expand, renew, and convert their facilities to meet ever-changing business goals. She has been with AOI since 1994. Her objective is to develop partnerships with our clients, realizing that we make their life easier if we understand their business needs. Hill holds a BS in Business Leadership from the College of Saint Mary.

Craig Janssen, LEED AP BD+C, President, Idibri, a Salas O'Brien Company, Dallas, TX

Janssen leads Idibri — a multidisciplinary team of technology designers, acousticians, and theatre planners — and is a frequent speaker on technological changes that impact group participation. He offers clients a framework to bypass the fads in favor of responding to the movements shaping environments. Janssen holds an HNC in Mechanical Engineering / Television Arts from the Durban University of Technology.

Delcine Johnson, President, Johnson & Pace, Longview, TX

Johnson leads Johnson & Pace — a multi-disciplined engineering, architectural, and surveying firm specializing in all aspects of site development engineering and project regulatory permitting. Johnson holds a Bachelor of Science in Business Management from the University of Texas at Tyler.

About Our Contributors

Lance Jones, PE, President, LSW Engineers Arizona, Phoenix, AZ

> Jones leads LSW — Consulting Engineers designing heating, ventilating, air conditioning, and plumbing systems for the built environment. Project types include correctional, municipal, courts, police and fire stations, theaters, and educational facilities. He received a BS in Mechanical Engineering from Montana State University-Bozeman.

Rebecca Jones, MBA, Chair, SafeworkCM, Lancaster, CA

> Jones leads SafeworkCM — a consulting firm that provides all aspects of construction management, project management, safety management, and construction inspection. Jones founded SafeworkCM in 1992 and has led the company to success using her unique brand of effective organizational development, solid business planning, and innovative marketing techniques. Jones received a BA in Asian Studies/Political Science from the University of Hawaii at Manoa and a Master of Arts in ESL from UCLA.

Grenee Martacho, Chief Executive Officer, Concord General Contracting, Phoenix, AZ

> Martacho leads Concord General Contracting — a practice offering a variety of construction delivery methods, including CM@Risk, Design-Build, and Competitive Bid. The company's portfolio comprises diverse projects in K-12, Higher Education, Municipal, Commercial, and Non-Profit sectors. Safety, quality, innovation, and growth drive Concord's culture. She joined Concord in 2007 and was most recently Vice President, leading marketing and business development and the firm's strategic initiatives.

Steve Osborn, PE, SE, President, CE Solutions, Fort Wayne, IN

Osborn leads CE Solutions — a structural engineering practice that provides exceptional service to public and private clients on various building types. Osborn founded the firm in 1998 based on his desire to start a different engineering firm centered on solid relationships, mutual respect, integrity, and ethical practice. Osborn holds a Bachelor of Science in Civil Engineering from Purdue University.

Marjanne Pearson, Founder, Talentstar, Santa Rosa, CA

Pearson founded Talentstar — a management consulting practice focusing on organizational resiliency and success strategies. Their clients are a remarkable design firm constellation that includes signature architects, emergent patterns, regional powerhouses, and corporate giants in the USA and Asia. Pearson has authored many articles and research papers published in various professional journals. Pearson regularly teaches a program focused on strategic resiliency in the new practice landscape for the Executive Education Program at Harvard's Graduate School of Design. Pearson received a BA in Linguistics from San Francisco State University.

Kevin Power, PE, President, KPE & EngTech, Omaha, NE

Power leads KPE / EngTech — a professional design and forensic engineering practice offering facility and infrastructure design, investigative engineering, and expert witness testimony. Power has provided services on thousands of assignments over a 30+ year career. Power holds a BS in Agricultural Engineering and has completed post-graduate Industrial and Management Systems Engineering programs at the University of Nebraska–Lincoln.

About Our Contributors

Michael Reilly, FSMPS, President, Reilly Communications, Boston, MA

Reilly leads Reilly Communications — a communication consulting practice serving professional service firms on media relations, marketing, message differentiation, and reputation building by creating content for external publications, social media outreach, and internal marketing. His firm develops successful, credible media relations strategies and results for clients through determined implementation. Reilly received an MS in Communications from Boston University and a BS in Journalism from Suffolk University.

Samantha Sannella, Senior Managing Director, Cushman & Wakefield, Toronto, ON

Sannella leads the Strategic Consulting practice at Cushman & Wakefield — a team focused on real estate and built environment strategies that foster productivity, increase effectiveness, mitigate cost, and reduce risk. They help clients solve the complex challenges encountered at the intersection of real estate and business. Sannella received a Master of Architecture from the University of Houston and a BFA from Louisiana Tech University.

Dawn Savage, FSMPS, Senior Director, Business Development, ICF, Sacramento, CA

Savage leads the Northern California Business Development efforts for ICF — a global consulting and technology services provider with more than 7,000 professionals focused on business analysis, policy, technology, research, digital strategy, and social sciences. Savage helps develop solutions to address our client's biggest disaster recovery challenges. Savage holds a BA in Economics from the University of California at Davis.

Dena Silver, retired President, M. Silver & Co., Raleigh, NC

> Silver and her husband/partner, Charlie — now retired — founded M. Silver & Company in 2000 to focus on strategic services with tangible results for the design, engineering, and construction industry. They specialized in facilitation, project initiation, partnering/team building, and lessons-learned sessions. They also provided strategic planning, research, facilitation, and implementation strategies, along with training on presentations, management skills, business development, and communication skills. Silver studied at Oregon State University and had a varied 30-year career in marketing and business development leadership for the general construction field.

Lee Slade, PE, Managing Principal/Board Chair, Walter P Moore, Houston, TX

> Slade leads Walter P Moore — an international structural engineering practice. During his almost 45-year career, he has filled multiple roles, from a graduate structural engineer designing and drawing to leading one of the top structural engineering practices in the United States. The company is a well-respected, diversified international engineering consultancy. Slade holds a BS in Civil Engineering from Rice University and is a graduate of Class V of the ACEC Senior Executive Institute.

Nancy Usrey, FSMPS. CPSM, Associate Vice President/Strategic Pursuit Director, HNTB, Dallas, TX

> Usrey leads the transportation sector design/build development efforts for HNTB — a global AE practice. Usrey helps pursuit teams develop and implement successful positioning strategies, effective work plans, and strategic win plans. She facilitates relationships between HNTB and their contractor partners, focusing on delivering premium service.

About Our Contributors

Usrey holds a certificate in Professional Services Leadership from the University of Maryland - Robert H. Smith School of Business and studied Architecture and Business at the University of Arizona.

Mark Valenti, CTS, retired President and Chief Executive Office, The Sextant Group, Pittsburgh, PA

Valenti — now retired — was the founder, CEO, and President of The Sextant Group from 1995 – 2018, a national independent technology consultancy. Valenti is an experienced leader with a demonstrated history of working in the information technology and services industry and has strong business development professional skills in advertising, strategic partnerships, team building, public speaking, and management. Valenti holds a Certificate in Audio Engineering from the University of Bridgeport and a BA in Economics from Penn State University.

Ron Worth, CAE, FSMPS, Assoc AIA, retired Chief Executive Officer of IAAO & SMPS, Kansas City, MO

Worth was CEO of two international A/E/C organizations: The International Association of Assessing Officers (IAAO) and the Society for Marketing Professional Services (SMPS). A trusted leader and innovative strategist, Worth created and implemented roadmaps that clearly defined organizational objectives, ensured the achievement of short and long-term goals, reflected the desired direction of the board, and drove profitable and sustainable growth. Now in private practice, Worth consults on organizational revitalization and development. Worth holds an MS in Business Operations from Bradley University and a BS in Architecture from the University of Kansas.

ACKNOWLEDGEMENTS

Find in the middle air an eagle on the wing and recognize the five that make the Muses sing.
William Butler Yeats

 WE EACH HAVE MANY PEOPLE TO THANK for their inspiration, mentorship, and perspectives that led to our writing of this book, and we are proud to share their influence with you.

From CRAIG PARK, FSMPS, ASSOC. AIA

As with my previous books, this book would not have been possible without the family, friends, and colleagues who supported, informed, and influenced this writing and the inspirational and innovative mentors and leaders who inspired me and framed my views of leadership.

No one deserves more thanks than my co-author, Barbara Shuck. She started us down this path, kept us on track, expanded on my original outline, and persevered with me through three parallel major life events — each of us moving to opposite sides of the country, experiencing life during the pandemic, and having significant job changes — that slowed, but never stopped, our progress toward publishing this book.

Barbara's interviews with our contributors encouraged them to share insights we might not otherwise have. Her thoughtful input into each leadership trait and her focus on tools for personal awareness, acceptance, and actions needed for leadership development completed our goal to create a book that provides the understanding, applications, and tools needed for visionary leadership.

I want to give special thanks to each of our contributors. They added unique value, insights, and focus to our concepts. They gave their time freely and provided ideas that further expanded our scope.

Added thanks go to Jennifer LaPointe, PE, LEED AP, Owner, Take Flight, LLC; Scott Braley, FAIA, President, Braley Training & Consulting; Stacey Huscher, Executive Director, Paradise Valley Schools Education Foundation; and Diane Rutledge, CPSM, President, Brand Transform for their cogent suggestions on voice, framework, and format.

Special thanks go to Tom Smith, FSMPS, retired CEO of BonTerra Consulting, past SMPS president, and Weld Coxe Marketing achievement award recipient, for your insights, careful edits, and content suggestions. Our book is so much better for your input.

The importance of mentors to leaders became a common theme during our research. Unexpectedly, through our interviews, I found that I share mentors and influencers with several contributors. You will find references to Patrick Bell, a highly-respected business consultant, Lou Marines, founder of the Advanced Management Institute, and Margaret Spaulding, author, and marketing consultant. As mentors and advisors, they each gave me a better understanding of the traits of successful leaders and what I needed to do to become a better leader.

Dr. Susan Harris, David Aitken, and Bill Truby — all faculty in the Advanced Management Institute's Leadership course — provided the foundation for my own leadership development journey when I completed their program in 1994.

The Society for Marketing Professional Services (SMPS) leaders played a significant role in my leadership journey, including Kay Godwin and Gwen Powell-Todd at the local level and Tim Barrick, Mike Reilly, and Ron Worth at the national level, who encouraged me to take the leadership challenge.

Acknowledgements

I also thank Randle Pollock, FSMPS, former national SMPS president, Fellow, and (yet another) Weld Coxe Marketing Achievement Award recipient. As Editor of the SMPS Marketer journal from 1998 - 2012, Randy initiated a decade-long series of cover articles entitled "Flying with Eagles." I was fortunate to interview several CEOs for those pieces. The insights from those interviews piqued my interest and understanding of the elements of successful leadership, which led to the eagle-related themes found throughout this book.

I have been fortunate throughout my career to work for professional practice leaders who provided opportunities and encouragement to improve my craft. My first employer, the late Hubert Wilke, was a great mentor and leader. I would not be here without his friendship and support.

I also want to thank Dennis Paoletti, Don Esters, Peter Devereaux, Charles Dalluge, and Mark Valenti. You each set great examples as leaders of highly successful organizations where I had the pleasure to serve.

As a volunteer in several A/E/C industry associations, I met and learned from innovative leaders, including Walt Blackwell and Randy Lemke of InfoComm (now AVIXA). Both were great leadership exemplars who gave me opportunities to lead national programs in the AV subset of the A/E/C industry.

My leadership journey began, like many, with the direction and encouragement of family. My father, Jesse Warren Park, Jr., a kind and gentle man with an unquenchable thirst for knowledge and understanding, taught me the importance of continual learning and the value of sharing ideas. It is to him that I dedicate this book.

And finally, I must thank my amazing and lovely wife, Margaret, for her encouragement and patience through this long and winding process. I am the luckiest man.

The Architecture of Vision

From BARBARA SHUCK, FSMPS, CPSM

I've always wanted to write a book. That old saying that a goal without a plan is just a dream proved very true until a fortuitous conversation with my friend, Craig Park. He has written books before and is a prolific author, which I've always admired. I was honored and thoroughly ecstatic when we talked about co-authoring this book on leadership. Boom. The goal turns into a plan, and the dream becomes a reality. First and foremost, I thank Craig for creating a hands-on, industry-specific, practical tool to help professionals understand and develop leadership skills. Craig, you're the best.

I've experienced many leaders in my life and have learned from all of them. Some of the best lessons have come through discomfort and hardship.

My father, Bill Bunten, was the first leader I experienced. He was a banker in Michigan and Kansas. While I didn't understand what he did, he embodied all the traits discussed in this book: vision, introspection, empathy, patience, wisdom, discipline, effort, agility, influence, purpose, perspective, trust, impact, values, courage, harmony, and character. He and my mother, Chuck (Charlene), made growing up a wonderful experience. Learning was not always easy, and there were moments of discomfort. I'm a grateful daughter.

The design and construction industry is not my first career. I had interesting positions in a trade association, a small graphic design firm, and printing, all of which involved writing, creating, sales, and entrepreneurship. As a novice professional, I experienced "we've always done it this way, so don't ask questions," from chaotic entrepreneurship to the challenges of being a business owner to hard-core sales, with brow-beating, intimidation, and ever-moving sales goals. I learned much about leadership in the first 10 years of my career.

Acknowledgements

I first experienced excellent leadership when I joined a construction company. My boss, Gordon Lacy, was empathetic, disciplined, and trustworthy. I will always appreciate his wisdom, courage, and character. Mental days off are healthy. His mentorship and introduction to the Society for Marketing Professional Services (SMPS) set me on a fulfilling career path. Thank you, Gordon. RIP.

Other bosses stand out for their leadership traits: Larry C., Jim G., Roy E., Jim D., Steve T., Ron E., Richard C., Bob W., Bob F., Steve W., and Jim R. I've also experienced many leadership traits with clients since I became a consultant. I believe in the Pareto Principle: 80% of my positive leadership came from 20% of the bosses and clients I have worked with.

And then there is the best leadership incubator that shaped my career: SMPS. Like many, I left my first meeting as a committee chair. The Arizona Chapter will always be my home group. I'm thankful for friends who taught me much about leading a group of people: Kristy B., Julie F., Lauren T., Ann S., Claudia H., Stephanie M., Rebecca T., Suzanne N., Jamie S., Christy S., and Julie S. are a few that come to mind. Apologies if I missed anyone. You are all precious friends and colleagues.

And, of course, I am thankful for my Nebraska Chapter leaders who supported me through the many years of Board service and then when I was Chapter President: Mike B., Mimi T., Michelle H., Quinn T., Terry H., Jodi V., Lisa S., Lisa K., Jeni M., Bart P., Bobbi L., and others who made my time in the Heartland unforgettable.

Beyond Arizona, I've been blessed with mentors and advocates that demonstrated all the essential traits and helped me sculpt my leadership skills: Tom S., Carolyn F., Kevin H., Frank L., Donna J., Dana B., Craig G., Chris R., Nancy U., Beth H., Dawn S., Mike S., Tim B., Mitch L., Andrea G., Paula S., Michele R., Janet L., Sarah K., Joy W., Stacy C., Ron W., Mike G., Antonio P., Tina M., Lisa B., Kevin D.,

The Architecture of Vision

Molly D., Natalie G., Marci T., Misty T., Natalie P., Shelley S., Jana M., Jen M., Jean K., and many others.

Special thanks to the leaders who served with me as Society President: Paula R., Brad T., Doug P., Tom T., Carla T., and Melissa L. Despite the discomfort, we sharpened, supported each other, and became a strong team. I am blessed to call each of you a very special friend.

My life's purpose is to glorify God through faith, family, friends, and work. My family has been a huge part of my leadership journey. To my children, Rochelle, Will, and Charlie thank you for your endurance and survival skills as I navigated long hours to meet expectations and deadlines. I'm very proud of the adults you have become, and you regularly demonstrate these leadership traits yourselves. You learn through mentoring, good leadership examples, and the discomfort and challenges. Yay, you!

And to my husband, Jerry, thank you for your patience. You joined our family just as my SMPS leadership path was gearing up and my career took off. I don't think we knew what a ride it would be! And now that you're retired, and I'm finally putting some dates on landing this career plane, it's exciting to think about what's ahead. I'm looking forward to creating a new path forward together.

Thank you to all who have given me insights into this book. I'm a better person because of you.

ABOUT THE AUTHORS

So flies an eagle flight, bold and onward, leaving no trace behind.
William Shakespeare

CRAIG PARK AND BARBARA SHUCK first met in 2002, when Craig was the SMPS national president-elect, and Barbara was the SMPS Arizona Chapter president-elect. They worked together on several AZ Chapter programs, including several *"Flying with Eagles"* panel programs focused on leadership perspectives from A/E/C industry leaders.

Craig and Barbara served as national and host chapter chairs, respectively, for the 2003 SMPS national conference, *Build Business: The Next Wave*, in Scottsdale, AZ. The conference was very successful and a fond memory for many of the attendees. Their paths led them both to Omaha, NE, where, again, they co-presented at SMPS NE Chapter events and remained active in national programs and committees.

Fast forward to Summer 2019, over lunch in Blair, NE, Barbara and Craig discussed the need for comprehensive leadership development programs for the A/E/C industry that included all aspects of a professional service firm — with a perspective from the marketer's point of view — and decided to write this book.

Since then, they have co-presented on the themes of the book *Inspiration, Innovation, and Integrity* at SMPS Regional Conferences throughout the US. The audience reaction and informal surveys during those presentations confirmed their belief in the importance of this writing.

About CRAIG PARK, FSMPS, ASSOCIATE AIA

Known A/E/C industry-wide for his unique mix of left-brained creative and right-brained analytics, Craig takes an individualized approach to consulting, coaching, and mentoring. He focuses on helping his clients identify and execute the measurable steps that help them reach their goals quickly and smoothly.

Craig is a sought-after speaker, author, and advisor for his insights into new marketing, technology, and leadership development. He is a repository of business and technology information supporting the business growth goals of individuals, industry associations, and professional service firms.

Craig's mission is to help his clients build value-centered leadership, content marketing visibility, and strategy-focused results-driven growth that generates raving fans and clients for life. Craig's process empowers your team with the strategic leadership, marketing, and technology tools needed to succeed.

For over 40 years, Craig has helped firms — ranging from 20 to over 1000 people, spanning a single office to over thirty branches and generating from $2M to $500M in annual revenue — grow and succeed. His approach engages and challenges each organization to build a technology-enabled, leadership-focused, enduring professional practice that differentiates the practice and serves as the foundation for a culture of success.

Craig's private consulting practice helps his clients to identify gaps and opportunities and improve outcomes using an agile results-focused approach. Craig's work has been widely published in A/E/C-related journals and magazines, and he is a regular speaker at industry events.

Craig is an architect by training and a technologist by practice and passionate about developing strategic business, marketing,

About the Authors

and development frameworks designed to help his clients succeed.

Craig is an active member and volunteer for the American Institute of Architects (AIA), the Society for College & University Planning (SCUP) and the Association of Physical Plant Administrators (APPA).

He was named Educator 2000 by the National Systems Contractors Association (NSCA) and received awards for this technical designs from the Audiovisual Integrated Experience Association (AVIXA).

Craig is a Fellow, former national President of SMPS, a Distinguished Life Member, and the 2007 Weld Coxe Marketing Achievement Award recipient, the Society's highest honor for career achievements, leadership, and lasting contributions to the A/E/C community. He was also the 2005 recipient of the SMPS SF Chapter's William B. Hankenson Lifetime Achievement Award.

About BARBARA SHUCK, FSMPS, CPSM

Barbara Shuck, FSMPS, CPSM, is a veteran A/E/C strategist, writer, thought leader, innovator, trainer, and mentor. She gets marketing and business development in the design and construction industry. She uses more than 35 years of proven expertise to help clients focus on what they do best: delivering superior services to valuable clients.

Barbara's career spans more than 30 years of communications and client service. She worked in the printing and publishing industry for more than ten years before landing in the design and construction industry, where she has built a formidable reputation as a generous guide, eager to help technical and marketing professionals improve their knowledge and skills. She worked for construction, engineering, construction management, and architectural firms in Kansas, Arizona, and Nebraska before becoming a marketing consultant who serves A/E/C clients across the United States.

Today, Barbara helps A/E/C firms build effective marketing and communications programs. She advises, educates, and coaches marketing and business development teams, including proposals, interviews, research, planning, promotions, and management.

Barbara uses a proven storytelling framework to help clients with internal communications, initiatives, and external efforts that win work through compelling and persuasive content and message. She is a Donald Miller StoryBrand program fan and became a Guide in 2020.

Having presented to more than 250 audiences in the past 25+ years, Barbara knows how to connect with audiences and provide engaging, interactive learning experiences. Audiences include the Society for Marketing Professional Services (SMPS) chapter and regional and national programs.

In addition, she has taught workshops for numerous design and construction associations, including ACEC, AIA, SAME, ENR, PSMJ, APWA, and SWE, and in college classrooms and online. She is a Past

About the Authors

President of SMPS, a Fellow, a Certified Professional Services Marketer (CPSM), and a Trustee for the SMPS Foundation. She was the 2022 Weld Coxe Marketing Achievement Award recipient, the Society's highest honor for career achievements, leadership, and lasting contributions to the A/E/C community.

Barbara has a Bachelor's in Communication Arts and French and a Master's in International Business (marketing emphasis), along with career expertise in marketing research, planning, business development, proposals, promotions, and management.

www.ingramcontent.com/pod-product-compliance
Lightning Source LLC
Chambersburg PA
CBHW071852290426
44110CB00013B/1121